COMMUNICATION AS ORGANIZING

Empirical and Theoretical Explorations
in the Dynamic of Text and Conversation

LEA'S COMMUNICATION SERIES
Jennings Bryant/Dolf Zillmann, General Editors

Selected titles in Organizational Communication (Linda Putnam, advisory editor) include:

Haslett • *Communicating and Organizing: An Integrated Frame*

Kramer • *Managing Uncertainty in Organizational Communication*

Nicotera/Clinkscales/with Walker • *Understanding Organizations Through Culture and Structure: Relational and Other Lessons From the African-American Organization*

Parker • *Race, Gender, and Leadership: Re-Envisioning Organizational Leadership From the Perspectives of African American Women Executives*

Taylor/Van Every • *The Emergent Organization: Communication as Its Site and Surface*

For a complete list of titles in LEA's Communication Series, please contact Lawrence Erlbaum Associates, Publishers at www.erlbaum.com

COMMUNICATION AS ORGANIZING

Empirical and Theoretical Explorations in the Dynamic of Text and Conversation

Edited by

François Cooren
Université de Montréal

James R. Taylor
Université de Montréal

Elizabeth J. Van Every

2006

LAWRENCE ERLBAUM ASSOCIATES, PUBLISHERS
Mahwah, New Jersey   London

Lawrence Erlbaum Associates, Inc., Publishers
10 Industrial Avenue
Mahwah, New Jersey 07430
www.erlbaum.com

Cover art by Benita Sanders

Cover design by Kathryn Houghtaling Lacey

Library of Congress Cataloging-in-Publication Data

Communication as organizing : empirical and theoretical explorations in the dynamic of text and conversation / edited by François Cooren, James Taylor, Elizabeth J. Van Every.

    p. cm. — (LEAs communication series)

Includes bibliographical references and index.
ISBN 0-8058-5812-1 (cloth : alk. paper)
ISBN 0-8058-5813-X (pbk. : alk. paper)
1. Communication in organizations. 2. Organizational behavior. 3. Management. I. Cooren, François. II. Taylor, James R. III. Van Every, Elizabeth J. IV. Series.
HD30.3.C6415   2005
302.3'5—dc22   2005052984
                                            CIP

Books published by Lawrence Erlbaum Associates are printed on acid-free paper, and their bindings are chosen for strength and durability.

Printed in the United States of America
10 9 8 7 6 5 4 3 2 1

To Gail T. Fairhurst and Linda L. Putnam

Contents

Contributors

Boris H. J. M. Brummans, Université de Montréal

François Cooren, Université de Montréal

Carole Groleau, Université de Montréal

Senem Güney, University at Albany, SUNY

Joël M. Katambwe, Université du Québec à Trois-Rivières

Daniel Robichaud, Université de Montréal

Jean A. Saludadez, University of the Philippines, Open University

James R. Taylor, Université de Montréal

Elizabeth J. Van Every, Montréal

Richard J. Varey, Waikato University, New Zealand

Preface

For communication researchers who are asking what discourse analysis is and how to go about doing it, this book supplies some answers. There has been an increasing fascination among communication researchers, information scientists, and management scientists with the role of discourse in the constitution of organization over the past decade or so, such as the work in conversation analysis or, in a quite different tradition, the exploration of narrative and storytelling as the basis of organizing. Other approaches such as dialogism, rhetoric, and the theory of communicative action could also be cited. What has been missing, however, is a synthesis within which these multiple streams of reflection on the role of language in organizing are seen as complementary dimensions of a single problematic, rather than somewhat awkward partners, or perhaps more accurately, competitors.

This volume addresses this need. Throughout, the contributing authors adopt an approach to the explanation of organizational phenomena that is grounded in discourse. A single assumption has guided us: Organization emerges in the interplay of the textual world of ideas and interpretations and the practical world of an object-oriented conversation. Because we wanted to illustrate the applicability and utility of a discursive approach to understanding organization, each chapter not only develops a theoretical dimension of the central theme, but illustrates, through practical examples, how those concepts can be put to work to develop effective research. The result is a diversity of approaches to the analysis of organizational discourse—ethnographic research, account analysis, conversation analysis, and action research—that will serve as an illustration of the many opportunities that discourse analysis opens to the enterprising student. Although the volume has not been designed to be a textbook, our aim has been to make the various ideas and analyses easily accessible to senior undergraduate and graduate students and researchers in a range of disciplines, including management science, social psychology, pragmatics of language, sociology, information science and system design, public relations, and organizational studies, as well as to practitioners in organizational communication. It could very easily, for example, furnish the material for a course or seminar on organizational discourse analysis at both the introductory and advanced levels.

Following an introductory synthesis of the book's principal themes in chapter 1, the individual contributions are grouped into four parts. In Part I, "Integration, Differentiation, and Ambiguity," four authors use the concept of collaborative sensemaking to explore processes of organizational change, conflict, and integration. Noting the need for more empirically based research on "the local enactment of organizational roles whose actors participate in the making and sometimes in the collapse of shared meaning that sustains their organization," Güney (chap. 2, p. 19) reports on her research in a large technology development organization. Saludadez and Taylor (chap. 3) take the position that organizational forms emerge through the sensemaking process carried on in conversation that is in turn "framed and informed by organization," (p. 37). They explore this circular dynamic in their analysis of the accounts given by scientists of their participation in the formation (and occasionally, collapse) of collaborative research networks. In their analysis of filmed excerpts of managerial conversation, Katambwe and Taylor (chap. 4) develop an original approach to the empirical analysis of managerial conversation, one that emphasizes "the centrality of text as an agent responsible for authoring of the organization's goals, objectives, and structures," (p. 56). Ambiguity, they find, is inevitable as people confront the necessity of resolving the paradox of simultaneous organizational unity and diversity.

The concepts of "Agency and Narrativity" are taken as the focus of Part II. In his chapter (chap. 5), Cooren reconstructs the general problematic of agency as a "hybrid phenomenon" and suggests that we need to acknowledge the interplay and the contribution of both human and nonhuman actions. In chapter 6, Robichaud in turn proposes what he terms a truly relational reconceptualization of the notion of agency based on the ontology of Charles S. Peirce. In their analysis of naturalistic data based on the Greimassian theory of narrativity, Taylor and Cooren (chap. 7) demonstrate the potential application of that theory and the concept of worldview to a sequence of conversation in which the organizing role of communication is transparently shown.

In Part III, the communicational concept of "Coorientation" provides a conceptual framework for the analysis of the intimate relation between language and the daily accomplishment of ordinary activities that give an organization its reason for existing. Taylor (chap. 8) uses it to develop a communicative answer to the question "What is an organization?" He claims this is reconstituted in ongoing conversation, mediated by language, and cooriented to a mixed social and material world of experience. Groleau (chap. 9) takes collective object-oriented human practice as the theme of her critique and comparison of coorientation and activity theory, pointing out their commonalities and considerable differences.

The concluding chapters suggest some implications of the theoretical and analytical perspectives developed in the book for organizational analysis in general. Varey (chap. 10), from the point of view of management studies and managing practice, explores the theoretical and empirical advantages in the adoption of the notion of accounting as constitutive of organization. Brummans (chap. 11) reflects on the relation between agency, communication, and organization by centralizing

ethics and suggesting how the ideas presented in the book can both contribute to
and benefit from such a perspective.

ACKNOWLEDGMENTS

This book has come about with the collaboration of many institutions, colleagues,
students, friends, and relatives. First, we wish to thank Linda Bathgate and Sara
Scudder of Lawrence Erlbaum Associates for their unconditional support during
the whole project. Thanks to their expertise and leadership, the editing process was,
from the beginning to the end, an enjoyable and rewarding experience. We know
how much we owe them. Deep gratitude is also owed to the Université de Montréal,
and especially its Department of Communication, whose support over the years has
been invaluable. This department has created a wonderful place to work, one where
collaboration among scholars is encouraged and indeed nurtured. If our department
is now "on the map" in organizational communication at the international level, it is
first and foremost thanks to the staff and colleagues who make this institution such
a special place to do research.

Our thanks also go to all the members (students and faculty) of the Language, Organization, and Governance Laboratory (LOG), created in 2003 by Daniel
Robichaud and Chantal Benoit-Barné and now directed by Daniel Robichaud.
Through our weekly sessions (titled OUREPO, for Ouvroir de Recherches
Potentielles, or Workshop of Potential Research), we have been able to present and
test most of the ideas presented in this volume. Our special thanks to three LOG
members, Chantal Benoit-Barné, Hélène Giroux, and Alain Létourneau, as well as to
two precious LOG collaborators, Robert E. Sanders and Anita Pomerantz (both at the
University at Albany, SUNY). Their work is not represented in this volume, but their
ideas infuse its reflections at many points. We would like to also thank Gail T.
Fairhurst and Linda L. Putnam, to whom this book is dedicated, for their insightful
and helpful input throughout the development of the project. Through their invariably informed critique and unfailing encouragement, Gail and Linda have helped us
develop and make generally known the interpretive approach we advocate in this
book. Our gratitude also goes to Consuelo Vasquez, a PhD student in our department,
for being a very big help during the last stages of the proofing process.

We cannot, equally, fail to mention the remarkable generosity and support of a
number of other universities that have welcomed us as invited scholars. Their re-
searchers and students have contributed to the development of our ideas. These in-
clude (in no special order) the Universities of Waikato (Ted Zorn, David McKie,
Juliet Roper), in New Zealand; Amsterdam (Wim Elving, Betteke Van Ruler, Klaus
Schoenbach), Tilburg (Hans Weigand, Aldo de Moor), and Delft (Jan Dietz), in the
Netherlands; Boulder, Colorado (Michele Jackson, Gerry Hauser, Bob Craig, Stan
Deetz), and South Florida (Eric Eisenberg), in the United States; Uberlândia
(Valdir Valadão Júnior), São Paolo (Margarida Kuntsch), and Paraná (Adriana
Machado Casali), in Brazil; Helsinki (Yrjö Engeström), in Finland; Madrid
Complutense (José Luis Piñuel, Antonio Lucas Marín), in Spain; Odense (Lars

Christensen), in Denmark; Toulouse (Anne Mayère), Bordeaux (Valérie Carayol), Nice (Yvonne Giordano), and Lyon (Michèle Grosjean), in France; and Lüneburg (Egbert Kahle), in Germany. It has been in the teaching opportunities and collegial conversations that these exchanges afforded that we were pushed and encouraged to refine and modify our ideas. More concretely, we wish to acknowledge the financial support of Bell Canada, through its Bell University Laboratories R&D program, the Canadian Foundation for Innovation, the Centre for Interdisciplinary Research on Emerging Technologies at the Université de Montréal, the Deutscher Akademischer Austauscchdienst (the German Academic Exchange Service), the SEAMEO Regional Center for Graduate Study and Research in Agriculture (SEARCA), and the Social Sciences and Humanities Research Council of Canada (SSHRC 410-2004-1091). Finally, on a more personal note, François would like to thank Nancy, his wife, and his two children, Nina and Émile who are such a wonderful source of happiness.

CHAPTER ONE

Introduction

François Cooren
James R. Taylor
Université de Montréal

Elizabeth J. Van Every
Montréal

In analyzing the conceptual foundations of organizational communication research, Deetz (2001) observed that "gradually, since the early 1980s, scholars in communication departments as well as a large number of non-U.S. scholars and some scholars from other academic units have focused on organizations as complex discursive formations where discursive practices are both 'in' organizations and productive of them" (pp. 5–6). One logical implication of this shift, he pointed out, is that the production of the field as an academic discipline—and indeed organizational communication as a distinct phenomenon that merits our attention—is itself a discursive accomplishment. Sauce for the goose, he is saying, is sauce for the gander. We have to come to terms with the need to look at ourselves as a domain of organizing and accounting in the same way—through the same lens—as we do for the object we are studying, organizations.

He then argued that, when we make this move, the academic field of organizational communication could be seen as divided into contrasting research orientations, depending on whether the emphasis is primarily on (a) consensus or dissensus, and (b) "élite/a priori" or "local/emergent" constitutive processes of organizing. Deetz (2001) then identified four resulting tendencies (it would be an exaggeration to call them more than that): (a) *interpretive* (premodern, traditional), (b) *normative* (modern, progressive), (c) *critical* (late modern, reformist), and (d) *dialogic* (postmodern, deconstructionist).

One could quibble with the classification scheme but a cursory scan of the current literature would suggest that Deetz was on to something. Corman and Poole (2000), for example, organized the chapters of their edited collection of essays by themes of interpretive, postpositivist, and critical. If we retain "critical" and "interpretive" and equate "postpositivist" to "normative" then three of Deetz's (2001) categories appear. On closer reading, however, it turns out that none of the authors invited to explicate the categories are very comfortable with them: The borders between them, they argue, are too fuzzy. Taylor, Flanagin, Cheney, and Seibold (2001), while "lamenting the resulting lack of a clear disciplinary identity" (p. 115), also echoed some of Deetz's categories in their listing of emphases of research: ethnographically oriented, focused on rhetoric and narrativity, critical and feminist approaches. However, they too emphasize the "permeability and the ready receptiveness to ideas" that they see as characteristic of the field. May and Mumby (2005) equally noted the current "paradigm proliferation" (p. 8). They identified no fewer than six dominant perspectives that both echo and extend Deetz's list: postpositivism, social constructionism, the rhetorical tradition, critical theory, postmodernism, and feminism. Miller (2002), for her part, reinforced the idea that the field is "highly interdisciplinary, both in its roots and in the resources drawn on in current research" (p. 196), but she developed a different classification scheme based, like Putnam, Phillips and Chapman (1996), on contrasting metaphors of the relation of communication to organization.

We undertook the writing of this book with a different idea in mind. What is missing in the current literature, we believe, is a synthesis within which these contrasting streams of reflection on the communicative basis of organizing—and the science of organization—are seen to be complementary dimensions of a single problematic, rather than somewhat awkward partners, if not, for the most part, competitors.

This volume attempts to address this gap. It is based on one elementary idea, that organization emerges in the interplay of two interrelated spaces: the textual-conceptual world of ideas and interpretations and the practical world of an object-oriented conversation directed to action. To adopt this position, however, is to supercede the kind of divisive categorization Deetz proposed.

Consider the first of his dimensions: consensus–dissensus. Scholars, he argued, can be grouped according to whether they see the organization as essentially consensual or dissensual. An emphasis on consensus is consistent with notions of coordination, centralized planning and strategy, conflict resolution, socialization of employees, training, reward systems, and, ultimately, in a recent manifestation, reengineering. It is a conservative image, emphasizing tradition and rationality. An emphasis on dissensus, on the contrary, assumes that "struggle, conflict and tensions" are the "natural state" of organization (Deetz, 2001, p. 15). It highlights, and aims to develop a consciousness of, "suppression of basic conflicts" and "domination of people."

As the reader will discover, the chapters of this book present a very different picture of organizational work, one that assumes communication to be the route to the establishment of both consensus and dissensus. We see cooperation and collaboration, on the one hand, and conflict, tension, and domination, on the other, as copresent elements in the organizational experience, and a consequence of how communication really works.

Deetz's system of classification assumes an either/or logic. Our emphasis in this book is on both/and thinking. Güney (chap. 2, this volume) uses her ethnographic research to illustrate the tension that develops in a very large high-tech company when distinct, although in principle complementary, development teams collaborate to develop a new product. Consensus and dissensus are so intertwined that it is hard to separate the threads. Saludadez and Taylor (chap. 3, this volume) present evidence of the same contradictory pressures in interdisciplinary teams of scientists, working in Southeast Asia. Katambwe and Taylor (chap. 4, this volume) go even further in their chapter, arguing that both consensus and dissensus are indispensable to the life of the organization. Both, they claim, must be constructed in communication. They develop an analysis of a filmed record of managerial interaction to illustrate how what they call association and dissociation emerge out of communication and why both may be essential to the continued vitality of the organization.

The conventional consensus–dissensus dichotomy may seem logically inescapable to the extent that we are limited to two-person interaction. The two either agree or disagree (the relationship is bipolar, although perhaps multidimensional). However, the moment a third person is taken into account, consensus and dissensus may be simultaneously present. Caplow (1968), in fact, argued that this ambivalent outcome is inevitable in triads. As he observed, the most significant property of a triad "is its tendency to divide into a coalition of two members against the third" (p. 2). If, as he believed, "triads are the building blocks of which all social organizations are constructed," then all forms of complex organization will inevitably be characterized by both consensus and dissensus. Even in congregations of many members, all participating in the same discussion, as Katambwe and Taylor show, interaction patterns resolve to the triadic form—*I* (first person, or speaker); *you* (second person, or targeted listener); and *he, she,* or *they* (third person, or to whom they are referring).

The resulting image of organizational interaction is of an essentially fluid and open-ended process of organizing, in which inherited positions of strength are exploited creatively by the participants. Structure is certainly present, built into the context, but it is also emergent. As coalitions form and dissolve so does the configuration of power (Groleau, chap. 9, this volume; Taylor & Cooren, chap. 7, this volume).

Similarly with Deetz's second dimension: *élite/a priori* versus *local/emergent*. The researcher, he claimed, can either begin by thinking of the organization as an established patterning of interaction that reflects preexisting codes, rules, cultures, and hierarchies of influence, power, and wealth (it is "a priori") or as a spontaneous organizing that unfolds continuously in the local communication activities of people (it is "emergent").

The authors in this volume once again go beyond the either/or assumption implicit in Deetz's scheme to adopt both/and thinking. Groleau observes contradictory pressures in every activity system, underpinning a dialectic of transformation and change, on the one hand, and systemic continuity, on the other. Taylor and Cooren discover in the recorded conversation of an ordinary organizational transaction both the shadow of the a priori, established understandings of social roles and, simultaneously, the emergence of local and emergent patterning of interaction.

TOWARD A PRAGMATIC PHILOSOPHY OF RESEARCH

In another respect, however, the authors in this volume take Deetz's cautionary remarks very much to heart, when he observed that we must apply the same lens to analyze ourselves as a research community as the one we adopt for the organizations we study. If there is one principle that all those who have participated in the preparation of this volume share, it is that communication is not simply information transmission, nor the neutral conveyance of observations and ideas. Communication is about *acting*—having an effect—fully as much as all the other purposive activities in which we engage as human beings (Cooren, chap. 5, this volume; Robichaud, chap. 6, this volume). This principle is vividly illustrated in several chapters (Güney, chap. 2, this volume; Katambwe & Taylor, chap. 4, this volume; Saludadez & Taylor, chap. 3, this volume; Taylor & Cooren, chap. 7; Varey, chap. 10). As Brummans (chap. 11, this volume) observes, the scientific community is never merely a network for the dissemination of the results of findings. It, too, is an arena where ambitions are realized, and competing ideological camps engage in a contest to establish their authority.

In the classic picture of science, investigators manipulate technology (mostly symbolic in the social sciences) to make discoveries; the resulting knowledge is disseminated within the scientific community through papers, talks, and informal correspondence and is eventually applied (if it is) in different fields of practice. However, that "knowledge" is, in fact, when we stop to think about it, a socially embedded form of accounting: an attempt to explain the way the world is for a given community. To cite Varey (chap. 10, this volume), "practical accounting is the construction of worlds of meaning in the course of social interaction." By focusing on the dynamic of accounting, our attention is recentered on relationships between people, in our own field fully as much as in other organizations, rather than uniquely on the mediating modalities of a subject–object relationship. Knowledge is no longer seen as something that one actor communicates to another, nor as something incorporated into the ability of an actor to mold or manipulate an object (Brummans, chap. 11, this volume). Instead, knowledge is seen as what must be constructed by people working together. It is both a precondition of their interaction, and emerges in it, and out of it, to become the basis of their collaboration. It is, thereby, problematic: It depends on the dynamics of the interaction.

Brummans (chap. 11, this volume) situates the work we are reporting on in the volume within the pragmatic tradition associated with pioneers such as Peirce,

James, and Dewey. In this respect, it is worth citing Peirce, who originated the term *pragmatism*. Here is what he wrote in 1877: "The sole object of inquiry is the settlement of opinion. We may fancy that this is not enough for us, and that we seek, not merely an opinion, but a true opinion. But put this fancy to the test, and it proves groundless ... The most that can be maintained is, that we seek for a belief that we shall think to be true" (Peirce, 1955, pp. 10–11). He also went on to write: "Unless we make ourselves hermits, we shall necessarily influence each other's opinions; so that the problem becomes how to fix belief, not in the individual merely, but in the community" (p. 13).

The chapters of the book illustrate the kind of ongoing dialogue that we believe to be consistent with our belief that knowledge, including scientific knowledge, is a product of "influencing each other's opinions" in the continuing quest for the "fixation of belief" in a community of which we are part. Peirce was very far from advocating a kind of inquiry that is lacking in rigor, and we share his unfailing commitment to the touchstone of the empirical. However, he also accorded fully as much credit to the speculative, creative side of research (which he called *abduction*) as he did to inductive and deductive methodology. The reader will discover in the chapters of this volume the kind of blend we understand him to have had in mind: continually returning to describe and analyze, using empirical methods, that which we are trying to explain, but also striving to enunciate original theoretical intuitions that will encourage us to look at the world in new ways.

The volume is thus a report of our collective hands-on investigation into the life of organizations. We privilege a variety of methods: conversation analysis, ethnography, account analysis—all in their way delving into the dynamics of organizational discourse. However the book is also an exploration in the communicational theory of organization: from the managerial theory of accounting (Varey, chap. 10, this volume), to narrative theory (Taylor & Cooren, chap. 7, this volume), to worldview (Taylor & Cooren), to the relational bases of agency (Robichaud, chap. 6, this volume), to coorientation (Taylor, chap. 8, this volume), to activity theory (Groleau, chap. 9, this volume) and to the moral basis of agency (Brummans, chap. 11, this volume). Although the emphasis may shift from chapter to chapter, all of them grow out of the authors' involvement in empirical research and theoretical development. Taken together they illustrate, we hope, what is meant by a pragmatic approach to inquiry.

SOME DOMINANT THEMES

The chapters of this volume are organized into four sections to emphasize thematic convergences and facilitate reading. Nevertheless, the principal themes taken up for treatment in the volume actually cross-cut all of the chapters and provide the real unity of the whole. As we examine them in turn, the reader will, we hope, have a better idea of what is to come.

Integration, Differentiation, and Ambiguity

In chapter 7, Taylor and Cooren explore the structuring role of narrative in human communication. They present in some detail a rich theory of narrative inspired by the writings of a little known French theorist, Algirdas Greimas. A narrative, Greimas proposed, is initiated by the interference of two narrative paths, one of which (that of the protagonist) is the point of view privileged by the narrator, and the other (that of an antagonist) presents, to the protagonist, an unwanted disturbance that must be dealt with. The alternative point of view, the one that is not privileged, remains a shadowy virtuality: It could have been the focus, but then that would have been a different story—a story that was not told. As Brummans (chap. 11, this volume) argues, and as Greimas found, there is thus a moral decision to be confronted: whose values take precedence—whose story are we listening to? Narrative always presupposes a backdrop of established conventional values that justify the actions of the protagonist in opposing the moves of the antagonist.

In everyday life, this choice of perspective, which view is to be privileged and which is not, presents an issue to be pragmatically resolved in the cut-and-thrust of organizational conversation: Whose story is going to get told—given precedence? As Güney (chap. 2, this volume) observes, sensemaking—translating one's experience into an account of what is happening—never occurs in a vacuum. It is rooted in what people see as the raison d'être of not merely their organizational status, but of the roles and activities that give them and their community meaning: their investment in their work. Values are at stake, but so is their existence as socially validated actors.

To illustrate, she reports on an ethnographic study she conducted in a major high-tech corporation, that she calls Deep Purple. Asked to collaborate on the development of a new product, two divisions of the corporation experienced a sequence of conflict-laden episodes during which their spokespersons fell back on their respective statuses (program manager vs. senior engineer) to resist the imposition of a compromise solution. When negotiations broke down, their rear-guard maneuvers threatened the collaborative process with total collapse. Güney found that the representatives of the two design divisions proved incapable of making sense of their collaborative project beyond the agendas inherent in their respective positions. Güney documents, on the basis of her own observations, how these two teams oscillated between dissensus and consensus until they were finally obliged, by an application of *force majeure*, to come to a decision. She thus highlights the grounding of sensemaking in professional identity, a relationship that emerges in the course of professional collaboration involving different domains of work and expertise. In keeping with the both/and dynamic, Güney shows how such interunit processes require the parties who are involved to navigate a course between what separates and unites their respective agendas and identities.

As Weick (1995) and others have pointed out, how one makes sense of an organizational situation is influenced by one's organizational roles and functions. Taylor and Cooren (chap. 7, this volume), citing Greimas, see those roles and functions as composing a space, both material and cognitive. It is material because actors achieve a sense of identity through the objects they relate to, and value. The subject–object relationship is itself framed materially by the configuration of the space they are accustomed to navigating within (Suchman, 1996), and the way they schedule their time (Gomes da Silva & Wetzel, 2004). They develop modes of sensemaking that explain and justify their activities within that composite space. The result is an adapted (and adaptive) practice that is resistant to interference, if only because it is adaptive. Linking to another, and perceived to be incompatible, space configuration is thus menacing, especially when it is imposed from outside (as it was in Deep Purple). The result, as it manifests itself in the overt sensemaking of actors who represent their communities, is what Greimas calls a *polemic*. The protagonist comes to see the other agent's agenda as an obstacle to be overcome. Making sense, Güney argues, often consists of relating a given situation to who you are and what you are in charge of doing in an organization. Drawing on reflection on macro-actors for her analysis, she shows how these spokespersons, so typical of organizational settings, are worth concentrating our attention on because they are speaking not only for themselves but also for the organizational group they represent. The ambiguity engendered by a forced collaboration renders their room to maneuver problematical. The more spokespersons ground their acts on their official roles of representative of their group, the harder it becomes for them to enact their roles as sensemakers and facilitators of organizational sensemaking, and the more difficult it is to find a rallying point with what has now been identified as an antagonist.

This same interplay of agendas, the essence of sensemaking (emphasis on "making"), informs the research of Saludadez and Taylor (Chapter 3). They describe interdisciplinary collaboration among forestry scientists in three Asian nations: Malaysia, Thailand, and the Philippines. There too they find alternative, and sometimes competing, agendas operative in the working out of how to collaborate. There too the narratively based accounts of how collaboration had worked displayed varying levels of ambiguity. The authors delve somewhat further into the sources of effective collaboration by their emphasis on the grounding of people's sensemaking in practices that are situated in time and space, directed toward objects that are salient in that community. Worlds of sense are *enacted* worlds, in which Greimas's assumption (not dissimilar from that of Weick, 1995) that subjects and objects are mutually defining, is confirmed. Because the object world is circumstantial, both spatially and temporally, the negotiation of cross-situation identities means reconciling more than cognitively grounded accounts. It means reconstructing the relationship of subject to object, materially as well as symbolically; in effect reconstructing the circumstances of collaboration. Like Güney (chap. 2, this volume), and Robichaud (chap. 6, this volume), the authors highlight the relational construction of meaning.

Katambwe and Taylor (chap. 4, this volume) address the same theme of reconciliation involving opposing agendas, and the play of organizational sensemaking, in a slightly different way. They argue that organizational integration and differentiation (Lawrence & Lorsch, 1969) should be treated as what they call "two sides of the same coin." By analyzing in some detail the dynamic of a managerial discussion, where there are different agendas and different interests in play, these authors show that the resulting conversation can be seen as an activity in which participants enact both differentiation and integration, and on a continuing basis. Although the tension is never resolved, it is mitigated by a complex language game in which participants align and realign themselves with others in conversational patterns of association and dissociation.

Like Güney, Katambwe and Taylor highlight how roles, statuses, and organizational identities, the usually taken-for-granted tissue of relations that they call the subtext of the conversation, may surface to become a bone of contention, if for no other reason than that this tissue of relationships, defining as it does relative power and status, functions as a kind of organizational constitution.

Using excerpts from a meeting that took place between top managers over problems of succession and organizational structure, Katambwe and Taylor show how direct and indirect expressions of rights and responsibilities allow interlocutors to navigate between integration and differentiation. The resulting sustained level of interactive ambiguity allows each member to mark that which differentiates the membership in terms of individual rights and responsibilities (including his or her own), while reaffirming what is supposed to be achieved collectively (i.e., integration). Members are delicately balanced between independence and cooperation, centralization and decentralization, flexibility and coordination. Organizational communication implies navigating between unity and diversity, between integration and differentiation.

The Indispensability of Agency to Organizing

The issue of agency, in one guise or another, arises in almost every chapter of the book. As Robichaud (chap. 6, this volume) points out, the idea that agent is a synonym for actor has a long history in Western thought (e.g., Giddens, 1984, still uses the two terms "interchangeably"). However, the usefulness of this way of defining agency, consistent with construing the individual as the locus of action and knowledge, is less apparent when the perspective is communicational. This is especially true for researchers who are committed to understanding organizational communication, because the building block of organization is inherently relational: how to stitch together individual efforts to weave a tissue of concerted action—not a sum of individual acts but a tying together of them. How this weaving is accomplished, practically and theoretically, is a topic addressed by several authors in this volume. They all mobilize the concepts of agent and agency, but in distinctly different ways.

Suppose, like Giddens, Cooren asks in chapter 5, we discard notions of macro and micro. Then we will have to concentrate on the "flatland" of human communication. How are we to explain the persistence of structure in a flat landscape? The answer, Cooren argues, is to take account of agency, and how it is inscribed in the material and symbolic world that constitutes the environment in which our activities unfold. Only by taking the reality of material agents seriously can we possibly account for the multiple ways our everyday actions are channeled into predictable patterns, usually without our even being conscious of the channeling. Cooren then offers an abundance of examples drawn from his ethnographic research to illustrate how "structure" is built into—part of—a hybrid material–symbolic world. If we are to act at all, we can only do so by patterning our interventions to both conform to and exploit the rutted paths the environment offers us.

Cooren is asking us to think about agent in a new way, as that which acts, whether its embodiment be human or nonhuman. An agent is that, in other words, which has an effect on our behavior. It may be inscribed in a human policeman, but it might equally well take the materialization of a stoplight or a sign or a speed bump. The issue is not the ostensible intention of the police agent (human or nonhuman), a psychological state, but the capacity he, she, or it has to communicate an effect. As Cooren observes, this is the lever that enables us to explain that most indispensable of all organizational characteristics: acting at a distance and over time—*tele*acting. If our intentions can be inscribed into material objects that have durability and transportability (Innis, 1951) then these latter become capable of acting for us, even when we are not physically—or even consciously—present. The effect persists, even when the effecter no longer cares, or even exists. Our actions have become *imbricated* (Taylor, 2001b): translated into media with organizing properties. And organization can grow larger.

The difference between little organizations like family get-togethers and voluntary work groups, and the behemoths that inhabit the global environment, is not that the principles of communication have changed, but that the material media of communication are different (Latour, 1986). The larger conglomerates are different, and open the door to greater complexity, because they make teleacting not just feasible, but inevitable.

For Robichaud (chap. 6, this volume) the debate over whether agency is a concept that should be restricted to what humans do, and intend, or enlarged to include nonhuman embodiments, is beside the point. Robichaud proposes an alternative concept that he calls a relational view of agency and intentionality. Agency and intention can be lodged neither in the individual human being nor in the material inscription, because the concepts of agent and intention are inherently relational, rather than substantial. Taking Peirce's (1931/1960, 1992) relational ontology and Wittgenstein's (1953) externalist thesis as his basis, Robichaud then argues that we should consider the very notion of agency to be meaningless if its intentional structure is not taken into account. This intentional structure is conceived of as a network of connectedness arising out of the engagement of humans in a pluralistic environment. As Robichaud writes, "Intentions are not a property of human mental activities, but are properties of institutionalized nets of practices emerging out of the conversations in which we constantly redefine our connections to others, machines, nature, and texts" (p. 114).

The concept of nonhuman agency ceases to be paradoxical, once we recognize the role of institutionalized "types of agency" that define a priori how things get done in our world. To the extent that one can say, for instance, that "A's memo *informs* us of our boss's resignation," "this form *indicates* who needs to sign," or "my computer *warns* me that the battery is almost down," then agency is nonhuman. However, to say this does not mean that we have disposed of the question of intentionality. On the contrary, as Robichaud points out, recognizing these forms of agency consists in simultaneously recognizing that humans do send memos to other humans to provide them with information and directives, that humans design and create forms so that other humans can sign and fill them in, and that humans design computers so that they can inform users of potential troubles. In other words, the nonhuman agency illustrated by the preceding sentences consists of acts of delegation embedded in institutionalized practices that define how and why these nonhumans do what they do. And, as Taylor and Cooren (chap. 7, this volume) show, those institutional frames are ultimately grounded in narrative.

Brummans (chap. 11, this volume) addresses the question of agency from a different angle, in that he problematizes agency through the lens of positioning and ethics. Brummans argues that attributing agency to a specific entity (whether human, nonhuman, individual, or collective) is not only an epistemological act, but also implies a political and strategic positioning with ethical consequences. Echoing Deetz (2001), cited earlier, he invites us to consider how a school of research, such as his own, positions itself in the larger language game of the discipline. Brummans argues for an enlarged reflection on agency, communication, and organization, one that focuses on how agents get added to or subtracted from the portrait of a given disciplinary configuration. As he points out, this selection process has important consequences for whom and what is deemed to be invited, or allowed to participate, in collective activities, and who gets excluded.

Agency is therefore, according to Brummans, a central issue confronting organizational communication scholars. A focus on agency not only allows researchers to position our own field of study in the larger field of the social sciences but pushes us to reflect on our own practice as academics. Using Cooren's analysis in chapter 5 as data, Brummans shows how organizational controversies boil down to debates as to who or what is ultimately acting; that is, who or what is ultimately responsible for what happened or is happening in a given situation. To address ethical issues in this manner illuminates not only the corporate scandals where issues of responsibility are raised, but also the interplay between schools of thought and the politico-epistemic game so typical of academic life. Brummans thus encourages us to consider how much of our (societal, organizational, interpersonal) world is a contestatory field of debate centered on who or what is doing something. In other words, agency is not a "capacity to act" to be defined a priori. On the contrary it is "the capacity to act" that is discovered when studying how worlds become constructed in a certain way.

Groleau's chapter (chap. 9, this volume) is a comparison of some of the assumptions that underpin a theory of action called activity theory, which is similar in certain ways to the approach favored by the researchers in this volume, and coorientation theory (Taylor, chap. 8, this volume). The best known contemporary interpreter of activity theory is Yrjö Engeström of the University of Helsinki. Like Cooren, Engeström emphasizes the mediating role of tools, whether material or symbolic: technology. He too sees action as a hybrid phenomenon. In other respects, however, the emphasis in the two approaches is different. For Engeström, the issue is one of the relationship of individual (or team) actions, mediated by tools, and the system of activity within which they are embedded. For Engeström (1990), an activity system is what he calls a "molar" unit, in that individual actions are articulated with those of other actors (not necessarily physically present)—the institution and practice of Major League Baseball, for example. This leads Engeström to conceive of individual action as located within a community that is in turn a basis for normative constraints, or rules, and imposes a division of labor on its members. Where he differs is in his emphasis on the contradictions that inevitably arise in any complex system that, he claims, are the generative impulse leading to transformations of the system, as contradictions are resolved.

Like Cooren, Engeström (1990) emphasizes the channeling effect of history— a history that is embedded in multiple ways not only in the physical, but equally in the symbolic environment that frames activities. Where their explanations differ, on the other hand, is in the emphasis they place on communication. Engeström's agent (or subject) is the privileged point of view for examining a system. For Cooren, on the other hand, action is that which is "shared between actors." Action, Cooren is saying, is grounded in a relationship. To be an agent is not only to act, but to act for. A relationship is forged in the acting for, and the product of all the imbricated relationships is the organization: a chain of agents. Any member of an organization, in turn, is empowered in that, because the organization exists, he or she is thus entitled to act, work, and talk in its name: act for it, represent it— re-present it, make it present. It is precisely the appropriation of one actor's action by another, Cooren argues, that constitutes the web of organizational relationships. The power to act is the very basis of organization, the intrinsic motivation for its presence as a social agent. Because relationships are dynamic, so is organization, and so is the distribution of power.

Sensemaking and Accounting: A Coorientational View

A third theme that runs through most chapters centers on how people account for their own and others' actions—"make sense"—and how such accounts both reflect and inform communication. Sensemaking in a collaborative process, Güney (chap. 2, this volume) argues, for example, requires that actors be able to rise above their designated positions to engage in a genuine negotiation if they are to arrive at a framework that will provide a platform for future collaboration. Both Robichaud (chap. 6, this volume) and Brummans (chap. 11, this volume) focus on how people manage to account for their own and others' actions. Building on a Peircean logic, Robichaud, for example, points out that meaningful action is fundamentally triadic, in that action–reaction only becomes knowable by the intervention of sensemaking: making a link that is inherently interpretive. Brummans similarly argues that academics situate themselves, and are given greater or lesser credibility, by the accounts they construct.

In chapter 10, Varey presents a somewhat different perspective on sensemaking that reflects his own commitment as a professor of management, and specifically of the managerial field known as accounting. Varey points out that management has tended, traditionally, to be conceived of as the science of the "command and control" of human and technical resources. It is a conception of communication and organization that has been dubbed the *conduit metaphor* (Putnam et al., 1996; Smith, 1993), because communication is reduced to the linear transmission of information and reproduction of intended meaning. This limited but persistent portrait of what managerial work entails tends to overshadow another dimension of managerial communication, its performative character.

Communication, as other chapters have illustrated, does not consist of merely offering a representation of the world; it is also about performance, acting. Varey explores this critical difference from the perspective of *accounting*, a term that he uses to indicate how members' activities can be understood as contributing to the creation of a world, and not simply as reaffirming it in a representation. Mintzberg's (1973) and Gronn's (1983) landmark studies, for example, have made us aware that the work of managers is accomplished through talk. In this chapter Varey highlights what he calls the *accountable* dimension of their communicative work. Through accounts, managers not only claim to represent a given reality, but they actively participate in its construction by providing their own credible explanations of what is done and what should be done.

Accounts are used to build positions that fulfill programs of action and reaffirm agendas. The manager's role, as Varey points out, thus consists of trying to control the meaning of a situation; that is, to find in the varieties of accounts being offered a justification of collective activities, and a portrait of a situation that gives a preferred line of action, and its consequences, legitimacy. Because people with competing agendas constantly attempt to influence one another with regard to how to behave and what to think, the manager thus becomes someone who must be aware of the relational dimension of communication, and of how to establish relations with others as well as how others relate to him or her.

Varey enjoins management scholars and practitioners to pay attention to both the textual (representative) and conversational (performative) dimensions of organizational communication. Practically speaking, this shift means that managers move beyond the role of controller to that of steward; that is, to a role that consists of taking into account the different communities of practice that constitute their organization: to, in effect, referee which accounts (or texts) are given precedence. The manager's role therefore has to be conceived as integrative: observing and reworking in conversation the many different accounts originating from various communities of practice to synthesize what can be considered by members the organizational text or account. The leader must, to echo Katambwe and Taylor (chap. 4, this volume), manage differentiation in the search for integration.

The command and control dimension of managerial work does not altogether disappear in this image of management (the organizational text and its integrative authority still exist), but managing is transformed into dealing with the contested and negotiated accounts that pervade the organization. Understood as an accounting practice, management keeps its central concern for adequate description (the textual dimension), while attempting, through conversation, to manage the relations that are being established there. Managing becomes a difficult feat—maintaining a balance between control and integration. There is almost certainly no unique solution to this kind of ambiguity.

In chapter 8, Taylor offers a synthesis of these threads by explicating a concept that he terms *coorientation*. Communication, he argues (following Maturana, 1997), exists in the borderland between two orders of reality (that Maturana calls "ontogenies"): a material world (the body and its extensions, in a way) and a symbolic world (the domain of sensemaking). Sensemaking, accounting, and knowledge are all instances of the construction of a representation (or, to use Wittgenstein's [1953] term, *picture*), in language, by means of which we humans become observers of ourselves. By being observers, we are enabled to be simultaneously both in and out of the world of sensory experience. Out of this tension arises the capacity to construct subject–object relationships, like those described by Robichaud (chap. 6, this volume), as something that we understand: a "thirdness," to use Peirce's term. But language is inherently an interactive medium, a medium of exchange. The symbolic realm is thus also a social realm. The construction of sense and meaning occurs as an ongoing project, involving both the endless search for a persuasive text and the negotiation of its construction in conversation. This dynamic is what is meant by coorientation. The remainder of the chapter is devoted to an examination of the mechanisms that language offers by which the coorientational dialogue is maintained, as Katambwe and Taylor (chap. 4, this volume) illustrate.

The complexity of the process of identity construction is in turn examined by Taylor and Cooren (chap. 7, this volume) in their analysis of the dynamic of an ordinary business conversation conducted in a New York high-rise office building. Human communication of the kind that is typical of management and the conduct of affairs more generally, evokes background understandings of two-party transactions, where the "parties" are categories, such as doctor–patient, lawyer–client, salesperson–customer, or parent–child. But how such categories get played out in a given conversation is not predetermined: It depends on the ingenuity of the people who are interacting. What remains to be explored in future research is the longer term dynamic of background–foreground: how our deep assumptions about society both inform, and are transformed by, over time, the conversations of the people who make up the society.

Coorientation theory is one way of linking the subjective, social, and the objective, material worlds within a single framework. But as Groleau (chap. 9, this volume) points out in her critique of activity and coorientation theories, that leaves open the question of emphasis. Engeström focuses on action, giving its discursive framework a secondary importance. Those who associate with coorientation theory are far from insensible to the embedded-in-action nature of human discourse (indeed, they insist on it), but their emphasis tends to be elsewhere, in the organizing dynamic that language-in-use makes possible. Both perspectives, Groleau argues, should be part of a larger view of how organization gets constituted.

What Is Shared in Common by All Those Who Contributed to the Book

What the reader encounters in this volume is not the presentation of a particular theory. The background assumptions, the empirical involvements, and the diversity of origins of the participants militate against any kind of standardization. Instead, we hope what the reader will discover is an invitation to enter a dialogue in which there is ample room for diversity. We remain committed to both/and, not either/or, thinking. Yet we also recognize there has to be a broad substratum of shared background assumptions: a rock-bottom platform. Those background assumptions include the following.

We are committed, for example, to always starting from, rather than arriving at, communication as the essential premise of every inquiry. Thus, we never begin by looking at knowledge, as originating in the individual and his or her particular situation, and then, subsequently, asking how it gets transmitted in communication, as many authors do. From a communicational perspective, we concentrate on knowledge, what it is, and what it does.

We are all committed to the idea that to be in communication is to be involved in a world that is both material and social, both concrete and abstract. This, of course, poses a challenge that we, as researchers, struggle to meet, each in our own way: What kind of theory of communication might be compatible with such a dualistic vision, and how can we use it in the conduct of empirical research?

Third, we also share an emphasis on the role of language in human communication. We understand that communication mobilizes many kinds of language, not just spoken and written. Nevertheless, language in the narrower sense of what we say and write is the dominating mode of sensemaking. In the absence of speaking and writing there would be no multinationals, and no great modern states. Language is indispensable to organizing "in the large."

This is the basis of a further commitment that we share, which is to understand the complexity of language as having more than one manifestation: as being both a tool for individual expression and self-assertion, and the enabler of forms of organizing that entail conversation and coorientation. This recognition of the duality of language-in-use imposes an agenda of research: to understand the dynamic of communication as both system and product. From this flows a further commitment, not just to study communication, but to always do so in an effort to understand that most dominant of all human accomplishments: complex organization.

Finally, we share a more diffuse but important commitment, to sustain, and even enhance, the openness of our discipline, which the authors cited at the beginning of the chapter emphasized. Of the 10 authors who contributed to the writing of this book, English is the first language for only 3 of them (Taylor, Van Every and Varey), and 2 of the latter have pursued their career at non-English-language universities (Taylor, Van Every). Three authors received their doctoral degrees at American universities (Brummans, Güney, and Taylor) but only one (Güney) now teaches in the United States. The countries of origin of authors (in alphabetical order) include Canada, the Democratic Republic of the Congo, England, France, the Netherlands, the Philippines, and Turkey.

We believe this is not an accident; the world of research has been, and is, changing very fast. Of the 30 authors who contributed to the 2001 *New Handbook of Organizational Communication*, for example, only one (Lars Christensen) had an affiliation with a non-American university. That is a fair image of where the field stood in the mid-1990s, when the chapters of the *Handbook* were being prepared. It is no longer the case. Globalization, we believe, means an infusion of new ideas and ways of thinking, different from, and yet complementing, the rich fabric of intellectual inquiry that the field has inherited from its founders. Hopefully, this book is an illustration of the kind of marriage of ideas we believe in.

Ours is a new discipline, comparatively, and as so many analysts have pointed out before, one that has exceptionally open boundaries. We think this is an advantage, and the chapters of the book illustrate in practice our willingness to reach out beyond the official limits of the field called organizational communication to collaborate with those in allied domains who bring to the table different cultural and intellectual habits of thought, and draw on sources of ideas that may initially seem unfamiliar but ultimately open doors to new ways of conceptualizing communication and conducting research.

Structure of the Chapters

Briefly, the chapters are the following:

- Chapter 2: Senem Güney explores sensemaking in a high-tech firm where interdivisional integration comes close to foundering because of the inability of interactors to overcome considerations of role and status.

- Chapter 3: Jean A. Saludadez and James R. Taylor address a not dissimilar pattern of intercommunity collaboration among Asian scientists involved in joint projects and find a mixed pattern of sensemaking, from successful to unsuccessful.
- Chapter 4: Joël Mulamba Katambwe and James R. Taylor analyze the conversation of a management council facing an organizational crisis to investigate integration and differentiation.
- Chapter 5: François Cooren uses his ethnographic fieldwork to illustrate and motivate a treatment of the role of nonhuman agents in the structuring of organizational communication.
- Chapter 6: Daniel Robichaud returns to the theme of agency, developed by Cooren in chapter 5, to place it within the pragmatic tradition associated with Peirce, and to reiterate the importance of relations of triadicity, or "thirdness," in understanding agency.
- Chapter 7: James R. Taylor and François Cooren explore the narrative bases of sensemaking, in both theory and practice, and make a link with the preexisting literature on worldview.
- Chapter 8: James R. Taylor presents a somewhat more elaborated defense of his notion of coorientation, and develops a justification of the centrality of text–conversation interaction.
- Chapter 9: Carole Groleau delves further into the concept of coorientation by contrasting it with the principles of activity theory, as propounded by Engeström.
- Chapter 10: Richard J. Varey takes a more theoretical look at the business of sensemaking, that he, in the tradition of Garfinkel, calls accounting, to highlight its importance in the daily practices of management.
- Chapter 11: Boris H. J. M. Brummans offers an overview of the place of the approach elucidated in this volume within the encompassing field of organizational communication to argue that all research is in the end grounded in values.

PART I

INTEGRATION, DIFFERENTIATION, AND AMBIGUITY

CHAPTER TWO

Making Sense of a Conflict as the (Missing) Link Between Collaborating Actors

Senem Güney
University at Albany, SUNY

The framework of organizational sensemaking (Weick, 1995, 2001b) is built on analytical concepts that illuminate local and emergent phenomena among organizational actors, who continuously engage each other to create apparent order out of not so apparently connected instances of their everyday actions. This interpretive framework, with its emphasis on the processes of creating and sustaining an organization through the work of interacting actors, has understandably had a significant influence on research in organizational communication (Cooren, 2004a; Manning, 1992; Miller, 1999; Taylor & Van Every, 2000; Weick, 1983, 1989; Weick & Browning, 1986).

The interpretive framework of organizational sensemaking shows us the structure of organizational processes as systems of shared meaning. This framework has provided analysts with a powerful tool to investigate instances of interactional crises in organizations, in terms of what Weick (1993) called the "collapse of sensemaking" in high-reliability organizations, such as the organization among crewmembers in a cockpit or in a firefighting team. We still need to see, however, more empirically based research on the local enactment of organizational roles whose actors participate in the making and sometimes in the collapse of shared meaning that sustains their organization. This chapter reports such empirical research.

Conflicts during organizational decision-making processes are instances in the everyday life of an organization where the apparent order among the actors is visibly challenged. During moments of conflict, organizational sensemaking may come close to the point of collapsing. We may assume that actors involved in these moments would interact to re-engage each other to become collectively heedful (Weick & Roberts, 1993) toward cues connecting past and ongoing events to establish a shared meaning for what is going on around them—if they intend to resolve their conflict. A shared effort at organizational sensemaking, in other words, is a fundamental communicative strategy to work through conflict. The question of whether this communicative strategy is as easily practiced as it is theorized remains to be answered.

This chapter investigates how actors accomplish the task of making collective sense of their actions when emergent threats to their apparent order arise. I examine the interactions between two organizations within a corporate structure in the process of product definition, as these organizations collaboratively develop a high-technology product. My goal is to show that sensemaking is an emergent activity that cuts across the communicative work of actors with distinct official roles—representing distinct perspectives and expectations—in the designed organizational structure (Weick, 2001c; Wenger, 2002). Weick (1995) discussed identity as a fundamental pillar of organizational sensemaking. There is, however, a lack of empirical research that shows how the official roles of organizational actors affect their collective construction of who they are and what they are doing together in the process of sensemaking. This chapter is intended as a beginning to fill this gap in the current literature.

Taylor and Van Every (2000) argued that organization is the site and consequence of communicative work among "macroactors," who speak not only for themselves but also for the organizational group they represent. I take this definition of organization and examine how macroactors enact their emergent sensemaking role in local contexts of organizational life. My findings indicate that established structures of organizational processes pose barriers against the recognition and enactment of the sensemaking role. The harder it becomes for macroactors to carry out their roles as sensemakers and facilitators of organizational sensemaking, the more they ground their representative acts on their official roles. In cases where the official roles place representative macroactors in radically dissenting positions in a conflict, communication between the conflicting groups continuously steers away from resolution and follows the direction of forced integration. If the conflict persists long enough, such forced integration leads the interactions between the participants to a point where their collective sensemaking completely dissolves.

In the following sections of this chapter, I will outline the organizational context of the ethnographic case that provides the empirical grounding for this study. This outline is followed by an examination of two organizational roles that come to represent two different sides—with their different organizational perspectives and expectations—in a conflict between two organizations. I then describe the specific events in the case that shed light on the issues under investigation. The chapter continues with my observations on how these roles are enacted in ways that undermine the sensemaking process between two organizations and paralyze their negotiations. I conclude my discussion with the implications of these observations for our understanding of collaborative action and sensemaking in organizations.

ORGANIZATIONAL CONTEXT
OF THE ETHNOGRAPHIC CASE

Data for this investigation come from my fieldwork conducted between May 2001 and December 2002 in a large corporation of technology development, which I call

Deep Purple.[1] My fieldwork focused on the collaborative activity between distinctly existing organizations within a common corporate structure. I conducted a significant part of my participant-observations, on-site interviews, and phone interviews with members across different sites in Hotville—one of the four development sites for Deep Purple server systems. I visited Snowfield, which is about 1,100 miles north of Hotville, with a group of members from Hotville for 4 days in October 2001. During this visit, I observed a series of meetings between members from the Hotville and Snowfield sites and interviewed members from Snowfield. Events that led to the meetings in October 2001 provide the empirical evidence in this chapter.

Hotville has the landscape of a midsize city that is a cross between a college town and a high-tech boom town in the southwestern United States. Snowfield is a small Midwestern town where the major sources of employment are computer development, health care, and dairy farming. The differences between the Hotville and Snowfield organizations of Deep Purple, however, were not simply related to their regional distinctions. These two organizations under a common corporate frame had quite distinct presences as development organizations within Deep Purple and as producers of Deep Purple brands in the market. The Hotville brand of server products was pushing to establish a leading position in its market segment with its high-performance hardware. These products responded to the computing needs of customers like the U.S. Defense Department and multinational technical research institutions. The Snowfield brand was leading the market with smaller machines that provided the capability to integrate different software applications. This innovative capability significantly increased the shelf life of these products and appealed to customers like small and midsize businesses.

At the time of my fieldwork, Deep Purple development organizations were in the process of implementing a corporate strategy to create a common family of server systems among distinct brands that were being developed in four different sites. The Hotville organization was about to launch what members called the "breakthrough system" Royal Fleet PT in December 2001. The Royal Fleet product family was being collaboratively developed between the Hotville and Snowfield organizations under the strategy to create a common family of Deep Purple servers. The "high-end" system[2] Royal Fleet PT—the first product to be launched as part of this common family—was still mostly associated with the Hotville organization, because high-end servers with high hardware performance were the mark of the Hotville brand in the market.

In September 2001, as the Hotville organization was heavily immersed in the December launch of Royal Fleet PT, members from the Hotville and Snowfield organizations began negotiations to define the features of next-generation products in

---

[1]All names used in this text are pseudonyms.

[2]Server systems come in three categories of products: high-end, midrange, and low-end/entry-level, which indicate different levels of sophistication and computing power.

the Royal Fleet family. Royal Fleet PT+ was the next-generation high-end system that was to be launched in 2004. In the first 2 weeks of product planning negotiations, interactions among the collaborators from Hotville and Snowfield took an unanticipated turn. Members from the two collaborating organizations held radically different positions about the definition of next-generation products. These different positions grew into a conflict about whether the position of Hotville or that of Snowfield would dominate in the product definition process. Before giving more specific details on the events that took place around this conflict, I focus briefly on the roles of program management and senior engineering in the development of Deep Purple systems.

TWO KEY ROLES IN THE ORGANIZATIONAL STRUCTURE OF DEVELOPMENT ACTIVITY: PROGRAM MANAGEMENT AND SENIOR ENGINEERING

Organizations are constructions of functional units with members who are supposed to work together for the achievement of a common goal. In high-technology development, these functional units are so numerous and their work processes are based on such sophisticated knowledge that their coordination for the development of a final product is an organizational function itself. Performing this function is the role of program management in Deep Purple. Program managers oversee the development process of a hardware system and make sure that the final product—with the committed features in the product plan—is released to the market on time and within budget. The role of coordinating and monitoring the work of different functions is designed as the official role of program management into the organizational activity setting of technology development.

In technology development, some functional units are involved in the definition of innovative concepts for products, whereas others get involved in the implementation of defined concepts. Innovations are expected to give products the edge to reach the ultimate goal in this extremely fast-paced and competitive industry: higher market share. In a development organization, senior engineers and their teams commit significant amounts of their time and professional knowledge to come up with designs that improve the technical sophistication of products. The official role of senior engineering exists to create and maintain technological innovativeness to keep the products at the leading edge in the market.

The distinct organizational roles of program management and senior engineering position the actors of these roles within intersecting and yet significantly conflicting spaces in the established structures of organizational processes like product definition. Senior engineers enact the role of pushing for more sophisticated, and inherently more time-consuming and expensive, definitions for products. Program managers carry out the role of defending boundaries that are imposed by schedule and budget on product definitions. Development of innovative technology requires the enactment of both roles, which are, ideally, given a brief period to interact at the early phase of product definition. During this phase, senior engineers propose new designs for new-generation products and program managers make the case for the required resources to develop the proposed designs. Negotiations over product definitions are based on the presentation of technical data that represent various possibilities and constraints for the development process to the executive decision makers. Once the executive decisions are made, interactions among different development groups about what they are (expected to be) building together are supposed to phase out so that the development activity can begin.

The enactment of organizational roles, like the roles of program manager and senior engineer, takes actors outside the formal contexts of interaction between these roles. Project status meetings, which are formally structured as contexts of interaction to "present technical data," for example, reveal intense clashes between different positions about the ongoing development activity. Actors engage in these moments to perform their roles representing different organizational perspectives and expectations. Sustaining collaborative action becomes increasingly more difficult when the actors' representations of what they are (expected to be) doing together founder on the official definitions of organizational roles that represent radically different perspectives about the ongoing development activity—like the roles of program manager and senior engineer. The ethnographic case in this chapter evolved around a moment of deadlock in the interactions between Anthony, the hardware system program manager of Royal Fleet PT+ in Hotville, and Greg, the leading senior engineer of a firmware[3] design team in Snowfield.

COMMUNICATIVE EVENTS IN THE ETHNOGRAPHIC CASE

During the first 2 weeks of negotiations to define Royal Fleet PT+, interactions between Anthony and Greg brought to the surface a radical disagreement between the Hotville and Snowfield organizations. Members of the Snowfield organization were pushing for a change in the product plan of Royal Fleet PT+ to include the innovative firmware function NuevoHyp in the product definition. A firmware design team led by Greg in Snowfield was developing the NuevoHyp function, which had achieved successful results in the low-end servers of the Snowfield brand. Building NuevoHyp into a high-end product, with a design that had more similarity with the Hotville brand than with the Snowfield brand, however, would mean testing this innovative function in a new and different environment. Both the members of the Hotville firmware design team and Anthony were against this proposal. They argued that such a significant shift in the product definition would put serious strains on their already short resources and jeopardize the development process. This

---

[3]In server technology, firmware—which is also called engineering software—is an interface function between the hardware and the operating system. This function helps minimize the impact of hardware design changes on the use of a particular operating system.

might risk the timely release of Royal Fleet PT+, which carried the promise of stellar success and high revenue for the Hotville organization and for the common family of Deep Purple servers.

Interactions on the phone and over e-mail about the definition of Royal Fleet PT+ between the members of the Hotville and the Snowfield organizations came to a complete stop when Greg refused to continue discussions with Anthony. Anthony was excluded from the list of recipients in an e-mail invitation from Snowfield that called for an urgent phone conference with higher level development executives from Hotville, Snowfield, and Oldnorth.[4] Anthony found out about this invitation from a development manager who came to his office with a printout of the e-mail note and asked Anthony what was going on. Anthony later got himself invited to the urgent phone conference about Snowfield's proposal to include NuevoHyp into Royal Fleet PT+. Follow-up phone conferences were held for a week between the different sites. At the end of this week, senior executives decided that representatives from Hotville and Snowfield needed to meet face-to-face to come up with a resolution.

Representatives from the two organizations held face-to-face meetings that ran 8 to 10 hours a day from the early morning of October 15 to the late afternoon of October 18, locked in a conference room—almost literally—in Snowfield. The day-long data presentation and discussion sessions were arbitrated by Anthony and John, a distinguished engineer from Snowfield who was working on the software strategy for common servers. During 4 days, members of design teams from Snowfield and Hotville presented technical data and argued for their different positions about which firmware function should go into Royal Fleet PT+. The meetings started in an extremely tense atmosphere, which did not disappear throughout the 4 days. The key participants were operating under the threat "to decide what to do or lose their jobs." Corporate executives communicated the seriousness of this threat in phone calls when they told the two sides not to leave the conference room before they reached an agreement about the definition of next-generation Royal Fleet products, and specifically about the definition of Royal Fleet PT+.

During the meetings, participants from Snowfield sat on one side and participants from Hotville sat on the other side of a large conference table, and no one, except for Anthony and John, changed the location of their seats during the 4 days of meetings. At some moments, Anthony and John sat side by side at one end of the table; at other moments, Anthony sat with Hotville members and John sat with Snowfield members. Anthony had a stress ball that he would throw to a participant, either from Hotville or Snowfield, to give that participant the turn to speak. There would be some curt laughter when Anthony threw the ball, and then the catcher would start talking. At one point on the second day of the meetings, Anthony threw

---

[4]Oldnorth is another Deep Purple development site, which is about 1,800 miles to the northeast of Hotville. The history of server development in Deep Purple and the geographic proximity of Oldnorth to the corporate headquarters make this site the residence of many corporate executives.

the ball to Greg. Greg did not move to catch the ball and it fell on the floor. The project manager on Greg's team, Stan, picked up the ball, looking at Greg, whose gaze was fixed on the slide that was up on the projector. Greg was paying no attention to the ball. Stan put the ball on the table in front of Greg, who began talking without shifting his gaze from the slide to look at either the ball or at anyone in the room. The emotional intensity of the interactions during the data presentations, which was reflected in this moment, characterized the encounters between the participants from Hotville and Snowfield during the 4 days.

At the end of the fourth day, John presented a summary of the cases made by the two sides to an audience of executives. This audience included the vice president of hardware strategy for common servers, the director of the Hotville firmware design group, the director of software strategy for common servers—who was also the director of the Snowfield firmware design group—and the director of the hardware program management of common servers. Anthony was also there. John's presentation laid out the advantages and risks—based on technical data that had been brought up by the development teams from Hotville and Snowfield—about including NuevoHyp in the next generation of the Royal Fleet server family. John's summary put forward a slightly different version of the original Hotville view over Snowfield's alternative proposition. The summary recommended the introduction of NuevoHyp into the common product line through low-end servers, unless the executives were willing to take the risks imposed on the schedule by developing Royal Fleet PT+ with a new feature. The executive decision makers adopted the recommendation to develop Royal Fleet PT+ without NuevoHyp and to include this new feature in the collaboratively developed low-end Royal Fleet servers, which were to be launched later than Royal Fleet PT+.[5]

COLLABORATION AND EMERGENCE OF ORGANIZATION

Organizations collaborate to achieve innovative solutions out of their existing ways of doing business. The fundamental advantage of collaboration is to create a framework for collective action among organizations so that they can achieve outcomes that they would not be able to achieve if they acted alone. The price of this advantage for the participants is to engage in complex discursive processes like negotiating a joint purpose, developing joint modes of operating, managing perceived (and real) power imbalances and accountabilities, and communicating across remote locations with different languages and cultures (Huxham & Vangen, 2000). The framework of collaborative action is discursively constructed as participants come together in local contexts of communication to negotiate the routines, procedures, and structures that delineate their roles and define their

---

[5]A couple of months after this decision, the next-generation low-end Royal Fleet servers in the development plan "died a budget death" and NuevoHyp did not become part of the collaboratively developed product line until the generation of products that came after the Royal Fleet family.

goals in the collaborative process. Communicative events—like project meetings where progress reports are presented, work sessions where product definitions are finalized, and urgent conference calls where disputes over plans are laid out—provide the local contexts for representing and negotiating who can legitimately make decisions or speak on behalf of the collaboration (Hardy, Lawrence, & Grant, 2005). Agreement on who represents what is not only a fundamental issue that the collaborating participants need to negotiate (Lawrence, Phillips, & Hardy, 1999), but collaborative action is in fact sustained through the ongoing discursive work of this negotiation.

Collaboration depends on the participants' ability to maintain a cooperative relationship without relying on the forms of control that normally guide organizational action (Hardy et al., 2005; Lawrence, Hardy, & Phillips, 2002; Phillips, Lawrence, & Hardy, 2000). Hardy et al. (2005) argued that market and hierarchical mechanisms of control do not operate within collaboration, even though these mechanisms might have prompted it to form. The ethnographic case in this chapter evolved in the context of the corporate initiative to build a common line of products between previously distinct Deep Purple brands. The Hotville and Snowfield organizations undertook the collaborative development of Royal Fleet servers because of this corporate initiative that responded to competitive market trends. Corporate decision makers, in other words, had formally defined the collaborative enterprise between Hotville and Snowfield in terms of what needed to be done (representing hierarchical control) to achieve what end (representing market control). Participants in this enterprise, however, were having difficulties sustaining their collaboration, even though they were acting under the mechanisms of control that were established to guide organizational action within their corporate structure.

According to Wenger (2002), organizations are social designs directed at practice and exist as dual structures, à la Giddens, reflecting the duality between the designed and the emergent. The designed structure defines organizations as institutions based on official definitions of roles and qualifications, distribution of authority, and relations of accountability. Institutions provide a "book to go by" for organizational actors through procedures, rules, policies, and so on. The emergent structure forms out of the practice of organizational life, as actors' response to the institutional "book." Wenger (2002) pointed to an inherent uncertainty between design and its realization in practice, because practice does not take place as a result of design, but rather as a response to it. Practice, in other words, is not realized by actors' strict reliance on design but by the continuous adaptation of their actions within the constraints and resources of design. Wenger's conceptualization of the duality between design and practice does not simply underline their coexistence as two distinct sources of organizational structuring. In Wenger's framework, organization happens where these two sources meet as they interact and influence each other. What Wenger described as design, which is reflected through the institutional book, parallels what Taylor and Van Every (2000) called the textualization of organization, referring to the construction of organization through communicative acts and artifacts. Taylor and Van Every's concept of co-orientation captures the duality that Wenger described to exist between the designed and the emergent sources of structuring. According to Taylor and Van Every's framework, the ongoing communicative work of coorientation between the relatively permanent structure of text and the relatively unpredictable processes of conversation becomes the locus of organizational action. Wenger showed us that organization emerges from the meeting of design and practice. Taylor and Van Every, on the other hand, located that meeting place in communication.

Collaborators, working to create new solutions out of existing ways, are frequently faced with situations that are hard to resolve by relying on the existing designed structures of their collaborating organizations. Constructing an emergent structure becomes the primary source of control and predictability over the collaborators' actions. The act of building an emergent order to give predictability to an otherwise unpredictable world is the act of organizational sensemaking (McDaniel, 1997). Actors engage in organizational sensemaking in their effort to construct the structure necessary for the continuity of their collective actions. Sensemaking becomes the overarching frame of interaction (Goffman, 1974) among actors in the practice of their organizational roles to construct an emergent structure for their collaboration.

Developers of high technology work within an activity context that is constantly (re)structured by the interaction between two opposing sets of parameters for successful achievement—whether that achievement is the work of one organization or of a collaborative enterprise. Technology development is a process of giving functionality to the most innovative product concept. One set of parameters for a successful development effort focuses on realizing competitive innovation. Developing an innovative product does not result in a successful achievement, however, unless the product is completed within budget and released on time to establish competitiveness in the market. The other set of parameters for success then focuses on the completion of the product according to plan. Neither set can singly represent the action framework to be constructed for the development process. Developers constantly negotiate and fine-tune the definition of the framework for their collective action that is grounded in the tension between two oppositional forces— one pulling in the direction of experimentation for innovativeness and the other pulling in the direction of boundary setting for effective manageability.

Using Wenger's (2002) terminology, we can argue that a development organization is a social design directed at the practice of creating innovation within particular technical and organizational limitations. This practice is built on interactivity between official roles, representing different organizational perspectives and expectations. The institution of a development organization grants the actors of these roles the representative authority to oppose each other within the designed structure of certain organizational processes. The institutional book description (Wenger, 2002)—or the organizational text (Taylor & Van Every, 2000)—in Deep Purple for the role of senior engineer gives the actor of this role (Greg from Snowfield in the case here) the representative authority to push for the most superior innovation. The same text holds the role of program manager (Anthony from Hotville) accountable for the completion of a product within predetermined bounds. Conflict becomes an inherent part of the interaction between these actors in the enactment of their organizational roles. The designed structure of defining Deep Purple servers limits the encounter between these two roles—and the potential for conflict during this encounter—to specific contexts at specific moments in the life cycle of a development project. The structure that emerges out of the practice of development activity, however, produces unpredictable conversations between the actors and triggers unexpected communicative events, as happened in the case being considered here.

REPRESENTATION AND SENSEMAKING IN COLLABORATIVE ORGANIZING

The ethnographic case in this chapter shows a sequence of communicative events in which collaborating actors were faced with the threat of not being able to move their interactions past a point of paralysis. The growing opposition between a senior engineer and a program manager was not quite unexpected in the product definition process, because these organizational roles in Deep Purple represent oppositional sets of parameters for what makes a project successful. Factors influencing the practice of this opposition, however, turned interactions between two collaborating development organizations into a conflict that almost dissolved their collective action. I argue that interactions among the collaborating actors evolved into this conflict because of the actors' inability to recognize and enact their roles as sensemakers in the local and emergent contexts of their collaboration. Why these actors—who were well qualified and motivated to successfully perform all aspects of their roles—had trouble recognizing and enacting their sensemaking role is the question that I pursue in this analysis.

Organizational sensemaking is about taking organizational action as an ongoing accomplishment that emerges from actors' efforts to create order and make retrospective sense of what occurs (Weick, 1995). Sensemaking actors are involved in actively constructing their environment by paying attention to cues to explain what outcomes are plausible for their actions. Weick's analysis of the Mann Gulch fire disaster (Weick, 1993) has become a landmark piece in the study of organizational sensemaking. In this piece, Weick analyzed how the interactive disintegration of the role structure among 16 Forest Service firefighters created a sudden collapse of sensemaking in their organization and caused 13 of them to burn to death. Weick observed that the mechanisms that dissolved the organization among the firefighters in Mann Gulch—emphasis on making decisions within the bounds of strategic rationality, conceptualization of role structures as static states, and experience of panic—are the mechanisms that make organizations vulnerable to the collapse of sensemaking.

Weick (1993) used the events that took place during the firefighters' struggle for their lives in Mann Gulch to describe how interactions among organizational actors can damage their intersubjective construction of a shared meaning for their actions and cause disruptions in their collective sensemaking. One significant event that Weick used in his analysis is the moment when the firefighter who was leading the crew's uphill escape shouted "Drop your tools!" as he saw the fire rapidly advancing toward the crew. Weick described this as a key moment in the dissolution of organization among the firefighters, who were rapidly losing their collective sense of what was happening around them:

> A fire crew that retreats from a fire should find its identity and morale strained. If the retreating people are then also told to discard the very things that are their reason for being there in the first place, then the moment quickly turns existential. If I am no longer a firefighter, then who am I? With the fire bearing down, the only possible answer becomes, An endangered person in a world where it is every man for himself. (p. 637)

It is important to understand that identity construction is a fundamental pillar of organizational sensemaking to see the inner workings of the mechanisms that disrupt this process. Weick (1995) described identity construction in sensemaking as actors' ongoing interpretations of the environment to maintain consistent and positive self-conceptions (regarding the actors' fit in the environment) that are in line with ongoing events. Actors make sense of what is happening around them by asking, "What implications do these events have for who I will be?" This sort of questioning underlines the interplay between the identity actors adopt to deal with their environment and what they think is going on in that environment. Actors define the meaning of events in terms of their understanding of who they become, where they fit in, and who and what they represent while dealing with events.

If the process of organizational sensemaking is grounded in identity construction, the analysis of this process, and the analysis of the factors leading to the collapse of this process, should focus on the communicative acts that reflect actors' sense of the organizational roles they represent in their actions. Examining these acts shows us how sensemaking actors become macroactors by representing the goals, values, and purposes—the identity—of their organization and help construct a shared meaning for the ongoing organizational action. The role of making and maintaining this meaning is necessary for the actors to (continue to) make collective sense of the events in their environment.

In the ethnographic case in this chapter, we see a sequence of communicative events that began with the interactions between Anthony, hardware system program manager, and Greg, senior engineer of firmware design. The organizational text defining Anthony's role gave him the task of bringing new hardware into production. The same text put Greg in charge of designing new firmware. These roles defined who Anthony and Greg were, where they fit, and what they represented in the designed structure of processes in two different Deep Purple development organizations. A corporate initiative then mandated that these two organizations collaborate on the development of a common line of products. Greg, operating under this initiative, made a move to import NuevoHyp, which his team was designing in Snowfield, into the new hardware system Royal Fleet PT+, which Anthony was producing in Hotville. This move was in line with what Greg was expected to do, based on his official role, to keep being who he was and what he stood for as a participant in a Deep Purple development project. For Anthony to keep being who he was and what he stood for in the designed structure of development in Deep Purple, he had to produce Royal Fleet PT+ on time and within budget with the already committed features, and that meant he could not add a new feature to his product at that point. We can see that Anthony and Greg are positioned in an oppositional relationship within the structure of product definition in Deep Purple, because in the enactment of their organizational roles, neither can give in to the other without having to ask "Then who am I?"

The outbreak of the conflict between Anthony and Greg seems inevitable given the timing, the designed structure of the development process, and the relationship between different organizational roles within Deep Purple. What made sense for Anthony, as a program manager, was to tell Greg, "Not now." In return, what made sense for Greg, as a senior engineer, was to push for his proposal. However, the inevitability of this conflict does not explain why it was pursued so intensely and persistently to a point where it almost became detrimental to the collaboration between Hotville and Snowfield. Why did Greg need to break off communications with Anthony, vilify him, and escalate their conflict to higher levels of authority within the corporation? Why were the actors from Hotville and Snowfield—all experienced and competent members of their organizations—not able to sort out the issues at hand and come to a resolution without any drama? My analysis suggests that the conflict over whether or not to include NuevoHyp in Royal Fleet PT+ called into question and jeopardized Anthony's and Greg's representative authorities in the process of defining a collaborative product between their respective organizations within Deep Purple. This moment of questioning about these (macro)actors' organizational reason for being amounted to a matter of life and death for the organizations they represented within the interactional context of the corporate mandate for collaboration.

"DROP YOUR TOOLS!"—EASIER SAID THAN DONE

Weick (1993) discussed how organizations become vulnerable to breakdowns in sensemaking when actors focus their attention on decision making within strategic rationality. He argued that sensemaking organizations rely on the ability of their actors to operate within contextual rationality, which calls on the actors to be sensitive to their need to "create and maintain intersubjectively binding normative structures that sustain and enrich their relationships" (pp. 634–635). In development organizations, actors orient to product definitions as organizational texts that represent the development activity as a sequence of decision-making steps toward the achievement of strategic goals. Product definitions, in other words, textually construct the "shared vision," which the actors are expected to follow, as a predetermined sequence of fixed states, leading to intended goals. In the structure of the product definition process, communicative events are designed as platforms of establishing consensus among the actors on the textual constructions (in the form of plans, schedules, worksheets, etc.) of their strategic goals. In the practice of these events, actors engage in conversations to explain, justify, challenge, understand, and reify their "shared vision." They hold meetings to determine product plans and define courses of action to realize these plans. They hold work sessions to evaluate their current state against the predetermined checkpoints on their projected trajectories for the realization of plans. They hold project status meetings to report their progress on their projected trajectories. They write e-mail notes and make phone calls to work through problems, correct mistakes, and resolve disagreements that stand in the way of achieving the next step in the development process.

In the case analyzed here, collaborators from Hotville and Snowfield did interact in communicative events like presentations of product plans, exchanges of status reports, discussions of problems, and so on, during the process of defining Royal Fleet PT+. In one of these events, Greg suggested a variation to the next fixed state (represented through the product plan for Royal Fleet PT+) in the projected trajectory of collaboration between Hotville and Snowfield. This variation presented the possibility of an undesirable outcome from the perspective of Anthony, who assessed the risks involved in developing a new feature to be higher than what would be gained with this new feature. Anthony responded unfavorably to Greg. The level of intensity increased in the disagreement between Anthony and Greg, and they portrayed each other's positions as being strategically irrational. Greg shut off Anthony and took the proposal for a new feature in Royal Fleet PT+ to a higher authority in Deep Purple. Anthony defied Greg and got himself invited to an urgent conference call that Greg had set up with a higher authority. Interactions between Greg and Anthony became representative of the relationship between the Hotville and Snowfield organizations, which had to collaborate across the temporal, geographic, political, and cultural boundaries in their distributed work settings (Orlikowski, 2002). Through Greg's and Anthony's representative acts-in-interaction, members of their collaborating organizations came to view each other's positions as threats to their own in defining the next fixed state of their collaboration. When the actors' shared vision was built on the product plan (i.e., when the shared vision was constructed textually on strategic rationality, and not conversationally on contextual rationality), a persistent challenge to that plan quickly dissolved collective sensemaking and created a radical conflict. The two sides in this conflict could no longer maintain a shared sense of their actions through regular channels of communication and executive decision makers called for the emergency face-to-face meetings between the two teams that were held in Snowfield.

Conflict characterizes the storming phase[6] of team formation, where actors try to move toward a new collective understanding of their environment (Duchon, Ashmos, & Nathan, 2000). Conflict can work as a catalyst for the construction of a shared sense for collective action, if actors recognize the construction of this shared sense as what is required for the accomplishment of their goals. Development organizations thrive on their actors' efforts to realize the best among competing good concepts for products. Conflict becomes an unavoidable part of collective action in these organizations that thrive on competition. Collaborative development benefits from conflict so long as actors recognize organizational sensemaking as an inherent aspect of their participatory roles in the communicative contexts of negotiating over conflicts. It is especially crucial for (macro)actors representing distinct organizational perspectives and expectations of conflicting sides in a collaboration to be able to engage in and facilitate sensemaking between the collaborating organizations. This requires that these actors operate within role structures that are designed to be responsive to emergent events, rather than within role structures that are designed as static states.

Weick (1993) argued that actors in a group can sustain their collective sensemaking, even when the routines and interlocking between their roles within the group are coming apart, if each actor functions as part of a "virtual role system" (p. 640). According to Weick, imagining participation in a virtual role system enables the individual actor to assume whatever role needs to be fulfilled within a group that is disintegrating in the face of a crisis. In the case of the conflict between Hotville and Snowfield, we observe how the actors' responses to each other's different positions created a momentary paralysis of their routines and the projected interlocking of their organizational roles as participants in a development project. This case illustrates an expected and potentially constructive conflict-gone-awry because (macro)actors did not step beyond their official roles in their responses to the ongoing events. In this case, the actors' official roles were not designed to include a function of representing a shared meaning for their ongoing collaboration—which is the function that the actors were called on to enact to work through their conflict. Such a design—or organizational text—was not found within the existing role structures of Deep Purple development organizations and needed to be constructed through the actors' participation in conversations on who they were and what they were doing together as members of a collaborative enterprise. Actors in the development of Royal Fleet PT+ did everything other than engaging each other in the

---

[6]Storming refers to the second of four stages—forming, storming, norming, and performing—based on a commonly known model of group development from social psychology (see Duchon et al., 2000).

conversational construction of a shared meaning for their collaboration. Anthony and Greg continuously oriented to their company-mandated "strategic goal" of developing a common product in their organizational roles as a program manager from Hotville and as a senior engineer from Snowfield, respectively. During the phone calls between Hotville and Snowfield, the actors' only source for organizational sensemaking was the collaborative product plan, and it was being challenged because of the disagreement about NuevoHyp. The face-to-face meetings in Snowfield between the two conflicting sides were structured as a series of debates, where each side presented "technical data" to be judged at the end by a group of executives. The communicative events between the two sides were designed to—textually and conversationally—construct the collaborative environment as a field of competition between winners and losers, and not as a platform of interactions between participants in the construction of a new order out of the collective understanding of their different positions.

According to Weick's (1993) analysis of the Mann Gulch fire disaster, panic is another significant source of disruption in organizational sensemaking. In the case analyzed in this chapter, we do not see a complete disintegration of role structure among panic-stricken actors, as we see in the case of the Mann Gulch disaster. Deep Purple developers were not, literally, fighting a monstrous fire that was racing toward them. Panic among the actors in this case, however, came from more subtle yet comparably vivid indicators of emergency in the everyday life of their organization. Some of these indicators were flaming arguments about who was competent and who was not in fulfilling roles and responsibilities, calls to "put one's [company] badge on the table,"[7] and corporate executive dicta being yelled out during phone conferences to employees, telling them to "decide on what to do or else." Threats of losing high-prestige and well-paying jobs would be expected to create panic among organizational actors, even though this may not be the same kind of panic that people experience in literal life-and-death situations. The disagreement on whether or not to include NuevoHyp in Royal Fleet PT+ put the actors from Hotville and Snowfield under a high level of executive pressure to "agree on the plan." This pressure created an emotionally charged context of interactions between the two organizations. When Greg took his proposal to a higher authority in response to Anthony's objection, "the moment quickly turned existential," in Weick's terms, in the process of defining the collaborative product. The (macro)actors from both sides interpreted each other's communicative acts as moves to make them "drop their tools"—their organizational perspectives and expectations, which were grounded in their official roles and formed the only source of structuring for their collective actions. These actors found themselves in a corporate structure of interorganizational collaboration "where it was every organization for itself." The

---

[7]Among Deep Purple employees, this expression refers to the act of resignation on principle. Actors involved in the conflict over NuevoHyp exchanged this expression a few times during the phone conferences between Hotville and Snowfield and during the face-to-face meetings in Snowfield.

construction of the collaborative environment as "a disorienting and dangerous place" disrupted organizational sensemaking, created an intense conflict, and threatened the continuity of collaborative development.

The participants in the collaboration between Hotville and Snowfield could not sustain their organizational sensemaking to create a link between the designed and emergent structures of organizing to define their collaborative product. The official roles of organizational (macro)actors did not involve constructing a shared meaning for their collaborative enterprise within Deep Purple. The corporate mandate for collaboration grounded the actors' framework of collective action on fixed-state representations of product planning. This definition did not enable the actors to participate in the communicative construction of a collective sense for who they were and what they were doing together in the moment of conflict. With the increasing intensity of disruptions to organizational sensemaking, macroactors in this conflict framed their interactions on the oppositional relationship between their designed roles, representing different organizational perspectives and expectations, and failed to act on their emergent roles as sensemakers across these perspectives and expectations. In the following section, I conclude my observations on macroactors' role of organizational sensemaking and discuss the significance of identity construction for the enactment of this role in collaborative activity settings.

CONCLUDING REMARKS ON REPRESENTING THE SENSEMAKING ROLE IN COLLABORATIVE ORGANIZING

This book presents arguments and cases illustrating what Cooren, Taylor, and Van Every (chap. 1, this volume) refer to as a "both/and" approach to investigating the discourse-world of organizations, which has been traditionally studied with an "either/or" approach based on the dichotomous dimensions of consensus–dissensus and the established–emergent (see chap. 1). In this chapter, I have used an ethnographic case to demonstrate that organizing is an act of juggling between coevolutionary loops of discursive phenomena, rather than a balancing act on intersecting dichotomous dimensions. In the analysis of this case, we have seen how actors can stir the ongoing events away from the direction of consensus and build up an intense dissensus to be forced back into consensus, when they do not take on sensemaking and fail to construct a link between the established and emergent structures as complementary dimensions of their organizing. The sensemaking role is part of the practice of diverse roles with different, and sometimes oppositional, organizational perspectives and expectations. The enactment of this role depends on the actors' ability to rise above their designated roles and participate in the communicative work to define a unifying yet dynamic framework for their collective actions. This is the work of identity construction.

The communicative work of constructing shared meanings for collective actions within large, complex organizations goes under the label of coordinating tasks, roles, and responsibilities. Actors, under the semantic influence of this label, assume the existence of a grand scheme according to which they are supposed to coordinate their collective actions. In complex activity settings of high-technology development, actors also privilege the work that goes into constructing representations of such a grand scheme. The epitome of these representations is the product plan. The problem with focusing on coordination is that it leads to the interpretation of dissensus between different organizational perspectives and expectations as glitches to be fixed by a reinstatement of the grand scheme—the product plan. Actors who are focused on the coordination of the tasks at hand do not step above their designed roles and engage each other in the ongoing (re)structuring of what it is that they are doing together.

Identity construction, on the other hand, is not simply about establishing a source of coordination. It is about creating a framework that constantly provides the actors a sense of who they become and how they fit into the joint activity environment as a result of their participation in that environment. In this framework, dissensus and consensus are interwoven in the definition of "strategic goals" and "shared visions" for collaborative action. The ongoing and dynamic work of identity construction is about maintaining coorientation between the textual world of product plans and the conversational world of negotiating over these plans. When actors recognize that facilitating this coorientation is an inherent function that cuts across their diverse roles in the accomplishment of collaborative goals and visions, they are able to continuously act as organizational sensemakers—whether they are program managers or senior engineers representing distinct organizations in collaboration. It becomes difficult, however, for actors to recognize and act on their sensemaking roles when they operate under established structures of collective action that are not grounded in identity construction. In these cases, when actors' sources of coordination fail, they quickly lose their sense of how to deal with each other, find themselves trapped within corporate structures, and refuse to "drop their tools," even though doing that presents a good chance of getting out of their trap. We can still find solace in the fact that most organizational conflicts are not as deadly as forest fires.

ACKNOWLEDGMENTS

I would like to extend my thanks to Larry Browning and Reuben McDaniel for their support and guidance in the conduct of my dissertation research, which provided the basis for this chapter. I also thank François Cooren, Roger Gathman, and Robert Sanders for their invaluable insights. I will always be grateful to "Anthony" and "Greg" and to all the other participants who made my research with their organizations possible.

CHAPTER THREE

The Structuring of Collaborative Research Networks in the Stories Researchers Tell

Jean A. Saludadez
University of the Philippines, Open University

James R. Taylor
Université de Montréal

The traditional systems view of organization assumes that communication consists of an exchange of information in and out of an organization. Organizational structure is conceived to be unidimensional and fixed, and for this reason it is thought to be amenable to managerial design. In the communication perspective that is developed in this book, by contrast, organization is conceptualized as grounded in a social process of interpretation (Taylor, Cooren, Giroux, & Robichaud, 1996). Organization is created and recreated (Kersten, 1986; Mumby & Stohl, 1996; Taylor, 1993; Taylor et al., 1996) in and through the everyday sensemaking activities of its members (Weick, 1995). From this perspective, organizational structure is conceived to be multiple (Kersten, 1986) rather than monolithic (Mumby & Stohl, 1996); fluid or even fragmented (Boje, 1998), rather than fixed; socially constructed (Taylor, 1993, 2001) rather than static (Hawes, 1974; Putnam, 1983); context-sensitive (Taylor, 1993) and historical (Thatchenkery, 2001; Kersten, 1986) rather than acontextual or ahistorical; emergent (Taylor & Van Every, 2000) rather than planned or exported (Mumby & Stohl, 1996); and revealing itself naturally rather than consciously designed. According to this view, communication and organization are coconstructing (Cooren, 2001a; Cooren & Taylor, 1997; Taylor, 1993, 1995, 2001; Taylor et al., 1996; Taylor & Van Every, 2000). In other words, it is through the process of communication that organizational forms emerge. And communication is in turn framed and informed by organization.

At the core of this view of communication is the principle of a circular dynamic: from conversation to text (text being interpreted broadly to include verbal as well as written expression of ideas), and from text to conversation (conversation being understood as interaction grounded in, and concerned with, practice). It is the circularity of the communicative dynamic—what Giddens (1984) called its *recursive* character—that explains organizing. Situations, patterns of interaction, contexts, and motives are all sited in the everyday ongoing flow of experience and yet they only take on meaning when they have been interpreted, retrospectively, to become not merely an account of what happened but as what actually did happen (Varey, chap. 10, this volume), now transformed into the context of future interaction. As Gilbert and Mulkay (1984) wrote, "participants' observable accomplishment of actions at a specific point in time cannot be neatly distinguished from, or separated from, the kind of retrospective story-telling which is generated in interviews and other indirect methods of data collection" (p. 9).

As accounts, stories constitute a framework of interpretation that is for the people involved their view of the organization they live and work in, or deal with. The organization takes on reality for them only by its having been filtered through the lens of sensemaking. The organization is, for the moment, crystallized as an account. It is thereby transformed into a powerful agent that subsequently channels the activities of the same people whose interactions and interpretations went to make the organization in the first place.

The goal of the research that we report on in this chapter was to document, through the accounts of scientists who had participated in collaborative research networks, how, over time, these networks evolved to display contrasting organizational forms. The choice of research venue was, as is often the case in qualitative organizational research, circumstantial: An opportunity presented itself. The choice of site turned out, however, to be serendipitous because the circumstances of voluntary collaboration left the ensuing evolution relatively free of immediate institutional constraints. It should thus afford, we hypothesized, an unimpeded view of the effects of spontaneous organizing on the part of members. In the stories or accounts of our informants we would be able, we hoped, to identify some of the factors that led to either a continuing association or a failed networking initiative. In this context, organizational viability would be contingent on the contributions of participants and thus particularly illustrative of the role of sensemaking.

This chapter thus aims to accomplish three objectives: present the circumstances and goals of the research; identify, on the basis of participants' accounts, patterns of association that they saw as emerging to produce different outcomes; and propose factors that may account for the differences. The work we are reporting on is based on a doctoral dissertation submitted in 2004 at the Universiti Putra Malaysia by the first author, Jean A. Saludadez. Her work stimulated in turn an online conversation, beginning in 1999, that involved the second author, James R. Taylor. This chapter is the text that resulted from that exchange. In offering our joint account of the research, we also have been organizing by engaging in a collaboration and, by doing so, contributing, reflexively, to the organization of a research community represented in this volume by its texts (Brummans, chap. 11, this volume).

RESEARCH COLLABORATION AS A SITE
OF MULTIPLE STORIES

Research collaboration among scientists can be considered an ongoing conversation (Huberman, 1990). The relatively less constrained circumstances of cross-disciplinary scientific collaboration tend to generate an interactive process that is at once polyphonic (in that there are multiple interests and disciplines involved) and polysemous (with multiple and often quite distinct modes of interpretation grounded in their specialized knowledge and practices; Boje, 1998). This plurality of voices and knowledge claims (Putnam, 2001) found its expression in our research not only in what people wrote but also in how they articulated their concerns in their talk as they figured out how to work together.

Before undertaking doctoral studies, the first author, Jean, had been working in a division of the University of the Philippines Los BaZos that offers training in, and conducts research on, the management of research organizations. Thus, research collaboration was already a focal interest for her as she began her doctoral research in a Malaysian university. While exploring which field would best provide an empirical grounding for doctoral study, she received a memo from her scholarship administrator (an arm of an intergovernmental organization in Southeast Asia promoting regional cooperation through education, science, and culture) requesting scholars to align their dissertation research projects along environment-related themes. Earlier, reading over the Malaysian university's directory of products, services, and expertise, Jean had noticed there were many instances of collaborative research in forestry. Because forestry is relevant to environmental concerns, she decided to situate her doctoral study within the context of forestry research.

In the same directory she found an already completed project in forestry, noting the names of the researchers who were involved. She then made an appointment with the lead researcher of the project to question her about her understanding of collaborative research. While waiting for the contact to arrive for the appointment, Jean had an opportunity to also arrange a meeting with her interviewee's coresearcher, whose office was in the same building and who, coincidentally, happened to be her scholarship coordinator. The coresearcher suggested that if Jean wanted to be sensitized to the issues in forestry research collaboration she should attend a 3-day international seminar on emerging institutional arrangements for forestry research, to be held in Chiang Mai, Thailand, in 3 months time. He then (as Jean's scholarship coordinator) indicated his support should she decide to go. She did.

The Research Managers' Meeting

In Chiang Mai, Jean listened, observed, and occasionally questioned participants (those who sat beside her during sessions and at meal times) about their views on research collaboration. From Jean's perspective, however, the Chiang Mai seminar was essentially a managerial conversation, as the 80 or so participants were for the

most part research administrators and managers of forestry research institutions in
the Asia-Pacific region. For these research managers and administrators, the collaborative research network was a partnership that they treated as being formally
structured: desirable combinations of technical expertise directed to certain kinds
of problems. The "networkness" of the collaboration was seen by those involved in
the discussion, to the extent that it was treated as an issue at all, to boil down to no
more than information exchange. This pervasive functional perspective on communication is illustrated by the following excerpt, taken from the final report of the
seminar:

> Technological advance and the increasing complexity of sustainable forest man-
> agement suggest that no single institution would be able to have all the expertise,
> resources and skills within its walls and collaboration and networking will be-
> come imperative. Rapid developments in communication/information technolo-
> gies will facilitate the process. Strategic alliances of research organizations and
> clients could become an important arrangement for research.
>
> In this context, it is important to examine the ability of existing organizations
> to adapt to changes and develop partnerships. (Nair, Apichart, & Enters,
> 1998, pp. 5–6)

This text reiterates a point of view that can be found in a variety of versions in
the research collaboration literature (see, e.g., Bloedon & Stokes, 1994;
Bonaccorsi & Piccaluga, 1994; Dill, 1990; Parker, 1992; Ruscio, 1984; Van der
Meer, Trommelen, Vleggaar, & Vriezen, 1996), as well as in studies on collaborative networks such as invisible colleges (Crane, 1972) and technological communities based on information and knowledge flows (Debackere & Rappa, 1994;
Rappa & Debackere 1992). It portrays an image of a network as technically supported and managerially designed. Issues of spontaneous organization are not
thematized, and the role of communication in generating organization through
participant interaction is passed over in silence.

A Space for Researchers' Stories?

There is of course more going on in cooperative forestry projects (and other collaborative research networks) than "information exchange," but this additional dimension of communication tends to remain unspoken and unheard in the research
managers' official account, as the Chiang Mai seminar, and its proceedings, illustrate. Jean realized she needed to explore these other voices that were muted in the
Chiang Mai discussions but could prove to be crucial to the success of a joint initiative. It is not only research administrators and managers, Jean reasoned, who are
entitled to speak on behalf of the collectivity that they claim to represent. The actual
researchers have a right to be heard as well, she thought. The doctoral dissertation
had found its motivation and a direction to pursue.

Jean now made a second appointment with the lead researcher with whom she had had the initial conversation, this time to delve in greater depth into her own experience and understanding of collaborative research. Following this initial interview, she went on to question 29 other forestry academics and researchers, located in three Southeast Asian universities (one each from Malaysia, the Philippines, and Thailand), about their personal experience of collaborative research projects. Conversations followed with the researchers in their places of work and wherever else was convenient, including at a snack bar, in the car, and over the phone.

The collaborative research experiences of these Southeast Asian forestry academics spanned the gamut from past to ongoing research, from project membership to project leadership, from single-discipline collaborative research to interdisciplinary research, and from in-house or in-country to an international setting. Their research interests varied from the economics of forest insects to climate change, from micro-organisms to ecosystems, from biotechnology to biodiversity, from resin extraction to road construction, from production of timber to protection of forest areas, from mangrove to manmade forests, and from women's role in forest development to that of communities.

MAKING SENSE OF MAKING SENSE: HOW STORIES BECOME ACCOUNTS

The theoretical commitment of the research we now describe, as we have already indicated, led Jean to focus on how researchers made sense of their experience in working in cross-disciplinary collaborative ventures. Like Weick (1995) she assumed that "most organizational realities are based on narration" (p. 127). To understand and interpret their own experience the people she interviewed would, we hypothesized, have transformed it into an account—a story—of their interaction with colleagues (Varey, chap. 10, this volume). The data thus consisted of the story-based accounts of networking and its outcomes that she collected over the course of her interviews. Our task in this section of the chapter is to summarize those features of storyhood that we considered to be important, and relevant to understanding how and why the collaborative exercises sometimes worked, and sometimes did not.

The following appear to us to be the salient features of narrative that are most illuminating in understanding the stories we needed to analyze.

Stories Structure Time and Space

A story recounts a sequence of events (Ricoeur, 1984, cited by Boje, 2001) moving from an initial to a final state. Cooren and Taylor (1997) described a basic narrative diagram as consisting of "two states (initial and final) separated by an illocutionary transformation operated by an agent on a recipient through an object, a transformation generated by a speech act originating from the agent" (p. 235; see also Taylor & Cooren, chap. 7, this volume).

The initial state is constituted by a "precipitating event" (Bruner, 1991, cited in Taylor & Van Every, 2000) that establishes a task to be accomplished, a situation to be corrected, a need to be filled—a project or "thrust," in other words. The final state— the closure—indexes the completion of the mission that motivated the project and its evaluation as successful or unsuccessful. The identities of individuals emerge from their roles in the unfolding of the story and the nature of the project that engaged them. The entire sequence from initial to final state, as it is recounted in retrospect, thus implies making meaning and interpreting experience, the meaning being inscribed in the structure of the narrative sequence (Hardin, 2001). However, the narrative has a further effect: It structures *social time* (Gomes da Silva & Wetzel, 2004). Social time is qualitatively different from one field of activity to another, reflecting as it does each group's practices and ways of making sense. How stories are punctuated as sequences that unfold in the trajectory from initiation of a project to its conclusion is the basis of social time: when a task was taken up, what the stages of task performance were, and when it came to a conclusion. It is these elements that constitute a logic of social time. As Gomes da Silva and Wetzel (2004) observed, "each organization constructs its own rules and ways of structuring time" (p. 5).

By much the same logic, the people who share a common discipline and work in similar circumstances, using similar techniques and technologies, develop a structuring of their *social space*. As Suchman (1996) observed:

> work activities and workspaces are mutually constituted, in ways that are structured … the physical place of a worksite comprises a complex of equipment and action, of spatial orders produced in and informed by the knowledgeable practices of setting members … the place of the laboratory for those who inhabit it is organized not by spatial coordinates but rather as topical contextures associated with indigenous orders of equipment and practice. (p. 36)

By definition, collaborative groups, such as those that form the subject matter of this chapter, have differing conceptions and practices about how to construct time and space, depending on their disciplines. To transform themselves into a collaborative group they thus face the challenge of developing that new, interdisciplinary group's own mode of understanding time and space.

Stories Structure Organization

According to Cooren (2001b), "any organizational form is structured ultimately as a narrative" (p. 181). The building block of both narrative and organization is exchange, or "the act by which an actor becomes an agent for another actor" (Taylor & Van Every, 2000, p. 250). Such acts then imply a form of compensation from the person who benefited from the act: There is a transaction, with reciprocal obligations being undertaken.

Exchange—transaction—implies in turn relational structure: hierarchy and agency (Taylor & Van Every, 2000). However, it also confers value on action, and the people who undertake it. By extension, both disciplines and the people who embody them come to be recognized as positively evaluated by society, because it is the presumed beneficiary of their disciplined activity. As agents who are charged with a task that has value to society, actors—the researchers—acquire status as scientists. Status is further conferred on individuals by their relational positions within the network of actors with whom they are accustomed to interact in the conduct of their work. They are recognized by their position within the community of agents. There is interdisciplinary status as well: Some areas of research may claim to be, and may be recognized as, of greater salience socially than others (e.g., medical research). Establishing status is thus in and of itself an effect of sensemaking. In the context of interdisciplinary research, sorting out the status of contributors may be problematical, as we will discover in our analysis of results.

Stories, by identifying relationships (who is the agent, who are their helpers, who are the principals to whom they report and by whom they will be evaluated, who are their beneficiaries), construct a world of sense, create a familiar organizational context, and situate actors within it.

Again, as in the structuring of time and space, people's daily purposeful activities fit into a practical and conceptual framework of familiar relationships of cooperation, delegation, and responsibility to some authority. This sense of context is accomplished in the mutuality of acting and making sense of one's acts by accounting for them to oneself and others: by transforming experience into a narrative interpretation of it. The process implies dialogue between practitioners engaged in a collaborative venture. They need to construct, in their practices and their interpretations, the basis of a viable collaboration if they are to continue working together productively.

As Barry and Elmes (1997) pointed out, stories imply an author and a reader (or a listener). You make sense—you give an account—to someone. It is this reflexivity of communication that explains the evolution of organization over time. A story is an account of an experience (an already lived-through set of events) but, because it is a transaction involving an author and a reader or listener, it is not just a retrospective account: It is, in and of itself, an experience that will also have to be accounted for. It is at once communicational and metacommunicational (Robichaud, Giroux, & Taylor, 2004): directed outward from the conversation to describe a world and inward to interpret what is happening within the conversation. It is thus not just a description of organization; it is a constituent of organization.

The scientific team that stays together to produce a viable collaboration, in which each partner adds value, thus needs to create a conversation in which the roles of speaker–writer and listener–reader alternate so that, however variable the content of their discussions, the fact of the discussion itself constitutes organizing. How durable the conversation becomes, however, is contingent on how it figures in the respective accounts of the collaborators. Is the collaboration perceived to bring added value to each of the participants, for example? If it is, then the likelihood is that the working association will develop characteristics of a more permanent organization. If it is not, the initial collaboration runs the risk of petering out as time goes on, not necessarily as the result of a dramatic break, but simply through a fading of enthusiasm and a progressive distancing of the original partners.

The Role of Worldview

As we have seen, each discipline typically constructs social time and space in a way that is unique to it. Similarly, the discipline becomes endowed with what Katambwe and Taylor (chap. 4, this volume) call a text or at least a subtext that establishes who is responsible for what and to whom. It covers the relative statuses and roles of people. Many of these often unstated understandings are grounded in the formative practices and conditions of entry to a discipline or profession: university degrees, publications, research grants, specialized training in a particular technology, and so on. However, other factors enter as well, as the result of repeatedly collaborating with certain people one gets to know well. People come to be recognized as having special abilities, both as practitioners and collaborators.

All this is inscribed in an intertextual framework of shared understandings that is partly explicit, but often largely tacit. One could, justifiably, regard this as the worldview of the profession (Taylor & Cooren, chap. 7, this volume). When two actors, individual or collective, enter into a transaction that involves mutual obligations, each is likely to see the other as either contributing to or impeding his or her own objectives. Each half of the association is, as we have seen, part of an activity trajectory that is grounded in both practice and in sensemaking. The usual trajectories of the partners to the transaction are not, however, the same. Their respective worldviews are not merely different. Now each partner enters the other's world of practice and sense as an actor within that world, but the worlds are not identical. If their respective objectives are seen as contributing to the other partner's objectives, the association is positive. If not, it is at best neutral, and at worst, conflictual.

Suppose the association links a forestry engineer and a sociologist. The engineer's objective is to develop a more productive practice of forest management for a certain ecology and region. The sociologist's objective is to understand the nature of present practices and to see how innovative new practices, in line with the larger project's objectives, might come to be accepted in the communities that depend on the forest for their livelihood. Here it is clear that the sociologist's objectives are subsidiary in the sense that they contribute to the larger project, a project that is, however, primarily associated with the engineers' goals. So if each partner performs its task satisfactorily, if their respective agendas of research are complementary, and if a bridge is established so that each partner is in effect helping the other to reach their objective, the project has a higher probability of delivering on its mandate. The basis of a longer term collaboration has been created.

There are, of course, a few "ifs" in our account, as this extract from an interview illustrates:

A:	Did you study alone or with a group?
FA:	I had with me two people. One of them was a sociologist from the department of sociology of this university. Also the other one here was a forester.
A:	So the study was supposed to be an interdisciplinary work?
FA:	Yeah, it was supposed to be an interdisciplinary but the outcome, this [sociologist] ... I'm quite surprised because during data gathering [the person] didn't have the time.
A:	How about the forester?
FA:	We met regularly, we had discussions. Like when we gathered the data, especially in the field, we discussed together. Then we tabulated some of the data, collated the data, and discussions—what we saw, what we observed, you know. Every night, we discussed. Even during dinnertime, we ate together and discussed.
A:	This sociology person, did [the person] join with this discussion?
FA:	Ah, not, not, not all the time. But only during the first time that [the person] went sightseeing. But since I know already I never asked [the person] anymore. Just one and forget it. I do it myself for my research. I have also the sociology background, so I could also do sociological study.

A more constructive view of collaboration would see it less as a simple means–end association than a genuine partnership where one contribution may be less salient than the other, but where the interaction produces an inflection of the separate activities in the interest of constituting a hybrid science.

This "synergy" seems to be reflected in several accounts:

FA:	Among the purposes of the meeting are, of course, first is, just to say hello, what's going on. And then we discuss the progress of our work. We report what are the problems. What are the needs of the different study leaders, project leaders. And primarily to just come together and then brainstorm about what are we going to do next, what are the challenges, what are the problems that we faced. And then during these meetings we come up with ideas and discuss and decide what are the priorities given these are the things we have to do. And so during these meetings we sort of discuss activities and then decide and prioritize these activities. And then implement them. Although we have the basic frame-

work of the program, the details of this program we discuss them during our weekly meetings. Those are the purposes of our meeting.

Of course, I mean being scientists ourselves sometimes we do quarrel, quote unquote. I mean we just discuss things, which one is better, which one is not. But at the end of the day you have to agree to a middle line.

We met regularly. We had discussions. Like when we gathered the data, especially in the field, we discussed together. Then we tabulated some of the data, collated the data, and discussions— what we saw, what we observed, you know. Every night, we discussed. Even during dinnertime, we ate together and discussed.

HOW THE RESEARCH PROJECT WAS ORGANIZED

There were 30 interviews in all. All were recorded on tape (including one phone conversation). Interviews lasted from 30 minutes to 3 hours (usually in one sitting but in two cases the conversation resumed the following day). A typical question format was along these lines:

- What does research mean to you?
- How do you define research collaboration?
- How many research collaborations have you completed [without precluding present or ongoing research]?
- What [happened] at the beginning, during, and at the end?

Interviews ended when the understandings and experiences respondents were sharing began to repeat themselves. All interviews were transcribed using Ethnograph software. Most conversations occurred in the second language of the person being interviewed (English) but in the case of scientists from the Philippines (Jean's own language) the text had to be translated into English. Overall the result was more than 1,000 pages of transcripts. Because respondents had sometimes participated in more than one collaboration, the actual number of accounts of collaborations (35) was slightly greater than the number of interviewees. Printed transcripts were then cut and pasted onto 8 × 5 index cards to produce a one-experience, one-account equivalence. This classification process yielded 27 specific and 8 general accounts, and 25 in-house and 10 international accounts.

Because the goal of the study was to understand the processes of collaboration, the accounts were analyzed using thematic analysis. Steps included locating recurring terms (phrases, propositions), identifying associated terms, identifying opposing terms, exploring the discourse for recurrences of assumed causal patterns, and noting evaluative assessments (Carbaugh, 1986). One result of the analysis was the identification of a dominant theme: working together (and its opposite, not working together).

For the purposes of this chapter, however, we limit ourselves to identifying factors that explain why some collaborative projects were successful, and others either encountered difficulties or fell apart after a time. For this purpose, we use the earlier theoretical propositions of the communicational basis of organizing as our guide.

HOW THE RESEARCHERS ACCOUNTED FOR COLLABORATION

The first thing we identified as significant was how the researchers understood the importance of social time and space.

The Construction of a Common Time and Space

We begin with a partner story, that we identified as a "team spirit story" (A is the interviewer-author, FA the forest academic being interviewed).

A:	When you got into the program, you said, the program had already started, a year earlier, how was the condition at that time when you got involved?
FA:	We were all very high, so to speak. It was, I think, our group who initially, as far as I remember, started the term, interdisciplinary, holistic, integrated, participatory. We were all high, enthusiastic, very eager to do what we can to really attend to our specific fields of specialization and be able to integrate this field to the other field, our colleagues. We were all very excited. In fact, we meet almost every week …
A:	You were meeting almost every week. What was the purpose of the meeting?
FA:	Among the purposes of the meeting are, of course, first is, just to say hello, what's going on. And then we discuss the progress of our work. We report what are the problems. What are the needs of the different study leaders, project leaders. And primarily to just come together and then brainstorm about what we are going to do next, what are the challenges, what are the problems that we faced. And then during these meetings we come up with ideas and discuss and decide what are the priorities given these are the things we have to do. And so during these meetings we sort of discuss activities and then decide and prioritize these activities. And then implement them. Although we

have the basic framework of the program, the details of this program we discuss them during our weekly meetings. Those are
the purposes of our meeting.

A: Without these weekly meetings, what do you think would have
            happened?

FA: If we probably did not meet once a week, then perhaps the spirit
            of the interdisciplinary team of doing or addressing research
            might not have been as active as we had during that time. And
            therefore that weekly meetings that we have had helped a lot in
            making us even more close to each other. Even now, until now,
            we still meet, the spirit of that interdisciplinary team which we
            started still exists among us. It is not as close as we had had be-
            fore but again as I said, it becomes a standard among all of us
            that when we see each other the spirit still remains. We have
            had, we had worked together.

Compare this account with the following, taken from a collaborative team that
had been successful in the past, but had gradually fallen apart:

FA: So the [faculty/college] had four or five thrust groups which
            worked quite well for about, I think, 5 years or more, maybe al-
            most 10 years actually. We had it in the mid-80s. That type of
            collaborative research was good. It had a lot of advantages as
            well as disadvantages. I think outside people when they saw it,
            it was seen as a group effort and therefore a more integrated ap-
            proach to problem solving, which is good. I think, in the end it,
            sort of, started to break up because leadership started to slack.
            And then involvement of people also started to slack. And the
            talking and contributing to the synthesis of the whole thing
            started to fall back. And, in the end, it just decayed as it were,
            which was sad.

A   What is it that you expect from a leader of this kind of research?

FA: Well, for one thing, I would have thought that, there should be
            regular meetings for instance, of the group, just to keep every-
            one going as it were. I think the leader should, for instance,
            keep everyone pepped up as it were. When you have a leader
            who doesn't work, then, doesn't call for meetings and, when
            you ask for various things, [the leader's] not around, sometimes
            to sign various things, claims and other things, it becomes a
            problem. And of course, when you have this kind of project you
            need to report regularly. For instance, end of the year you need
            to come up with something. If we don't regularly remind mem-

bers, they can get distracted and do other things. So, I mean we used to have meetings every 2 months, or something like that, just to keep people on their toes, as it were. Well, after that it just flattened. I think, we haven't had a meeting the last 2 years, when one of them took over. We didn't have a meeting for 2 years. At the end of the project, it just went on.

Meeting together on a regular basis is a way of at least minimally reconciling research agendas to establish a calendar that situates each partner's contribution to the project, and thus give the project reality. Unsurprisingly, respondents saw this feature of time organization as a minimal condition for successful collaboration.

What about creating a common space? At least one respondent made clear how important that may also be:

There are two kinds of collaboration in the sense that sometimes, okay, it doesn't matter, you can do a lot of things here, but make sure that you put my name there. If not, I will not allow, that also happens that way. But I think in the real sense, we try to make the work a success story because we go to the field, we establish a plot, we measure the tree, not only us, you know, also there's a person who came. Of course the person cannot come every month, you know. So I think, in my case, I can say that's a real one, a real collaboration. The one we establish in [the area]. It's a result of collaboration. We established one-acre plot, beautiful, ready with all the fences, you know. Beautiful!

So in a way I cannot speak for others, but I think definitely in [here], the one I say, I myself experienced that, that is real down-to-earth collaboration. That means we collaborate, we work, together we share the results. That's the definition of collaboration.

Another respondent cited a similar experience:

A: How are you organized?
FA: Well, we appoint a project leader. Okay, the project leader will call a meeting when appropriate. For example, at the inception of the project, we write up on the compartment of the project in line with our expertise. Then, we discuss together and make a good proposal. And then, okay after [approval of funding], we plan what to do, we establish plots on site, so we have to call a meeting again. Normally, you don't have to be physically present, just send through e-mail and then respond accordingly. And then we go together and we establish the plot ourselves. The only thing that we did, we are not only research managers, we are actively involved. We planted the bamboo. We carry the bamboo up and down the hill. So very, very interesting in that sense, you know. And of course at the end of the day we have to

submit one report also. So the only thing that we are dealing
with is our narrow area of specialization, but also we have to be
knowledgeable about the other sections which our colleagues
are dealing with.

A: When there is a change in the design, how is it communicated?

FA: Well, okay, before we go to the field, so because the site is a bit
far from here, so you have to travel at the evening. So at night we
reach the place. So before we go to bed we have discussion and
there where we are physically present, there, discuss. Okay, this is
going to be our altered objective, or altered procedures. And the
students also, those who pursue their masters will be there, listening to us. Normally, things are going on rather smoothly.

Not all collaborative research is quite so hands-on. Often, what is more important is the quality of human relationships. Our theoretical interpretation of how organizations come into being placed the concept of transaction at the core of
organizing. Transactions, we proposed, entail reciprocal obligations. Reciprocity is
the sine qua non for more complex characteristics such as hierarchy. The agents
who figure in a collaborative venture need to know that their role is valued because
the benefits their work brings with it are receiving recognition. Only in this way is
their status affirmed, and their loyalty assured. Several interviews provided
illustrative support for our assumptions.

A: So you have experience working with people from other countries and with locals. I am interested to know whether you
found any difference working with people from other countries
or other universities and within the university?

FA: For myself, I didn't find any difference. I heard our national research council or our [faculty/college] before they accepted this
[foreign group] project, the first one, they had lots of discussion
because they said these foreigners would just come and we will
just be like their laborer, but not coresearcher. And they will
take lots of data and we don't know what they are doing, or
something like that. But from my experience, they are very nice.
Or I don't know if it's only this group or not. But they are very
nice and we share and we make plans together. We work together. If they have new equipment they share and the data we
have we share. And whatever they have, new software, they
share and the publication we always have both sides name. So, I
don't find any difficulty working with them.

A: In a collaborative work, what do you think is important?

FA: I think maybe the recognition that the researchers must work together as coresearchers.

A slightly different, and considerately less positive response, came from another respondent:

A: You mentioned earlier you have negative experiences in your collaborative work. What are those?

FA: Actually, two. And it involves the same person. If I'll talk about the late, the later one. It's foreign-funded. It's about gender. It's about women, globalization and women's livelihood in forest communities. It's got something to do with forest policies and all. So, I'm a case study writer there. There's a project leader (PL) there from [our faculty/college]. So, this is about social forestry and women, basically, transformations of forest communities, different kinds, like from logging to becoming integrated social forestry project sites. Different kinds of transformations in the context of globalization in general, whether at the incipient stage of globalization, or already in place or whatever. A good study. I think, this is a five-country project, and we're doing [our country] component. At that time, of course, the project leader was still my friend, so why should I even join if we are enemies already? But it got really that bad.

A: [How did the story go?]

FA: One of the problems that we met was really methodological. For example, one question I had was the selection of sites. We have four sites. We chose one of the sites in [a province] based on a case study the project leader [PL] published. [The PL] said this community represented concession from logging to community-based management. [The PL] was saying in the past, it became an integrated social forestry site. Okay, so we chose that community. And we flew to [that province]. When we arrived at the community just with the first few informants, we already knew, it was never an integrated social forestry site at all. It was really bad. The methodological flaw was fundamental. It's okay if it is in terms of interpretation or what. But it was data collection. Just at the site selection we already had problem. And then, here's a case where there were three parts of the research. The first part was a framework that was supposed to be developed. Okay, then came the case studies that would flow from the framework. And finally, there will be a conclusion. Unfortunately, one comment of the donor, disconnected. They don't flow.

A: So what happened?

FA: So, I wrote, I sent a memo to this project leader, a copy was furnished to the donor. It's the project leader and the donor who are in communication. So, I have to defend my name also. Of course, I regret having been so passive also. I was so conscious ... In [the PL's] memos ... "I'm the project leader, you're just a team member." So I kept quiet. But when the criticism was serious, I have to state what really happened. I was explaining to them [the donor], the reason why it's disconnected is because, the framework was written very much ahead. It was not something that was reiterated or what but it was written way before. And it was typed already long before I joined this. Not just that, the conclusions were also written already. And we did not, the members of the team did not participate in the framing of that initial framework nor of the conclusion. That's why our case studies are disconnected. They don't have connection with the framework nor with the conclusion. And because you're part of the team, and because [the PL] is lording it over, you are so stifled in terms of giving that kind of feedback within the team also.

A: What would be the effect if the leader is lording over people?
FA: Our favorite word is synergy, you know. We really have to "synergize," you have to work together. There must be a reason why it's a team. There must be a reason why we're a project, even if there are separate studies. Why is it a project? It means, the separate studies are connected. And yet, we're not able to integrate and interact ... I think a feudal set up will not work in research because it is a creative thing. It's like a symphony orchestra. You play your own music but somebody is the conductor there. But if somebody lords it over and plays [his/her] violin when it shouldn't be, it destroys the harmony ....
A: [What has become of the project?]
FA: Finally, the funding agency wrote, "since your contracts are separate, why don't you do your own thing?"

When collaboration works, however, it can be immensely gratifying.

A: So, in the end, what happened to the team and what happened to your output?
FA: Then the team continues as far as we are still formally together and even informally as stated earlier. And then the results we published them to some journals. We reported the findings to seminars and symposium. And of course we have our annual reports. And we are so happy that even if we already left the area, they [the upland dwellers] continued on the activities that we started. And that is one of the intentions of the program. We just have to provide the seed money, head start and let them

know that we will leave the place, so the responsibility will be theirs. Actually, what the people there were saying, if you've been to [the area], that is a big big watershed that during the summer months there are no greens. It's really denuded grassland. But in the middle of those big denuded grassland watershed, there is one area that at least planted successfully with mangoes, coconut and so on and grown with vegetables. They describe it as paradise in hell, if there is such thing as paradise in hell, because of the greenery that was established in the middle of so dry and barren area.

CONCLUSION

All of the segments we have cited qualify as accounts, in that they report a sequence of events, from a beginning (formation of a collaborative project) to a conclusion, from a point of view (that of the respondent). Respondents interpreted the meaning of their experience in collaboration without difficulty, and evaluated it as either positive or negative, simultaneously justifying (if only by indirection) their role in it, as well as that of others. Accounts that related issues of conflict exhibited, as we would expect from narrative theory (Taylor & Cooren, chap. 7, this volume), stronger story properties than those that did not, although all told a story of a sort. One, at least (the researcher who participated in an international team), inverted the conflict theme, from an expected exploitation by the visitors (negative polarity) to a mutually productive cooperation (positive polarity).

A closer reading of the accounts, however, reveals another feature of the storytelling facility. Making accounts of what is happening is iterative, an everyday practice. For example, consider the example of the researcher who found herself confronted with a site reality that clearly contradicted that of her project leader's account of it. That too had to be accounted for, and undoubtedly triggered an episode of sensemaking on the part of the respondent. But then other facts emerged: The site report had already been written! The project leader was feeding the sponsor biased information. Now, the project having faded into history, the respondent has classified her experience, in retrospect, as "feudal." The present account, in other words, is in fact an account of accounts. As the experience unfolded, each new account recursively (to use Giddens's term) incorporated elements of the previous, reinterpreting some and obscuring others. This is how accounts organize.

This confirmation of our initial hypothesis was in fact the most gratifying result of the inquiry. However condensed accounts may have become as the accounter began to distance himself or herself from the actual experience, one salient conclusion emerges from the interviews. Those that were successful uniformly mentioned meeting regularly, discussing progress, altering objectives, brainstorming about what to do next, coming up with ideas, coming up with information that was generated from research, participating in the framing, having a discussion before turning in at night, learning from others, and quarrelling "but at the end of the day agreeing to a middle line." As we had predicted, sometimes what is said is less important than the fact that the partners are saying it to each other (although not always, as Güney [chap. 2, this volume] has illustrated, although there the organizational context was different).

And, of course, we are ourselves accounters, reporting on what we learned: from a perspective. There had to have been a choice of which people to interview. The interviews were tape recorded, and transcribed, but, as Kvale (1996) observed, "Transcripts are not copies or representations of some original reality, they are interpretive constructions" (p. 165). Analysis meant a further winnowing of the potential sources of interpretation, and this chapter is itself an extra refinement of the material reported in the dissertation.

There is not, however, it seems to us, any way to short-circuit the interpretive dynamic. Neither a tightly controlled experiment based on deductively sourced hypotheses, nor an inductive statistical analysis of frequencies, offers any greater guarantee of authenticity. As Gilbert and Mulkay (1984) noted, "It is presumably always possible for the analyst, like the participant, to extract a 'definitive' version of events from even the most diverse of accounts" (p. 11). "But," they continued, "this process of reinterpretation to distill a comprehensive, ultimate version can produce firm conclusions only by disregarding copious interpretive uncertainties" (p. 11).

ACKNOWLEDGMENTS

We acknowledge the Deutscher Akademischer Austauscchdienst (the German Academic Exchange Service) for its financial support to the research as administered by the SEAMEO Regional Center for Graduate Study and Research in Agriculture (SEARCA).

CHAPTER FOUR

Modes of Organizational Integration

Jo M. Katambwe
Université du Québec à Trois-Rivières

James R. Taylor
Université de Montréal

A recurring theme in the literature on organizations is the contradictory pressures that management experiences in shaping their enterprise to deal with the contemporary world. Menz (1999), for example, remarked that "to remain successful an organization needs to both reduce and retain complexity" (p. 103). Pye (1993) commented that "managers will speak in one breath about, for instance, encouraging autonomy and responsibility for subsidiaries and then in the next, describe the tightening of controls by the center" (p. 163). She saw both difference and unity "as crucial dimensions of effective executive teams." It is not, she believed, an issue of either/or but of both/and, even though both/and thinking sounds contradictory and ambiguous. Achieving both/and is not, however, unproblematic. Markham (1996), for example, reported on the results of a field study where, on the one hand, management insists on worker autonomy, and, on the other, "explodes when the designers do not perform according to unstated expectations" (p. 390). The resulting double bind, she found, "functions to construct and reproduce a powerful, hegemonic system of control" (p. 391). Putnam, Phillips, and Chapman (1996) similarly remarked that "paradoxical situations cause tensions and feelings of paralysis" (p. 388).

Organizations, as they accommodate themselves to serve a varied clientèle, need to encourage the emergence of communities of practice characterized by diverse modes of thought, missions, technologies, and disciplinary backgrounds. At the same time they need to display unity of purpose in competing with other organizations and institutions, even if this means imposing limitations on the liberty of action of members.

In this chapter we explore the production of ambiguity as an output of managerial conversation. Following up on Markham's intuition we hypothesize that ambiguity is an inevitable consequence of being simultaneously different and unified. As Eisenberg (1984) and others have argued, ambiguity is "an inherent and sometimes necessary element of human interaction and social life" (Markham, 1996; p.

392). Our attention focuses on the discursive mechanisms that go into producing ambiguity. We illustrate by drawing on the filmed reproduction of a managerial encounter centered, reflexively, on its own modes of accommodating diversity and unity. We develop an original approach to the analysis of managerial conversation that emphasizes the centrality of text as an agent responsible for the authoring of the organization's goals, objectives, and structures. Given contradictory models of how the organization should function, each expressed in a complex text, we then turn to examine the conversational mechanisms by means of which contradiction is accommodated. Finally, the chapter concludes with some observations on the value of ambiguity as an integrative mode of organizing.

DIFFERENTIATION AND INTEGRATION: TWO SIDES OF THE SAME COIN?

Consider the following extract from the transcript of a meeting of senior managers, gathered to consider the future of the company they work for when their long-term president and owner takes his retirement, as he has announced he shortly intends to do.[1] (Sam S. is the president, John P. is responsible for human relations in the firm, and Jack L. is vice president for the largest region covered by the enterprise, a supermarket chain; he is also a longtime colleague of the chief.)

58	John P:	I think that the structure of the company has one single (0.5)
59		overwhelming purp- purpose and that is to facilitate
60		the achievement of company goals and objectives. (0.8) I'm been s-
61		eh. (1.0) I feel we have *not* esh-established our our objectives.
62		(0.5) And I think th*at's* gotta come first. (0.2) Where we going,
63		what do we wanna be.
64	Sam S:	This is exactly how I feel (0.5). Now listen to what I'm telling,
65		each and every one of you. (0.5) Evidently over the past four o'
66		five weeks, (0.5) a hundred or two hundred items (0.5) have to
67		be increased in price
68	Jack L:	<Seventy-two items> =
69	Sam S:	= Alright, well, I'm telling you what I heard. [so- .
70	Jack L.:	[(accumulated) on
71		four weeks, seventy-two items =
72	Sam S.:	= Okay. Let's (0.2) let's say it's seventy-two items. (1.0) So
73		here's what happens. I meet one of our managers having lunch
74		upstairs who's the manager of St-Lawrence and Cremazie. I
75		walked over an' say "Hello, how are you?" and everything else,

---

[1]For the interested reader, the full text of the transcript of the managerial conversation from which we take excerpts can be obtained in Cooren (2006). A videotape of the recording is included as a supplement to the book.

76		"How is it going?" He says "Very fine, sales are up thirteen or
77		(0.2) fourteen percent" but he says he's terribly dis*turbed*. (0.5)
78		They got in a wh:ole list of items that they have to increase the
79		prices on (0.5) and he's disturbed because now they'll be going
80		back to what they did in the past, raising prices an' (.) putting on
81		higher prices an 'everything else.
82	Jack L:	Mr. President =
83	( ):	=[hhuhh
84	( ):	[Could I..Could I=
85	Jack L:	=No, [just a minute
86	( ):	[Could I..could I..could I get =
87	Jack L:	=Will you wait a minute? Mr. President look, this is what- this's
88		*why* I want to talk about structure first. (1.0) It happens that I and
89		you communicate. (0.5) (Twice a day three time a day four
90		times a day- no matter what time of day it is eh? <
91	Sam S:	Ri[ght.
92	Jack L:	[We communicate, I communicate to you, you com'nicate to
93		me. And I brought up to you (1.0) this perplex thing. 'Cause I
94		have to have somebody to speak to too (.) outside of my peers
95		who we speak to, eh? So I communicate with this. ((*Spoken with*
96		*intensity and pointing finger*)) Have you got the same problem in
97		Toronto?
98		(1.0)
99	Jack L:	Do you know what's happening at Toron[to?
100	Sam S:	[No, (I don't).
101	Jack L:	((*Spoken with intensity and pointing finger.*)) Are you running
102		one company or two companies? Is the *struc*ture that's wrong? Is
103		it professional management's wrong? Is it a (box) wrong? *How*
104		do you communicate? *They* communicate an' listen to this an' an'
105		I this is why I say structure (.) is so important an' how we're
106		gonna do it an' feedback an' control. .hh *Th:ey* been raising
107		prices from the first week. We kept prices back four weeks, we
108		did- though we got a co-co*st* increases, four (0.2) three four
109		weeks 'go three weeks 'go, so forth, we kept back four weeks.
110		They've been e- every week, putting in the price changes though
111		they come in- the same problem with- They discuss it with you?
112		(.)
113	Sam S:	No =
114	Jack L:	= Have they communicated with you? =
115	Sam S:	= No.
116	Jack L:	((*Spoken with intensity and pointing finger.*)) = Have they
117		communicated with anybody here? (0.5) How many companies
118		are you running? (0.5) *What* philosophy do you want? That's

119   why my *first* thing on page *six* (0.2) page *six* and I want you to
120   go back and read it. This is exactly- I I am *very* glad you brought
121   it up. Because page six I say, for God sake, "the *objec*tives and
122   goals and corporate philosophy, the objectives and goals must be
123   spelled out." _*What* is your goals for Tor- ? Are you running one
124   business? Are you still running an- an Ontario business? You
125   wanna be the general manager here? Or do you want to act as the
126   President? Do you wanna act as a corporate- as a corporate
127   President for everybody or for one?

What is going on here, and how should we go about analyzing it?

Let us start with the obvious. There is a difference of opinion. It seems to center on an issue of "structure" versus "goals and objectives." John P. and Sam S. come down on the side of goals and objectives. Jack L. is passionately preaching the crucial role of structure, which he associates with feedback and control. (The passion is more evident, perhaps, than the consistency of his argument, because he also insists that objectives and goals and philosophy must be "spelled out" [Line 123]. However, the tenor of his talk makes it clear that he at least thinks he is defending a principle different from that of his superior and his junior John P.)

The second thing that is obvious is that the discussion is occurring within an organization—a "business." The participants take it for granted they have a right to voice more than a personal opinion. They are managers. Sam S., for example, cites a conversation he had with a store manager. Jack L. refers to "peers" (Line 94) and to privileged conversations with the president, on a daily basis.

We can thus confidently assert that we are listening in on a managerial conversation where the issue is confronting difference, presumably with the object of arriving at a common understanding (otherwise why bother to talk). The future of the company, both parties would agree, depends on maintaining an integrated vision of both goals and structures. The debate, and the differing points of view, turns on which to accord priority. Both are important, even if they seem to be in contradiction.

The question we address can thus be stated somewhat differently: How do organizations manage to reconcile diversity and the unity of point of view? This raises the larger issue of differentiation and integration.

The Differentiation–Integration Paradox

In 1969, Lawrence and Lorsch published a book with the subtitle "Managing Differentiation and Integration." They taxed their colleagues at the time of being overly preoccupied with "the one best way to organize in all situations" (p. 3). They accused them of having underestimated, indeed ignored, the complexity of modern organization, operating under diverse economic and cultural conditions and incorporating a wide range of objectives and technologies. As they observed, "The organizational requirements for an effective sales unit may be quite different from those for an effective production unit" (p. 2).

This creates a puzzle. If, "as systems become large, they differentiate into parts, and the functioning of these separate parts has to be integrated if the entire system is to be viable" (p. 7), then the question is raised as to how the organization is to achieve both differentiation and integration simultaneously.

It sounds paradoxical, because differentiation and integration are antonyms (at least in mathematical calculus). We show that, paradox or not, the achievement of both, simultaneously, is an outcome, when it happens, of communication, and not just a desideratum. We argue that both differentiation and integration have to be enacted in the conversation of members of the organization on a continuing basis.

Differentiation is not merely a cause of the managerial conversation—that which has to be dealt with—but equally an effect of it. It has to be constructed. Historically, the difference between sales and production, for example, emerged when industrial leaders such as Henry Ford found out they could control distribution of their products more effectively (and profitably) by running their own outlets, rather than farming the marketing function out to independents. However, what sales and production were, and how they would interface, was a puzzle to be resolved, year after year, by the people who worked in each of the many multidivisional organizations that subsequently subscribed to the practice.

Maintaining differentiation with integration, we argue, is not a once-and-forever achievement; both have to be renegotiated in the everyday jostling of running a business (or department of government, or nonprofit association). It was the challenge of discovering how the mix of integration and differentiation is constructed, pragmatically, in the course of a managerial conversation, that stimulated us to focus on exchanges such as the one we cited at the outset.

THEORETICAL COMMITMENTS

The approach we adopt to the investigation of the foundations of integration and differentiation in the conversation of managers is based on a number of theoretical innovations. In this section, we consider the principal concepts that figure in our analysis.

Text

There is first the idea of text. A *text*, as we define it, is a string of statements, whether vocalized (spoken) or written, which is focused on some topic, or unified in some other way by its coherence as the expression of a point of view. Consider the intervention of Jack L. Although he could be accused of clumsiness of expression, it is clear enough that the speaker meant his remarks to be understood as an argument for a principle, namely the primacy of "structure." That President Sam S. has his facts wrong serves Jack as a point of entry to his argument (and incidentally provides a refutation of the latter's preceding text). It also conveniently allows him to quickly turn Sam's reproach into an illustration of his superior's failure to maintain a coherent line of command. It is the skewing of the president's horizon of interest, by paying too much attention to one region and not enough to another, that illustrates his point: The company needs a clear and consistent reporting structure.

The "text" to which we refer is not, however, merely the expression of a personal point of view. That would fail to qualify it as organizational. It is part of a larger collectively produced corpus of texts, those of the management committee as a whole. Later in the recorded conversation of the meeting at the Palomino Lodge, Jack L. would return to make a concrete proposal about how he would like to see the company structured, one that emphasized clear lines of reporting. This taking of position would generate both support and opposition. In the process, the text became more elaborated. It enlisted allies and stirred opposition. Here, for example, is the intervention of Mel D., Sam S.'s son-in-law and the eventual inheritor of the title of president (although nobody knew that at the time):

167	Mel D:	Obviously (.) gentlemen, inherent in each of our reports, (0.5)
168		although we don't state it (.) in negative terms hh we're a:ll
169		try:ing to *look* at *what* the deficiencies (.) have been, what they
170		a:re, and how we're goin' to correct them. This is (.) what
171		everyone really wants to do deep down. [Nobody is=
172	Sam S:	[Absolutely.
173	Mel D:	=saying "Look so and so is incompetent." We might think it
174		each of- whoever they think is incompetent or degrees of
175		competence and so on, but *that* is secondary at the moment 'cuz
176		we're not now e*va*luating individuals. *All* we are saying (.) is
177		that the sum *to*tal (.) of everything that has been *do*ne (1.0) in
178		one way or the other has not (.) been satisfactory. So we're
179		trying to change.=Now (0.5) if we had a structure that (.) certain
180		types of policies ((*fist tap on table for emphasis*)) *must* be
181		cleared and spelled out > to the nth degree prior to
182		implementation, and a consistent follow up and discussion on
183		these policies (.) in *all* divisions, not only the Quebec Division,
184		the same applies to Ontario and everywhere else < then (.) these
185		things wouldn't *happ*en. So they'd be prevented from
186		occurring. But it's no use telling Jack right now "Don't you
187		raise these prices" because (.) for two weeks the President was
188		away? and there's four thousand other items that are happening
189		simultaneously? and it's physically impossible for any one
190		individual to consistently follow up and check and get
191		clearance? Therefore I sub*mit* that from *my* understanding, and
192		maybe it's limited, that un*less* we clearly spell o:ut, which is a

193   f:ar (.) *less* arduous task, the organizational structure, and *how*
194   we make decisions and *how* the reporting relationships will
195   function, to permit these things to happen. Once that's cleared,
196   then we gonna spend (0.2) a _*year*, if need be, on spelling out
197   the objectives. Now (.) if you say objectives is just broadly that
198   we wanna maintain a profit, we wanna reverse a trend, who is
199   against that? That we can resolve in ten or fifteen minutes, so I
200   s:ay (0.2) that we *leave* objectives until the other thing is settled

The corporate counsel, James D., had his lawyerly take on the same issue:

391   James D:=All our previous discussions, and we had some before we
392   came up here to Palomino, we thought (.) uh it was impressed
393   on us and many individuals raised the point that we should be
394   *try*:ing (0.2) > difficult as it is for all of us< to be *object*ive
395   about what we said in these reports (.) and to th:*ink* of the
396   organization (.) *not* in terms of the incumbency in any one
397   position but as to h:ow the organization itself (.) should be (.)
398   *best* structured from the point of view, and w:orry about the
399   b:odies to fill the positions afterwards. And that is what, if
400   we're going to be objective, we should be doing here (0.2) and
401   we're *d:odg*ing the issue because we're saying "Ah (0.5) it
402   might possibly point the finger at any one of us, and that's a-
403   too delicate area for us to discuss" =

Sam S., on the other hand, claimed to be baffled (Harry S. is the meeting chair for the occasion):

288   Sam S: No but I'm still confused
289   (0.2)
290   Jack L: Sorry if I am not
291   Harry S: (xxxx) the President
292   (2.0)
293   Sam S: I'm looking at your chart and uh, I felt that uh as I said, I started
294   out to say, the cobwebs have somewhat (1.0) lifted (1.0) and
295   when I look at this (.) chart so to speak and looking at it from
296   your point of view I see Vice-President Quebec, Ontario (0.2)
297   manufacturing, private label, market research. (0.5) Now are we
298   saying that the Vice-President (0.5) of my Quebec Division
299   (0.8) is the Vice-President over the Vice-President of Quebec
300   and Ontario Division?
301   Jack L: Yes, I'm tellin' *one* Vice-President is respons' for all this so they

302   have a man- you'll have a man (.) res[ponsible
303 Sam S: [A Vice-President for
304   Quebec?
305 Jack L: Yeah! If [he's (xxxx)
306 Sam S: [A Vice-President 'n Ontario=
307 Jack L: I *don't care* [*names*
308 Sam S: =[And we'll have another Vice-President (0.5) in
309   ch:arge of all of these three operations, beside you've added a
310   couple (.) uh of others. Now, we said the purpose of this
311   meeting i::s that we arrive at some under*stan*ding that removes
312   *b:arr*iers that makes it more uh practical, and more efficient to
313   operate. Now you can't call yourselves *all* Vice-Presidents but
314   *one* Vice-President is different to the other Vice-Presidents (0.2)
315   without saying what that is?

The issue of structure, in fact, would infuse the discussion of the participants throughout the entire encounter, although it would not lead to any concrete outcome—no consensus would be forthcoming. The "text," as a unanimous expression of the intention of management, was never finalized. They ended the meeting without a consensus.

Subtext

The second key concept we introduce in conducting our analysis is that of *subtext*, a concept we borrow from the work of Labov and Fanshel (1977). These authors distinguished between "what is said" and "what is done" (Labov & Fanshel, 1977, p. 71). What is said includes the text of the intervention, plus relevant paralinguistic cues (e.g., emphasis) and "implicit reference to other texts and propositions" (p. 71). What is done they described as the *plane of interaction*: "itself a multilayered complex of speech acts" (p. 71). Now the emphasis shifts from the speech part of speech act to the act part. It is here that the interactive system discloses its own structural underpinnings.

The reference to "speech acts" is the key to understanding the idea of subtext. According to speech act theory (Cooren, 2000b), communicating via the generation and interpretation of texts (conversing, orally or by other forms of technical mediation) accomplishes more than transmitting information or communicating an idea. It is how people influence each other's beliefs and actions. It is a way of expressing attitudes and motivating others to share them: doing by and in saying; an action as opposed to an expression register of speech (Austin, 1962).

Attitudes, however, have two potential spheres of reference. They may be explicitly directed to either the world outside the conversation, or, reflexively, the conversation itself and the organization it is instantiating, or both. The excerpt we cited at the beginning of this chapter illustrates the distinction quite well. Sam S., for example, states what he has learned as a fact that prices have been raised without his approval. He then indicates, by implication, what should now happen: Go back to the established policy of keeping prices down. His remarks are both outwardly and inwardly oriented: Both state a fact and indicate what somebody should do about it. Concurrently, it is clear, he is also asserting a relationship to his subordinates: "Now listen to what I'm telling, each and every one of you" (Lines 64–65), he begins. It is a relationship in which they have the responsibility to answer to him (not just listen to him). He is entitled, he assumes, to sanction their performance, positively or (as in the example) negatively. He is the company president. Implicitly, he is reminding them what the structure of the organization is.[2]

Jack L. briefly refutes the alleged "facts," justifies his own actions ("We kept prices back four weeks, we did- though we got a co-co*st* increases, four (0.2) three four weeks 'go three weeks 'go, so forth, we kept back four weeks" (Lines 107–109)), and then turns the conversation back to focus on itself. He contradicts neither the rights of the president nor his own responsibilities. Instead, he introduces a further tacit rule of behavior, namely that those having equivalent ranks and responsibilities must be treated equitably—another reference to structure. Sam S., by implication, has broken the rule.

We call these tacit assumptions about the rights and responsibilities of the various members of the organization (the tissue woven out of their relative powers and statuses) a subtext. Labov and Fanshel (1997) thought of a subtext as "general propositions" (p. 53). Each individual in an organization (even one as small as a single family unit), they reminded us, has a status. "Each of these statuses," they observed, "carries with it a set of role obligations and criteria for satisfactory role performance" (p. 55). This is what we understand Jack L. to have been doing: commenting on Sam. S.'s unsatisfactory performance of his key role of president, given his status (the converse is also true, of course, because the president has said he was unhappy, indirectly, with Jack's performance). Jack takes the offensive:

125 Jack L.: Are you running one business? Are you still running an- an
126 Ontario business? You wanna be the general manager here? Or
127 do you want to act as the President? Do you wanna act as a
128 corporate- as a corporate President for everybody or for one?

As Labov and Fanshel (1977) observed, participants in conversation "normally do not argue the propositions directly, but argue whether or not the events being talked about are instances of these general propositions" (p. 53). The interjection of Jack L. illustrates the principle: It is a comment on the performance of his boss—

---

[2]Katambwe (2004) termed this tacit communication of relative status and relationship the *taxemic* modality of speech. The root of taxemic is the Greek word for arrangement. The taxemic effect of speech is thus to arrange the statuses of speakers, to categorize or classify them, in other words.

more explicit than usual, but still indirect. Later, however, Jack L. would try to formalize his assumptions about the nature of each status's rights and responsibilities. He would present a revised company organization chart built around the concept of a new role, that of executive vice president, or, as we would now say, Chief Operating Officer. It was this proposition—an explicit reference to the subtext, this time—that elicited the evident skepticism of the sitting president, but it is significant that the latter would take it as normal that debating what we are calling the subtext should occur as part of the managerial discussion. The subtext is collectively owned, even where there is less than total unanimity as to its terms. By common understanding, it functions as a tacit constitution governing everyone's actions, including those of the president (indeed, first and foremost those of the president).

Summary

Managerial conversations such as the one we have been using to illustrate our theoretical basis have two possible points of reference. They may be directed outward to the external context within which the organization operates, or inward, reflexively, to the set of arrangements and relationships that effectively pattern the day-to-day interaction of organizational members. John P. and Sam S.'s preference for a discussion of "goals and objectives" exemplifies the first alternative; Jack L.'s insistence on discussing "structure" the second. In this discussion, the group preference turned out to be for an inwardly directed examination of the internal dynamics of the firm. The choice was manifested in the texts of the discussion.

Texts, however, are not just any string of language. They have coherence by their focus on a theme, and their form as, for example, an argument or a plea. When they are focused inwardly, their theme is the set of arrangements that exemplify what might be called the "systemic" regularities of the organization (Giddens, 1984), or how people tacitly perceive the statuses, roles, rights, and responsibilities of each of the organizational actors. This normally implicit charter of organization—its "Magna Carta"—is what Jack L. meant by "structure." Texts, however, may be authored (singly or collectively). Indeed authoring the organization by setting out its goals and objectives and its structure, is indispensable to the organization taking on an identity to which the individual members, as well as others in the society, can relate.

AUTHORING THE ORGANIZATION

Although each intervention in the managerial conversation can be analyzed as a personal statement, reflecting individual styles of speech and argument, collectively the group assembled at the Palomino Lodge was there to generate an organizational text.[3] That they were aware they had been delegated by their organization to author the policy of the company in the context of a change of president is attested to by a sequence that came near the end of their meeting:

```
1518  James D: There's another aspect I think we should discuss briefly (0.2)
1519            We have a very sad history (.) of leaking out (.) all kinds of (.)
1520            uh semi-official (scutterbug) (.) rumor through the organization,
1521            which (.) again I think does more harm than good.
1522  (  ):     You mean (xxxx) the President?
1523  James D: I beg your pardon?
1524  (  ):     (xxxx) the President?
1525  James D: No, I'm not concerned with that (0.5) ((people speaking at
1526            once)) But I do think that we we should have some consensus
1527            (.) as to what we want to say to our subordinates about what
1528            went [on here.
```

Consider the context of the discussion we have been citing. It is occurring within a very successful grocery and real estate enterprise, founded by Sam Steinberg, many decades before, and headed by him ever since. Now he is retiring. How to proceed? Two options offer themselves. One we have already encountered: Concentrate on the structure first, and then fit the people (including the new president when he arrives) into it.[4] On this score, the principal advocate of this strategy, Jack L., was fairly explicit on what he thought was wrong with the current regime and how it should be corrected. In the intervention we have already analyzed, he enumerated a number of propositions:

1. The president is in constant communication with the Quebec Division, and vice versa.
2. The Quebec Division communicated with the president with respect to the problems associated with increasing costs and raising prices.
3. The Ontario Division (Toronto) did not communicate with the president with respect to the problems associated with increasing costs and raising prices.

---

[3]In the broad sense, of course, every member of the organization is contributing to building a collective text that we can think of as that of the organization. All the members are in this sense "authors." They all represent their organization in their talk (Cooren, chap. 5, this volume). The difference in this case is that the participants in the discussion were self-consciously generating a text that they assumed would have "official" status. That it could be construed as official is a consequence, in turn, of their privileged status as managers, and that is also a reflection of an underlying subtext.

[4]The "he" is intentional. It is 1969, and in this family firm there would be no question of appointing a woman chief executive. Sam Steinberg had not been blessed with a son (he had three daughters, one of whom did possess executive experience). When he eventually chose a new president it would be the son-in-law, not the daughter. Of course, he himself stayed on as chairman of the board.

4. The president does not know what is happening in the Ontario Division with respect to the problems associated with increasing costs and raising prices.

If this is the text of his intervention, it speaks to a tacit subtext, which would read somewhat as follows:

- The president should have a clear and unambiguous philosophy of management.
- He should treat all divisions equitably, in the same manner.
- He should be informed about what is happening in all divisions.
- For their part, the divisions must communicate with the president, and keep him informed, particularly for what concerns pricing policies.

The other option was never quite so explicitly enunciated, although it was transparent enough, almost certainly, to those present: Go on as before, but with a new president in the driver's seat, with a large measure of discretion, and with the family—read Mr. Sam himself—still in the background, pulling the strings.

Let us now see if we can elucidate, using what we know of the company, what lies behind this discussion of alternative emphases.

First, Sam Steinberg was a family man. He built his supermarket and real estate empire from humble origins, running his mother's corner store in Montreal's immigrant quarter when he was still a boy. He never forgot his family obligations, and his brothers and later his nephew and son-in-law became part of his management team. He had imagination, drive, and a considerable fund of common sense, but doing it by the book, running a tight ship, was not the cornerstone of his success. Dealing with people on a one-to-one basis and sizing up the possibilities in an equivocal situation were. He took chances; he was savvy; he built. Now on the threshold of retirement, his company had become far too extended to be an enterprise he could run out of his pocket. Jack L. was probably well justified in accusing him of acting more like a general manager of one division than a president of them all.

Sam S. (familiarly referred to as "Mr. Sam") never enunciated his subtext in so many words in the discussion (as he himself observed at one point, he did not have to; he owned the company). But there are hints. They emerged in what was the most emotionally charged segment of the management meeting, where allegations were made that the family exerted an undue influence over the running of the company. The topic was broached by Sam's nephew, Arnold, who voiced the opinion that "n-nepotism (0.2) generates sa-satisfaction to any (.) particular individual for a very short period of time" (Lines 780–781). The theme was then taken up by Irving L., a comparative outsider:

824   Irving L: Well I tell you, I just wanna comment a little on this because uh
825   (0.2) I've had a lot of uh people uh come to me and talk to me

```
826              about this bec- may be because:e you know I'm a little younger
827              and only joined the company .hh uh some eleven years ago and
828              uh went through all this and in my case obviously it was no
829              great deterrent for me. .hh but uh let me just say this, that uh
830              there is an awareness (0.5) in the co- in many of the people in
831              the company that uh there is such a thing as an informal
832              organization at Steinberg's (0.8) which is directly linked to the
833              family (.) and there's an informal organization perhaps in every
834              company but this one happens to be directly linked to the family
835              .hh to the point wh:ere (.) there uh there (.) if you're sitting
836              among a group of peers (0.5) that the fact th', and I'm gonna
837              level here and tell you that the standard joke is (.) that the key
838              decisions are not made at the management committee (.) or with
839              the President (.) but at Friday night supper (1.0) and this in itself
840              is very indicative because I'm sure you've all heard the same e-
841              expressions used (0.2) and it's very indicative (.) as to how
842              people see the organization an' how they read it. They don't see
843              (.) equ:ality; if one fella happens to be Vice-President of this
844              and another fella Vice-President of that and they're both putting
845              forth their opinions, if one happens to be related (.) the feeling
846              is (.) that he's got an awful lot more to say (.) a) because he is
847              much closer, b) it's sort of his money involved and, c:) it's
848              because (.) he goes to the Friday night supper as opposed to the
849              other party (.) and I think that this (.) is the feeling among a lot
850              of the people (.) in the organization. They feel it definitively
851              has hampered in the past (.) and I might add (.) that uh perhaps
852              from my own point of view anyways is probably is less so now
853              than it has been (0.5) and it's been very severe in the past (.) in
854              my opinion.
855              (2.0)
856  Irving L: And I can tell you there's a lot of people they spend a lot of
857              time talking about this stuff (0.2) a lot of -time. And so I think
858              we have to recognize it and be aware of it.
859              (4.0)
860
```

Irving's observations elicited this intervention from the corporate counsel, James D.:

```
868  James D: No yeah but to to support everything that Irving is saying uh
869              there is also and I think Irving could, might call in on this (.)
870              there's a sort of uh (0.5) another:r feeling around (0.5) that (0.5)
```

871   a a certain amount of this has (.) definitely been taken care of in
872   a much better way in recent years with the appointment of other
873   non-family people to very senior positions. But running along
874   with that wh-whether we like to admit it or not there's a there's
875   one school of thought going around which sort of looks as us a
876   little bit like the Negroes in a cabinet (0.5) you know (.) that
877   really we're we're there more for show ((starting to laugh)) than
878   for performance. And that the real decisions are still made as
879   Irving says in the in the Friday night eh meetings whether that's
880   (0.5) has validity or not, that's what they believe=

Sam's response to the allegations is revealing:

792   Sam S: hh now uh (0.8) uh the only comment I would like to make at
793   this mom- this moment was that I read a Harvard report (0.5)
794   where it deals with families in organizations=
795   ( ):   =We all read it. ((People interrupting and agreeing.))
796   Sam S: Alright! So it tells you that after a period of twenty years there
797   is more family than ever before=and that hasn't affected the the
798   performances as I read it in these companies. (1.0) On the >
799   other hand < (0.5) I think that when we look around the table
800   over here, we talk about family, (1.0) well (.) I looked upon
801   Jack as a member of the family=I look up:on (.) Oscar as a
802   member of the family (.) I've looked upon Jack Ginser always
803   as a member of the family (.) and I think that they look upon
804   _themselves as a member of family.

In other words, not only did he run the company as an extended family, he believed it should be run on the principle of family organization.

Taylor and Cooren (chap. 7, this volume) argue that every thesis has an antithesis, and that thesis and antithesis are coconstructing. In the Steinberg Inc. managerial discussion the issue was quite explicitly "family organization" (Lines 647, 660) versus "professional management" (Line 685) leadership. But every organization is confronted with the necessity of reconciling two irreconcilable imperatives, integration and differentiation. The ambivalence may assume different guises, such as we have seen, but it will still be there, for precisely the reason that Lawrence and Lorsch (1969) wrote about. The authority lodged in the president is crucial, but so is the *marge de manoeuvre* of the subordinates.

So how can an organization be simultaneously a thesis and an antithesis? Obviously, by the continued coexistence of both: logically contradictory, but pragmatically reconciled by a sustained level of interactive ambiguity.

METHODOLOGICAL CONSIDERATIONS

If, as Labov and Fanshel (1977) found in their research, and our work confirms, references to the subtext are typically indirect, then a methodological problem is posed. Mostly, what these analysts call the "mode of argument" (p. 53) is oblique. As they wrote, "it is rarely possible to 'say what you mean'" (p. 53). Consider, for example, the following excerpt from the managerial discussion we are analyzing (Arnold S. is a nephew of the president and a senior member of management):

622   Arnold S:I think (.) there's been a number of very m:ajor decisions which
623   have been taken (.) uh (.) there seems to be an assumption (.)
624   that there's a-an eternal t:ap? that we turn on and the cash just
625   flows out. And frankly uh unfortunately we're at the stage
626   where just the reverse happens to be true where there is no more
627   cash. And unless we we follow these events very closely we
628   could find ourselves in serious trouble. Let me give you
629   another example: we at the present time (0.2) have four million
630   dollars invested in the restaurant business (.) four million
631   -dollars (.) There was *never* a decision made to invest anything
632   like that kind of money (0.5) by any one individual= I doubt
633   frankly that anyone in this room even _knew we have four
634   million dollars (.) invested in the restaurant business and that
635   doesn't include the buildings. This is I'm talking just about the
636   leasehold improvements and the equipment and the inventories,
637   four million dollars. Now that was no *planned* decision (0.5)
638   and yet it someh:ow with the loose kind of organization we
639   have, we find ourselves at the beginning of nineteen sixty-nine
640   with a four million dollars investment and we will lose this year
641   something like four hundred thousand dollars in that business.
642

Notice how very carefully he avoided pinning down responsibility for the unplanned (although "major" [Line 622]) decision. He put it down to "the loose kind of organization we have" (Lines 638–639). In fact, people knew who he was referring to, even though he avoided any specific attribution, as the immediately following intervention illustrates:

645   James D:You have given an example of what I was going to cite myself as
646   a combination of a) one-to-one decision-making and b) and f)
647   family organization. 'Cos if ever there was an example of the
648   *family* (0.5) and one-to-one decision-making (.) getting us in a

```
649          spot (.) that is it. (1.0) As every- uh certainly Bill knows this (.)
650          and I'm I'm sure uh Bill did it (.) and I did it (0.2) we were
651          against this whole thing. (1.0) We (.) vr' - I was most
652          vociferously against it (0.5) uh in principle > right from the
653          start=I said "If we're going to go into this kind of an outside
654          venture< (.) let us go out and get the best possible people we
655          can (0.8) and (1.0) let's not settle for any second best (.) let's not
656          go into the basis of (.) buying a company that is already (0.8)
657          not making money (0.2) but losing money." (0.8) That there's a
658          a specific (.) eviden- example of two barriers (.) where the one-
659          to-one decision-making is made (.) and at the same time (.) it's
660          the family organization=when I say organization (.) the family
661          (.) if you like (.) pulling rank (.) on the rest of the non-family
662          executives in the corporation an' saying "Well that's the way it's
663          goin' to be."
664          (2.0)
665  James D: An' an' an' in effect (.) the non-family part of the business had
666          absolutely nothing to say about that and what they did say (.)
667          was absolutely ignored.
668          (1.0)
```

"Family" is a code word for the president, Sam S. But even James D. is discreet, contenting himself with referring to (a) "family" and (b) "one-to-one decision-making" (Line 646). In a family firm, headed by the patriarch of the family and unique owner of the company, it could not have been too difficult for those present to dot the i's and cross the t's.

The methodological challenge posed by indirection is this: If what is important in the conversation is what people are doing, but what they are doing is only indirectly communicated by what they are saying, then what goes into decoding a spoken text calls on tacit knowledge—that of the analyst, as well as that of participants. A hermeneutic is involved (Giddens, 1984). The researcher-analyst cannot possibly possess the tacit knowledge of the people who were actually participating in the actual conversation. We can, at best, roughly approximate the missing subtext by what Labov and Fanshel (1997) called an *expansion*. In an expansion, the analyst brings to bear whatever additional knowledge is available to make sense of what is occurring. We know, for example, that Sam S. and Jack L. shared a common heritage as members of the same ethnic community and religion, and that they had worked together for decades in building a billion-dollar company. That history is relevant to the bluntness of Jack's criticism of his superior. Seniority and sustained performance confer certain idiosyncrasy credits, directness of speech being one of them, especially in the cultural context of the firm (Stohl, 2006).

Also in the analyst's favor is the recurrent character of talk. The participants in the discussion returned frequently to the same themes, and as they did it became easier and easier to understand what they were getting at in any single intervention. An expansion puts all this background information together.

Beyond this normally tacit contextual and intertextual knowledge, we can accomplish something in addition by focusing on the actual mode of interaction: how people choose to express themselves, straight-on or obliquely. It is this feature of conversational analysis that is directly related to our objective, which is to understand how conversation is able to construct both integration and differentiation from within. By "mode of interaction" we are referring to the constructive techniques that language affords for the assembling of a verbalized text. To see what is involved here let us again focus on part of the exchange between Jack L. and Sam S. (boldface type indicates exceptional emphasis).

87	Jack L:	=Will you wait a minute? Mr. President look, this is what-
88		this's *why* I want to talk about structure first. (1.0) It happens
89		that I and you communicate. (0.5) (Twice a day three time a
90		day four times a day- no matter what time of day it is eh? <
91	Sam S:	Ri[ght.
92	Jack L:	[We communicate, I communicate to you, you com'nicate to
93		me. And I brought up to you (1.0) this perplex thing. 'Cause I
94		have to have somebody to speak to too (.) outside of my peers
95		who we speak to, eh? So I communicate with this. ((*Spoken with*
96		*intensity and pointing finger*)) **Have you got the same**
97		**problem in Toronto?**
98		(1.0)
99	Jack L:	**Do you know what's happening at Toron[to?**
100	Sam S:	[No, (I don't).

Notice how Jack builds his case (remember that his aim is to reproach his boss for what amounts to a less-than-perfect performance as president). First he takes care to associate himself positively with his target. He presents the positive face of Sam S. He implies that the latter is open to communication, receptive, and actively engaged in the affairs of the company, on a daily basis ("We communicate, I communicate to you, you com'nicate to me" [Lines 92–93]). He simultaneously establishes his own credentials as a team player, someone who talks to his peers and consults his superior on a regular basis. Abruptly, he then switches from a normal tone of voice to a markedly more emphatic register (his voice rises and he points accusingly with his finger). Notice also that he simultaneously switches from an affirmative construction "I and you communicate" (Lines 88–89), "We communicate, I communicate to you, you com'nicate to me" (Lines 92–93) to the interrogative mood: "Have you got the same problem in Toronto? (1.0) Do you know what's happening at Toron[to?"(Lines 96–99). In employing a different mode of interaction, he achieves several things at once. First, posing his intervention as a question allows his interlocutor the possibility of an out: The latter could refute the implied assertion by saying that he was perfectly knowledgeable about what was going on in Toronto. The indirection introduced by the interrogative mood thus leaves some flex room for the interlocutor. Second, by employing the Socratic technique of a rhetorical question he is successful in eliciting an admission from his superior: "No, (I don't)" (Line 100). Jack in effect plays the role of prosecuting attorney. In managing to get this response, he nevertheless simultaneously, if implicitly, associates himself with his target, by distancing both of them from his opposite number in Toronto (the president talks to me, and vice versa, he shows, he doesn't talk to anyone there). On the other hand, he has succeeded in reproaching his boss for not having communicated with the other division. Finally, he has established, as we have seen, the groundwork for his proposal to restructure the management of the company to provide clearer lines of command and consultation. This latter achievement could not have been totally unrelated to his own ambition to be the person who replaced the departing president (which he ultimately succeeding in doing, although not immediately after Sam S. retired).

His "saying," in other words, is a "doing," however much he uses indirection to accomplish his action.

We have found it useful, in conducting analyses of this kind, to employ the terms *inclusion* and *exclusion* rather than integration and differentiation, which have a rather different connotation, in that they refer to the various practices and cultures that make up a large organization. In the managerial conversation we analyzed, each member of the in-group represented a community with its distinctive interests and practices. However, in the context of the conversation, each participant is in effect constructing borders, by allying the speaker with some others while distancing himself or herself from others: including, excluding. Thus Jack L. began by building an imaginary fence around himself and his superior ("We communicate, I communicate to you, you com'nicate to me" [Lines 92–93])—an inclusion—while drawing a boundary between his region and that of Ontario—an exclusion. On the other hand, on the issue of goals versus structure, the inclusion–exclusion division will prove to have a different contour. Here Jack L. will be aligned with Arnold S. even though they divide on a different issue (Mel is the son-in-law of Sam S., and will ultimately succeed him as president).

671	Jack L:	=only because I think we're getting some feelings out. For
672		three, four, five years, Mel and I have been saying very clearly,
673		yearly, we used to do it yearly, that the organization being (.)
674		*built* at corporate was much too heavy for our retail k:ind of
675		operation that we're into. .hh and we just talked against the
676		wind. As we talked it grew bigger and as we talked it grew
677		bigger .hh and (.) it- this costs us *time* and *money* and
678		*competi*tiveness because of this one kind of act=and we couldn't
679		make any change. We had no power=*I* had no power making

680   change, .hh *M:el* (.) didn't have the power because I know Mel
681   yelled as much I did, no power. Now where is there an
682   organization _responsibility? (0.5) and a function of a
683   management (.) in order to take this kind of v-view into fact and
684   see if we can *afford* what we're building. (0.5) Never was? Is
685   that, is that making manag- professional management as a
686   professional management exercising (.) decision-making? I
687   think we, we've failed=
688 Arnold S:=I'm (not sure) about that Jack. Which what you're saying
689   impl:ies (.) that there was duplication (.) that was unnecessary
690   building. [Isn't that what you're implying?
691 Jack L: [Mmh, yes, absolutely.
692 Arnold S:But surely the corollary to that (.) is that the duplication existed
693   at the corp- at the divisional level. You're saying that the
694   divisional level had to have what the corporate didn't. Wo' but
695   surely (.) in in a discussion (0.2) which is now coming out in
696   the in in work that Bill's group is doing (.) they're discovering
697   that the duplication is in fact taking place at the division (.) and
698   the *real* need is at _corporate? I mean all I'm saying Jack is that
699   in fact I agree that duplication exists.
700 Jack L: But Arnold=
701 Arnold S:=But you're assuming that duplication is at the corporate an' not
702   at the division
703 Jack L: *((Shouting.))* But (.) corporate started to build up (immaterial)
704   that was at the division. Now where should it be?=
705 Arnold S:=Maybe [xxx corporate who say the division grew up not=
706 Jack L: [xxx at corporate?
707 Arnold S:=even though it was at the corporate. (xxxx) Jack, I am agreeing
708   that some[one should have sat down.
709 Jack L: [Okay (0.5) Right! That's all what I am saying.

They resolve their head office–region difference by constructing a different in-clusion–exclusion boundary, this time dividing themselves from "someone [who] should have sat down" (Line 708). What might have made them adversaries, in one context, is now turned into an alliance by contrasting, textually, their "we-ness" with an unidentified but salient "they."

The discussion at Palomino was marked, above all, by opposing views on how the structure of management should work: haphazardly, at the beck and call of the president, or following strict lines of reporting responsibilities. It was a delicate issue, because it touched the statuses of those involved: their rights and responsibilities. The subtext of management was at stake. Labov and Fanshel (1977) predicted that in such a context the conversation will be characterized by a significant degree of indirection of speech: people saying things that convey, by inference, their meaning as to what they are doing, and what they really mean. The mode of integration, in other words, will be marked by ambiguity. People, after all, are conscious of the need to preserve each other's face, especially if they have to work together every day.

Estimating Ambiguity

This distinction between speech as saying and speech as doing suggests a method of research. If what people are doing in their saying can only be understood by inference—by exploiting background knowledge of the speech context to decode the meaning of the intervention—then the result is indirect speech. The degree of indirection then provides an index of the level of ambiguity that is present in the conversation as a whole.

Consider Jack L.'s intervention again from this perspective.

```
92    Jack L:    [We communicate, I communicate to you, you com'nicate to
93               me. And I brought up to you (1.0) this perplex thing. 'Cause I
94               have to have somebody to speak to too (.) outside of my peers
95               who we speak to, eh? So I communicate with this. ((Spoken
96               with intensity and pointing finger)) Have you got the same
97               problem in Toronto?
98               (1.0)
99    Jack L:    Do you know what's happening at Toron[to?
```

We examine this sequence of talk according to three criteria:

- The grammatical mood of the utterance (assertive, directive, interrogative, etc.).
- The absence or presence of indirection.
- The implied inclusiveness or exclusiveness (i.e., where the boundary is drawn between speaker, the person addressed, and others).

For example, the first utterance is phrased as an assertion and the meaning is transparent: It is direct. It is also inclusive (affiliative). The second utterance is similarly affirmative, and direct, but it is neutral on the dimension of inclusion (notice though that it connotes a hierarchy because it is Jack that "brought up … this perplex thing" [Line 93] to Sam). The third utterance is similarly a direct affirmation and takes the form of a justification—a self-reference. The final utterance, however, is more complex. Both parts of the intervention are phrased as questions: They are instances of the directive mood (directive in the sense that they are formulated in a way that compels a response: "Do you … ?," "Have you … ?"). Here what is said is clearly not what is being done (in the Labov–Fanshel sense of doing). Jack L. already knows the answer to his question, so obtaining an informative answer to it clearly cannot be his primary motive. The surface effect of the speech act, as a quest for facts, is secondary. There is thus another intention in play, namely to establish a fact: Sam S. and Toronto do not communicate with each other. However Jack L. already knows this as well. His primary intention (taking account of context) is thus neither to ask for, nor state, a fact; it is to accuse his superior of a bias. He thus implicitly distances himself from the actions of his boss, even though, in the sequence as a whole, he has already established their sustained conviviality. Both inclusive and exclusive, in the course of a single intervention, it is (one suspects, deliberately) ambiguous.

So this single intervention is in fact three acts packaged into one utterance. As a question, it is directive, indirect, and neutral. As an affirmation it is assertive, direct, and neutral. As a reproach (the tacit, or primary, act indirectly conveyed by the surface, or indirect, speech act) it is assertive, direct, and exclusive.

In effect, Jack L. has managed to produce both an integration (an inclusion of Sam S. and Jack L. within a single universe of communication, distinct from the other region) and a differentiation (in clearly distinguishing his own point of view from that of his cocommunicator, Sam S.). This is why we spoke earlier of the necessary coconstruction of integration and differentiation from within the conversation. Jack L. will go to the stake for his company, he is at pains to show throughout the meeting:

488   Jack L: When I put these things out I feel deeply about the organization
489   and where it's going and where it should go. An' I'm willing to
490   (.) subject my *own* personal goals at this point- though I 'ave
491   personal goals- to the good or welfare of the organization.

But he will also fight like a tiger for the autonomy of his region of authority.

This analysis points the way to how to analyze the level of ambiguity that is present in a given interactive discourse: the ratio of indirect to direct acts of speech. Limits of space preclude a more in-depth analysis of this potential, but it invites further research.

CONCLUSION: MANAGEMENT AS THE MAINTENANCE OF AMBIGUITY

Sam S., to judge by his performance in the managerial conversation we have been analyzing, was himself a master of ambiguity. He did not squash the insubordinate criticism implied in Jack L.'s intervention. In fact, he encouraged it and other such criticisms:

752   Sam S: When I started out the meeting I said each one of you in your
753   report there must be *something* that you *feel* and we recognize

754   that and this is one of the reasons we're here. So if there are in
755   tho:se those items that you (.) consider uppermost that you
756   reduce to writing and felt free to say so (.) what is uppermost in
757   your minds that you feel has some restraining influence I think
758   it should like Jack said (0.5) uh (0.7) *brought out*?

Although he could play the family card, he could also assume the mantle of a highly successful and respected businessman:

952   Sam S: Listen (.) foremost in my mind there's al:ways *been* (0.5) the
953   person's ability to cope with his job (0.2) at the _*point* when he
954   was no longer able to measure up to that job (.) he was replaced
955   and that'll go all the years that we've been in business. Doesn't
956   matter wh:at that relationship (.) happened to _be. (0.2) Now,
957   *however* it's viewed (0.5) from the outside (1.0) as long as I am
958   in the job in any case (0.8) family will always be given
959   consideration but *always* (.) subject to the person's ability to
960   discharge that responsibility.

Why is this ambivalence on his part significant?

Steinberg's managerial discussion was polarized between two seemingly contradictory texts. We could call them the "family organization" (Lines 647–660) and the "professional management" (Line 685) texts (these were in fact the terms used by the participants themselves). What we now want to suggest is that these alternative visions of the organization conform to what Taylor and Cooren (chap. 7, this volume) refer to as story versus antistory. Each text is in effect a vehicle for constructing a narrative account of the organization: its purposes and its legitimate agents. Authoring is going on.

In the family organization text there is a hero, Sam Steinberg. He exemplifies in his own person the values and personality of the company. His nephew enunciates the narrative quite straightforwardly:

1   Arnold S: Uh, this company has been uh directed u::h by, Sam Steinberg
2   for-for some fifty years now and the company has been built up
3   ar*ound his* leadership. And it's been built up uh on the
4   assumption that u:h (.) that nothing will happen to Mr. Sam
5   Steinberg in:n- for time in memoriam. If uh anything *did*
6   happen, that- we- we would be faced with a catastrophic
7   situation of- uh, in *my* opinion of a, of a most serious nature. I
8   put number one in- I put succession as number one because
9   (0.2) of this _catastr*ophic* situation that would result, I think that
10   everything else would pale by com*par*ison (0.2) in the event of
11   something happening to- to the President

If we were citing Max Weber here, we would be tempted to refer to this as the narrative of the charismatic leader. And, still inspired by Weber, we could also point out that, in addition, being head of the family connoted not just charismatic but traditional grounds that justified his exercise of power in the corporation. After all, that was how he treated everybody from store manager up, as he himself pointed out.

Now let us consider the antistory. Clearly, in Jack L.'s envisaged arrangement, the grounds of authority in a professionally managed company would be what Weber called "rational." It is worth citing Henderson and Parsons's (1947) translation of Weber on this score:

> In the case of legal authority, obedience is owed to the legally established order. It extends to the persons exercising the authority of office under it only by virtue of the formal legality of their commands and only within the scope of authority of the office. (p. 328)

In this scenario, Sam S.'s actions are an unjustified usurpation of power: ignoring the chain of command by chatting up store managers, neglecting Toronto while freely interfering in operations in Montreal, starting up in a restaurant business without consulting his management council, and so on.

How, in practice, do organizations effectively deal with these internal contradictions? They do not, we suggest. Instead managers maintain the ambiguity by resorting to face-saving indirection in how they interact with each other. The underlying contradiction is not resolved, but the organization nevertheless goes on, as long as there is sufficient slack to allow the contradictions to persist. The water never quite comes to a boil. On the other hand, it is never far from doing so. Ambiguity persists. And it is the ambiguity that contributes both to a sufficient level of inclusion to assure integration, and an adequate degree of exclusion to assure differentiation. It doesn't always work, of course, as Güney's research (chap. 2, this volume) demonstrates. But mostly it does.

We are not suggesting that ambiguity is necessarily a desirable state of organization. As Markham (1996) pointed out, it can be destructive, in submitting employees to intense psychological strain. It may also result in suppressing—occulting—information vital to the carrying out of the organization's mission, as the commissions of inquiry into both the *Columbia* catastrophe, and the operation of the intelligence agencies prior to the 9/11 outrage, illustrate. We are saying no more than that ambiguity is inevitable, and that the reason can be found in how communication works wherever people confront the necessity of resolving the paradox—pragmatically, not intellectually—of simultaneous unity and diversity. The functionalist goal of attaining equilibrium is forever unattainable, certainly in a globalized world, and perhaps in any world in which human interaction is central.

PART II

AGENCY AND NARRATIVITY

CHAPTER FIVE

The Organizational World as a Plenum of Agencies

François Cooren
Université de Montréal

With the interpretive turn in the 1980s (Burrell & Morgan, 1979; Putnam & Pacanowsky, 1983; Weick, 1979) and the discursive turn in the 1990s (Alvesson & Karreman, 2000; Fairhurst & Putnam, 2004; Grant, Keenoy, & Oswick, 1998; Keenoy, Oswick, & Grant, 1997; Oswick, Keenoy, Grant, & Marshak, 2000; Putnam & Fairhurst, 2001), there has been a growing interest in the study of the role discourse and communication play in the functioning of organizations (Putnam & Cooren, 2004). Despite the undeniable success of this perspective, some scholars still question what they claim to be the collapse of materiality into discursivity (Reed, 1999, 2000); that is, the tendency to reduce an organization to a discursive form. According to this realistic stance, discourse and communication cannot be considered the building blocks of organization, because this would amount to neglecting the material conditions of its production (Fairclough, 1995). For these scholars, one cannot scale up from discourse and communication to organization without mobilizing ideological structures, relations of power, and material realities, which are traditionally used to account for what transcends, determines, or shapes discourse and communication (Reed, 2000). We thus end up with the traditional micro–macro gap, which highlights the irreducibility of organization to communication.

Commenting on this debate, Putnam and Cooren (2004) noted:

> The epistemological choice these positions offer is either a socio-constructive approach to reality, in which discourse is seen as a "filter" through which members' interactions co-construct and co-constitute the organization, or a materialist approach, which conceives of discourse as reflecting something already constituted. (p. 385)

This chapter proposes to problematize this opposition by showing that questioning the material world–social world dichotomy amounts to reconceptualizing the way we approach the general problematic of agency. In other words, what I would like to propose here is a sort of agency turn, a turn that will enable us to see that the socioconstructive and materialist views both appear to be incomplete.

More precisely, I show how action in general (and organizational action in particular) should be considered a *hybrid phenomenon*; that is, a phenomenon that tends to mobilize the participation of entities with variable ontologies (material, discursive, human, nonhuman). As Latour (1996) observed, action is something that is shared between actors, whether these actors be humans, machines, tools, documents, signs, or architectural elements. To do is to cause to do (*faire, c'est faire faire*). According to this approach, we never leave the terra firma of interaction, but we then need to acknowledge the interplay and contribution of human and nonhuman doings. In other words, the socioconstructivists are right to start from interaction, but they need to widen the extension (and intension) of this concept to recognize that nonhumans also do things. As for the materialists, they are right to notice that humans are acted on as much as they act, but they need to recognize that using analytical shortcuts like "structures," "power," or "ideology" to account for what influences human action and discourse does not do justice to the complexity of the phenomena they study.

Through a series of illustrations taken from fieldwork conducted in different organizational settings, I show how humans are actually very good at producing technological and textual devices that can in turn work in their name, a process that Taylor and Van Every (2000) named *imbrication*. The dynamic that needs to be better understood thus turns around the concept of appropriation. By appropriating the action of other actors, one can act from a distance and across time, a phenomenon that appears crucial for whoever wants to understand how managers and employees in general achieve coordination by maintaining a relative and distant control over their own and other's work. This teleappropriation can be considered the key phenomenon by which collective actors emerge and their identities can be reinforced.

This chapter is divided into four sections. In the first, I show how the world as we know it can be said to be filled with agencies, a position that requires a reconceptualization of such key terms as *agents* and *agency* if we really want to understand how societies and organizations manage (or fail) to function, how control is operated, or how resistance can occur. According to such a redefinition, the term *agent* means what or who appears to make a difference, whereas *agency* simply means making a difference. This forces us, as organizational analysts, to (a) take into account what entities with variable ontologies appear to be doing in a given situation; that is, what difference they seem to make as well as how their actions can be appropriated or attributed; and (b) pay attention to what humans say or write when they ascribe agency to these very entities, whether they are documents, machines, or even organizations.

The second section highlights two important features that can be ascribed to these redefined agents. As noted by Taylor and Van Every (2000), one possible definition of agency involves the fact that an agent acts or speaks on behalf (or in the name) of a principal, a phenomenon that explains how one can act from a distance (i.e., teleact). Recognizing teleaction as a key organizational (and social) feature of agency thus leads us to another of its important characteristics: representation. In keeping with our focus on agency, representations are here mainly understood as actions: the acts of making present something or someone. Acting in the name of others thus amounts to making these others present, a sort of "presentification" that, as we will see, tends to solve the conundrum of the mode of being of societies and organizations. According to this approach, a collective entity like a group, organization, or society exists through all the entities that act or speak on its behalf.

This reflection then leads us to the third section, which addresses more specifically the questions of the mode of being of organizations. Like any collective entity, an organization is identified, defined, and delimited through the different agents that speak or act in its name. In this sense, an organization, let's say a corporation, in the legal sense of the term, can be made present through its logos, by-laws, stock certificates, ledgers, board of directors, minutes, organizational charts, buildings, annual reports, CEO, vice presidents, commercials, public relations, workers, treasurers, secretaries, machines, corporate seal, texts, and operations, to just name a few elements. As we will see, all these entities, at one time or another, can be said to act, work, or speak in the name of the organization they represent (i.e., make present). In a world full of agencies, an organization's identity can thus be understood through all these entities that can act and speak in its name. The organization, in this specific sense, is a kind of monster, a Leviathan, to the extent that its mode of being can be extended to whomever or whatever ends up representing it by teleacting (see Callon & Latour, 1981).

Although this last reflection is valid for any kind of collective entity (whether a group, a band, a couple, an institution, or society), what remains to be shown is what makes organized forms (i.e., organizations) so particular. Although a group is not necessarily organized, an organization requires, at least on paper, this dimension.[1] This brings us to the fourth and final section, which addresses the process of organizing; that is, the process by which collective entities are "put together into an orderly, functional, structured whole" (the American Heritage Dictionary, 2000). As shown, our reconceptualization of agency helps us in this matter to the extent that different types of agencies are typically created and mobilized to fulfill organizing (to just name a few, organizational charts, contracts, ledgers, surveillance cameras, statuses, checklists, orders, memos, supervisors, supervisees, programs, procedures, etc). Like organizations, organizing can thus be understood as a hybrid phenomenon that requires the mobilization of entities with variable ontologies, which contribute to the emergence or enactment of the organized form (Taylor & Van Every, 2000; Weick, 1979, 1995).

---

[1] In that specific sense, one could say that society is, of course, an organized form even if we usually refrain from saying that it is an organization. This might be mainly because society, as an entity, cannot truly be said to have very defined objectives or one single raison d'être, a dimension that we normally find in what we call an organization (see Taylor & Robichaud, 2004). In a way, the raison d'être of society is always an open question: It is a matter of discussions, debates, and even fights between agents who put themselves forward as speaking on its behalf.

THE WORLD AS A PLENUM OF AGENCIES

Before addressing the main question of this section—to what extent we can say that the world as we know it is filled with agencies and only agencies—we need to first explain how we define such key terms as action and doing. As Deetz (2001) rightly reminded us, to define means to "make final," or worse, "to kill" (p. 4), because it consists of delimiting (always arbitrarily) what is inside and what is outside the concepts defined. To avoid "killing the bird" (p. 4), the solution might be to account for how it lives in our everyday world; that is, how it grows and evolves before taxidermists end up stuffing it to make it look like it is alive. For these "birds" that we call action and doing, this could then consist of showing that the way we account for reality amounts (at least implicitly) to ascribing agency to more entities than we usually are ready to consider.

Imagine the following situation. You are the CEO of a newly created company and tomorrow you have an important appointment at 9:00 a.m. with a representative of a venture capital firm in Manhattan. Having spent the day working on your PowerPoint presentation, you drive back home exhausted by a long day of work but with the vague feeling of being finally prepared for D-Day. Just before going to bed, you look into your PDA to check the firm's address you had added 1 week ago: 500 5th Avenue, corner of 42nd Street. Looking at your subway map, you figure out how to get there and how long it is going to take to make it to this appointment. The day after, you finally arrive at your destination: a 60-story skyscraper, built in the 1920s.

On entering the building, you notice a sign inviting you to check in at the concierge's desk. You follow these instructions and go to the desk. There, the concierge asks for the reason of your visit, has a camera take a picture of your face, and invites you to say your name so that it can also be recorded while the picture is taken. Having submitted to all these security procedures, you proceed to the lobby and quickly check the name of your potential investor in the list of companies on the left wall: New York Venture Capital, Inc., Suite 3503. Once you have arrived at the 35th floor, you follow an arrow to the right that leads you to your final destination. At the front desk, a secretary politely asks the purpose of your visit, checks your information on her calendar, and invites you to sit in the waiting room. Five minutes later, a representative of the firm comes to introduce himself and invites you to follow him to a conference room. While you nervously hook up your computer to the video projector, three other representatives settle around the conference table. The show can now begin!

Why describe this (relatively mundane) event? Simply to illustrate that such a description implicitly or explicitly requires the attribution of agency not only to humans but also nonhumans. Indeed, if we review the actions described during this exercise, we realize that we had no problems saying that:

- A sign *invited* you to check in at the concierge's desk.

- A camera *took* your picture and *recorded* your voice.
- An arrow *led* you to your final destination.

As we see, this relatively short list accounts for the sign's, the camera's, and the arrow's doings, but some other types of contribution are also hidden in the description. Here they are:

- What you wrote in the PDA *reminded* you that the appointment was at 500 5th Avenue, corner of 42nd Street
- The subway map *indicated* how to get to your appointment
- The list of the building tenants in the lobby *informed* you which floor you should go to.
- The presence of your name in her calendar *confirmed* to the secretary that you indeed had an appointment at 9:00 a.m.

As we see in this second list, ascribing agency always is a matter of perspective (or worldview, as Taylor [1993] would say). In saying that you looked into your PDA to check the firm's address you had entered 1 week ago, no agency was apparently attributed to this electronic instrument. However, and this is one of Latour's (1994) crucial teachings, this description precisely passed over in silence this tool's contribution by focusing solely on your action (i.e., checking). But checking would not have been possible had what is written in the PDA not made any difference in the situation. What difference does it make? A big one, if we consider that the address you entered in it reminds you of a piece of information that is quite important, given the circumstances: the location of your appointment.

Certainly, informing is an action that cannot be performed by the address written in the PDA alone; it requires some contributions upstream and downstream. Upstream, it of course required that you enter the address 1 week ago after your phone conversation with the representative of the firm. As for downstream, it required that you, the human agent, get to the appropriate date and read the information you had put in today's 9:00 a.m. slot. This is the other contribution of Latour's (1994) work: Action is something that is always shared with others: "Faire, c'est faire faire" (to do is causing to do). The same thing is true for the other contributions: The subway map can indeed indicate how to get to your appointment because, upstream, it was designed to do so by a series of topologists, cartographers, printers, and publishers who put their energy and abilities into the production of this device, and downstream because you happen to know how to read maps and understand the information it contains.

To consider the world as full of agencies and only agencies—what could be called, in reference to Garfinkel (1988), a plenum of agencies—thus requires that we take into account all the human and nonhuman entities that, day by day, contribute to its building and organizing. This does not mean that we fail to account for the human contributions, as some critiques of this ontological stance seem to imply

(McPhee & Seibold, 1999). On the contrary, recognizing the nonhuman participation in the processes we analyze implicitly amounts to acknowledging the humans' contributions, whether upstream or downstream. All these devices, objects, tools, and machines that indeed do things in our world, in fact, represent competencies, skills, techniques, imagination, and creativity that are quite unique in the animal realm.

To say that the address you wrote in the PDA reminded you where to go, that the arrow on the sign led you to your final destination, or that the presence of your name in her calendar confirmed the appointment to the secretary does not completely pass over in silence the human contribution; it is just a way of describing the world that happens to highlight the nonhuman contribution in those different situations. Without what is written in your PDA, you would not know where to go tomorrow; without the sign on the wall, you would be lost on the 35th floor; without the calendar, the secretary would have no way to discriminate between you and an unwelcome intruder. It is therefore in this chain of actions that organizing lies, and not only in the humans' sensemaking practices, as some interpretive scholars tend to reduce this phenomenon (Eisenberg & Riley, 2001).

Certainly, we just saw how sensemaking practices are important in this chain of actions, but they are just one part of the equation. We are far from the phenomenological perspective implicit in Berger and Luckmann's (1966), Garfinkel's (1967), Schutz's (1973), or even Weick's (1979, 1995) works, to the extent that we do not reduce the organized world to the way people make sense or interpret it. People do display competencies, abilities, interpretive skills, and intelligence, but organizing cannot be reduced to these dispositions, because doing that amounts to bracketing out what precedes or follows these sensemaking activities. We are in a world full of agencies and only agencies to the extent that understanding how this world works or fails to work consists of accounting for whatever happens to make a difference in a given situation, which is what we call agency.

When something or someone makes a difference, this difference can be accounted for by a verb that describes what the human or the nonhuman happens to do in the present situation. The annual report that *summarizes* the company's results, the tray that *collects* the paperwork on the desk, the lamp that *lights* your office, the elevator that *brings* you *up* to the floor you selected, or the memo that *informs* you *about* the organization's new policies are all different types of contribution that should be differentiated (Cooren, 2004b), but to the extent that they *contribute* to given processes, nothing should prevent us from saying that they represent agency. It is for this specific reason that nothing should also prevent us from saying that the annual report, the tray, the lamp, or the memo are actors or agents. They are agents or actors to the extent that they do something in a given situation.

This idea of selection also introduces the question of how humans in general tend to speak about and conceive of the world around them. As an illustration, let's take a look at an article taken from the Toronto *Globe and Mail*, on Friday, March

26, 2004, which commented on a decision of the Supreme Court of Canada regarding the Roman Catholic diocese's responsibility for a priest's years of sexual abuse. Here is how the article reads:

> A Roman Catholic diocese in Newfoundland is liable for hundreds of sexual assaults committed against young boys over a 30-year period by one of its priests, the Supreme Court of Canada ruled yesterday.
>
> A 9-0 majority said a diocese is much more than a faceless, landholding entity. It is instead a central authority intimately linked to the lives of parishioners, especially in isolated areas where its priests enjoy godlike status.
>
> The court concluded that the Roman Catholic Episcopal Corp. of St. George's is both directly and vicariously liable for the failure of two successive bishops "to properly direct and discipline" Rev. Kevin Bennett during his prolonged sexual rampage.
>
> "All temporal or secular actions of the bishop are those of the corporation," Madam Justice Beverly McLachlin wrote. "This includes the direction, control and discipline of priests, which are the responsibility of the bishop."

As we see here, the Supreme Court of Canada did not hesitate to implicitly attribute some form of agency to a Roman Catholic diocese in Newfoundland. From the priest who committed the alleged sexual rampage, to the diocese he belonged to, through the bishops who supervised him, the nine judges of the Supreme Court of Canada selected the institution itself as the ultimate entity responsible for what happened.

Like any act of selection, this is a matter of decision, here the judges', because it consists of delimiting where one should end in the chain of agents. The chain could have stopped at the priest's level, but it was judged that the Reverend Kevin Bennett's misconducts would not have continued to occur over 30 years had the successive bishops not failed to "properly direct and discipline" him. In other words, the Reverend Bennett being under the bishops' authority, these latter could be considered liable and responsible for his acts and through them, the diocese they represented. We actually find here something that Taylor (1993) had already pointed out in his book, *Rethinking the Theory of Organizational Communication: How to Read an Organization*, that is, the common etymological root of the terms authority and author. Technically, when you have authority over individuals, it means that when they act in the context of this authority, it is as if you were acting (i.e., teleacting), because you have to respond (hence, have responsibility) for what they do.

This logic of agency is precisely what we mean when we say that action is something that is shared. Although the diocese tried, through the bishops who spoke in its name, to dissociate itself from the priest's action, and thus to stop the chain of actions at the priest's level, the judges of the Supreme Court of Canada decided to incorporate the bishops and the diocese itself in this picture. Technically, everything happened as though it had been decided that it was, in fact, the diocese itself that had failed to prevent the molestation of the young boys for 30 years. Note that the last sentence does not amount to putting forward a nihilist position, unless you consider that the Supreme Court of Canada's decision is nihilist. Indeed, as the article reports, Madam Justice Beverly McLachlin who represented the Supreme Court of Canada did not hesitate to write in her judgment that, "All temporal or secular actions of the bishop *are those of the corporation*" (italics added). Note also that saying what she did does not consist of exonerating the bishops' or the priest's responsibility, but on the contrary, extends their responsibility to the diocese they, in their own way, represented.

TELEACTION AND PRESENTIFICATION

Having recognized why it seems reasonable to widen the extension of such key concepts as agent, actors, and action to what nonhumans do, we can now draw one of the conclusions of this epistemological gesture. If indeed it appears possible to say that things do things, we suddenly seem better equipped to address questions that have puzzled generations of sociologists and organizational scholars. For instance, how is it possible to analyze local interactions, while accounting for phenomena that appear to transcend their localness? Can this so-called micro–macro gap, which traditional approaches seem incapable of filling, be finally addressed, as Latour (1993, 1999) claimed, with the nonhumans' interventions? This is indeed our position. Once we have recognized that action is something that is always shared, it seems nonproblematical to account for interactions while recognizing that these latter always participate in something that transcends them.

To illustrate this phenomenon, let us look at a mundane example taken from fieldwork done in one of Manhattan's tallest skyscrapers. Denis and Frida are inspecting a construction project that has just been completed in the company's premises where Frida works. Denis, who is the building manager, was in charge of completing this job for Frida's company and he is now checking with her if there is anything that needs to be fixed, redone, or added. Although their interaction lasts for about 10 minutes, I select only a brief passage in which Frida and Denis speak about a sign that is apparently missing on the office door. Just prior to that excerpt, she mentioned that she needed more information about blinds that could be installed in her office and that a lock needed to be put on a door. Here is the excerpt:[2]

```
266   Frida:                                          [Yah and uh Oscar
267            would like to have also a company name on the door you know
268            that
269
```

---

[2]To preserve the individuals' anonymity, their names, as well as the company's names, have been changed in the transcript.

270 Denis: On this ((pointing backward))
271
272 Frida: Yah we paid for that [That's our door
273
274 Denis: [On this *door*? ((pointing backward))
275
276 Frida: On [our door ((pointing forward))
277
278 Denis: [No your door ((pointing forward))
279
280 Frida: Yeah
281
282 Denis: [Oh okay
283
284 Frida: [Baker Turner Co
285
286   (0.2)
287
288 Denis: Okay wait a minute now. Hold it ((starting his voice recorder))
289
290   ((sound of the voice recorder))
291
292 Frida: They're two people with two different names ((looking at the
293   camera))
294
295 Denis: Phil, we need a lock seven for the mechanical room up in Baker
296   Turner (0,5) Also we need to uhm (0.3) uh National blinds I got to
297   call him for the blinds. And we got to get a hold of uhhh the sign
298   guy. They want a sign on their front door

As we see from Lines 266 to 284, Denis and Frida are negotiating that a sign needs to be installed on the office's door. After checking what door she is speaking about (Lines 270–280), Denis acknowledges that the sign needs indeed to be installed (Line 282), asks Frida to "hold it" (Line 288), starts his voice recorder (which also happens to be his cell phone), and records the different jobs that have been agreed on since the beginning of the inspection (Lines 295–298).

Let us now examine the characteristics of this interaction. Apparently, it seems local to the extent that it takes place during a specific period of time (around 10 minutes, the time it takes here to inspect the completed job), in an office located in a Manhattan building, between a manager (Denis) and one of his numerous tenants (Frida). This interaction can be said to be local because it can be located within a specific period of time and within a delimited space. But is it really that local? In Lines 266 to 268, we notice, for instance, that Frida positions herself as speaking on behalf of Oscar, her boss. According to her, "Oscar would like to have also a company name on the door" (Lines 266–267) and she ends her turn by saying "you know that" (Lines 267–268) to remind Denis that he is supposed to already know that information. What happens in this brief passage? Why could not we say that, through Frida's statement, it is, in fact, her boss's wishes that are expressed, or even her boss who is speaking? By mobilizing Oscar in the discussion, one of the things Frida is doing consists of positioning herself as his agent and Oscar as the principal whose interests can be represented in the interaction. Although locally enacted, this interaction can be said to mobilize actors that are not physically present but whose interests, objectives, ideas, and so on, can be represented. Although he might be completely unaware of it, Oscar may be said to be teleacting through Frida's mentioning his wishes.

Teleaction thus presupposes a central phenomenon, which is representation, that is, the act consisting of making present, of presentifying something or someone in the interaction. Through Frida's statement, it is also Oscar's wishes—the fact that he would like to have the company's name on a door—that are made present. Although locally achieved, interactions can thus be said to constantly mobilize entities—here, Oscar and his wishes—that were not initially considered to be present in the discussion, but that can be literally brought into it by the interactants.

This example illustrates how teleaction can occur through the way humans represent other entities in the interaction, but nonhuman entities can also do this job very well. Let us look, for instance, at what is happening from Lines 288 to 298. After acknowledging that a sign is indeed missing on the door, Denis asks Frida to "hold it" (Line 288), or to keep in mind for a moment what she was about to say. He then starts his voice recorder and begins to record the different things to be done, which have just been identified during the discussion: A lock must be installed, Denis needs to call the blind company, and a sign has to be put on the door. An hour later, when Denis will finally be back in his office, he will check what has been recorded on his cell phone and be able to communicate the information to his secretary so that action can be taken regarding the problems identified during the inspection of Frida's office.

As we see here, teleaction is nothing mysterious, because it consists mostly of transporting through technological devices or human memory what happened in one locale to another locale. When Denis is back in his office, his recorder will remind him of what needs to be done, an action that is, of course, shared with other entities upstream and downstream. Upstream, we can say that it is also Denis-in-Frida's-office who is reminding Denis-in-his-office of what needs to be done, whereas downstream, we can highlight that the act of reminding can also be attributed to the recording itself, and that this action also requires that Denis-in-his-office understand and recognize what Denis-in-Frida's-office recorded 1 hour ago (in other words, the act of reminding requires that the person who is reminded understand the message and recognize it as valid, in this case, coming from oneself). It is in such chains of action that the micro–macro gap can be solved and not in the almost magical intervention of social structures, as we will see later (Cooren, 2004b; Cooren & Fairhurst, 2004). In connection with what was said in the first section, we live in a world of agencies and only agencies; that is, if we can indeed dislocate the local, it is because things that happened in the past can be transported (by memory, by machines, by documents, by wires, etc.) from one locality to the other.

THE MODE OF BEING OF COLLECTIVE ENTITIES

So far, I have tried to demonstrate that a better way to account for the world as we know it is to speak in terms of agency, a reconceptualization that led me to insist on such key phenomena as presentification (or representation) and teleaction. We live in a world filled with agencies—what, in reference to Garfinkel (1988), we could call a plenum of agencies—but recognizing this implies that we open the door, conceptually speaking, to the ideas of acting from a distance (teleacting) and rendering present things that might at first sight be considered absent (representing) through various means. It is through these key phenomena that local interactions can transcend themselves, establishing links with past and future events or situations as well as remotely located entities. We live in the terra firma of interactions (and only interactions), but through representation (by language, memory, and technology essentially), entities from the past or from a remotely located area can teleact, or make a difference, in any given situation.

What remains to be shown, however, is to what extent this ontological position enables us to account for collective entities like societies, groups, and organizations. After all, if we do live in a world filled with agencies, we still need to understand what the mode of being of these collectives is, which precisely appear to transcend interactions. However, in fact, it is here again that the phenomena of teleaction and presentification or representation take on their full meaning. Collectives do exist—as we will see, they even act—but it is always through something or someone, a phenomenon that we could call, for lack of better words, incarnation, embodiment, or even materialization. As we know, the term incarnation etymologically comes from the Latin root *carne*, which means flesh. Incarnation, in the somewhat restricted sense I propose, thus refers to a phenomenon that consists of giving flesh to something, a definition close to the one for embodiment, which consists of "giv[ing] a bodily form to" something. As for materialization, it refers to a phenomenon that consists of "tak[ing] physical form or shape" (American Heritage Dictionary) to something that was initially devoid of it.

If we do acknowledge that one key phenomenon to understand the world as we know it is representation or presentification, we can then notice that a collective entity can be *made present* through a variety of entities that appear to materialize or incarnate it. In this specific sense, a corporation—in the legal sense of the term—is made present (a) through specific texts like logos, by-laws, stock certificates, ledgers, minutes, organizational charts, annual reports, memos, and brochures; (b) through spatial elements like buildings, gardens, gates, fences, offices; (c) through various artifacts and technologies like computers, robots, pieces of furniture, the corporate seal; and also (of course) (d) through the various humans who eventually represent it, whether they are CEOs, vice presidents, accountants, secretaries, public relations, or simple employees.

As we see here, collective entities, as noted by Callon and Latour (1981) more than 20 years ago, are not at all mysterious if we recognize that their mode of being irremediably passes through the various entities that actualize them, that give them flesh. However, acknowledging that then forces us to recognize that collectives are *variable geometry entities,* or entities with a mode of being that is never finalized or defined. They are, as Callon and Latour (1981) rightly noted, Leviathans, or monsters with several heads, multiple mouths, numerous ears, and a proteiform body (see also Law, 1991). To convince ourselves, let's go back for a moment to our building manager in Manhattan. Does he represent the branch of the real estate firm he is working for? Yes, certainly, at least for the tenants who keep calling him to complain about problems or ask for special favors, or for the contractors who work for him on several renovation projects all year long. For them, he surely represents or incarnates (at least partially) the firm that is in charge of managing the building operations. They are reminded of that incarnation each time they sign a contract for jobs to be done in the building. However, do we exhaust this organization's mode of being by acknowledging this type of incarnation? Certainly not.

Indeed, this organization has several other modes of being that no list can truly exhaust. For instance, it exists through its offices located in the second floor of the building; through its secretaries who invariably pronounce the firm's name as they answer the phone; through its blue-collar employees (electricians, painters, plumbers) who work every day in the building, fixing things and renovating spaces; through its receptionists and security guards who make sure that no unidentified intruder penetrates the skyscraper; through its numerous texts and documents (contracts, leases, work orders, memos, signs, etc.) that often bear its name; and through its computers and the different tools and machines that employees use in their daily work. All these entities (whether they are human, technological, or textual) constitute the organization in one way or the other because they all represent it in one way or another.

It is to this extent that collectives can be said to not only exist, but also to act. Let's take the example of the real estate firm one more time to illustrate this point. When the secretaries answer the phone by pronouncing the company's name, one could say that they mark that the callers have indeed reached the firm's offices and that they are indeed speaking to it. By responding to the phone, the secretaries can be said to be speaking and receiving information, complaints, and requests on behalf of the firm for which they work. In other words, they are literally its voice and ears. The same reasoning works for other entities, like for instance the contracts, the purchase orders, or any type of document that might represent the organization for one specific type of activity. Here is, for instance, an excerpt from an interview conducted with one of the secretaries, Olivia. During this interview, she was asked to speak about her daily routine in the organization. In what follows, she speaks about some specific types of documents she regularly has to process.

93	Olivia:	What else do we do here?
94		
95		(3.0)
96		
97	Olivia:	(We) process a lot of construction bills
98		
99	François:	Okay how does it work to process them. For what do you do?
100		
101	Olivia:	Oh we have to do up an AIA contract (.) for any contract (0.2)
102		_ any work over ten thousand dollars requires an AIA contract
103		
104	François:	What is an AIA
105		
106	Olivia:	Hum it states the work that's being done in the uh (1.0) *particular*
107		*space*
108		
109	François:	Okay
110		
111	Olivia:	And it keep- it's a big contract (.) Let me see if I have one right
112		*hee:re*
113		
114		(1.8)
115		
116	Olivia:	I have a blank one here that I have to deal with
117		
118		((grabbing the contract in her desk tray))
119		
120		(2.2)
121		
122	Olivia:	This is for our plumbing company I just didn't do it yet
123		
124		((opening the document on her desk))
125		
126		(2.0)
127		
128	Olivia:	It states out uh the unit prices.
129		
130	François:	So who has to fill that? The the [people=
131		
132	Olivia:	[*This* we fill out (.) the

133   [contractor will=

134

135   François: [Oh you fill this out

136

137   Olivia: =then come and *sign it* (0.08) like he's done already for me::

138

139   François: Okay

140

141   Olivia: And then we ha::ve a lien waiver

142

143   (1.0)

144

145   François: O[kay

146

147   Olivia: [uhmm (1.0), which protects the building in the event that we
148   don't pay and they can't put a lien on the building

149

150   François: Okay

151

152   Olivia: and *thi::s* (0.4) is our Capital Improvement Certificate (.) so that
153   if there's (0.2) _any work that's capital, which this plumbing

154

155   François: Uhm hm

156

157   Olivia: _Uuh this contract is actually for the bathrooms

158

159   (0.4)

160

161   Olivia: So that's all brand new work

162

163   François: So it's im[provement of the building=

164

165   Olivia: [capital improvement

166

167   Olivia: =*Yeah_* (1) so *this* t- (0.5) uh exempts us from the tax=
168   ((showing the Capital Improvement Certificate))

Several passages are interesting with regard to the way she talks about her work. For instance, having said that they process a lot of construction bills (Line 97), Olivia mentions that they have to generate AIA contracts (AIA stands for American Institute of Architects), which, as she says, "*states* the work that's being done in the uh (1.0) *particular* space" (Lines 106–107, italics added). Having grabbed a copy of an AIA contract from her desk tray (Line 118), she then shows it to me by saying, "it *states* out uh the unit prices" (Line 128, italics added). As we see here, Olivia does not hesitate to say that this contract does specific things, here stating the work that is being done and the unit prices. This document's agency thus appears implicit in her account.

Even though this is not mentioned in her answer, one could also say that this contract officially "defines [the] contractual relationships and terms involved in (...) design and construction projects" (as mentioned by the AIA). Like any contract, this document commits its signatories (here, the contractor and the owner of the building) to do specific things. Olivia mentions, for instance, that the plumbing company has already signed it (Line 137), which means that, once the building owner signs its section, the plumbing company will be considered committed to completing a specific project defined in the document. There is nothing magical in these commitments and the binding capacity of this document. By generating this type of document, the organization can be said to create an agent that will do things on its behalf.

Note that the effects of representation and teleaction here are quite fascinating. The signature represents and commits its signatory, who herself represents and commits its organization (here, the plumbing company). It is therefore through this work of appropriation that the plumbing company can be said to not only exist, but also act. It exists because it is made present through this document (and many others) and it acts to the extent that this document does something on its behalf. This type of teleaction is confirmed by the way Olivia speaks about other documents. For instance, she does not hesitate to say that the lien waiver she is showing me "protects the building in the event that we don't pay and they can't put a lien on the building" (Lines 147–148) or that the Capital Improvement Certificate she is holding in her hands "exempts [them] from the tax" (Line 167).

As we see in these two short excerpts, Olivia (and whoever understands how forms work in general) has no problem attributing to nonhumans a capacity to do things, here protecting and exempting. Certainly, she could have also said, "*The building* is protecting *itself* with this lien waiver in the event that we don't pay" or "*We* are exempting *ourselves* from the tax with this Capital Improvement Certificate." These alternative accounts are, of course, valid, but they do nothing else than confirm what was claimed previously; that is, that agency is something that can be shared upstream and downstream. As illustrated through these examples, collective entities exist and act through many different agents, including documents.

THE MODE OF BEING OF ORGANIZATIONS

This, of course, does not mean that entities are all equal in their capacity to act and speak in the name of the collective they represent. For instance, we know that some voices appear to matter more than others, a phenomenon that has been widely studied by organizational communication scholars (Buzzanell, 1994; Deetz, 1992, 2001; Mumby, 1988, 2001), but it would be a theoretical and practical mistake to reduce the organization's voice to the ones of its CEO and vice president, like it would be a mistake to reduce the organization's activities to the ones that are officially recognized as such by its official representatives.

The *Globe and Mail*'s article quoted previously is a good illustration of this phenomenon. As it reads, the Supreme Court of Canada ruled that The Roman Catholic Episcopal Corporation of St. George, Newfoundland, was "liable for hundreds of sexual assaults committed against young boys over a 30-year period by one of its priests." In other words, the Supreme Court of Canada, through its main representative, Madam Justice Beverley McLachlin, and through the court decision she wrote in the name of her eight other colleagues, considered that this diocese was indeed responsible for its two successive bishops' repeated failure to intervene. As we noted before, she wrote that, "[a]ll temporal or secular actions of the bishop are those of the corporation" and she specified that, "[t]his includes the direction, control and discipline of priests, which are the responsibility of the bishop."

This explains why representation and teleaction can be sometimes subjected to so much control. Given the monster-like mode of being of any organization (especially, of course, multinational corporations), we can indeed understand why the capacity to speak and act on behalf of a collective body is the object of scrutiny by people in a position of authority; the people who could be considered the legal authors of what is done under their supervision. If the world is indeed a plenum of agencies, what characterizes the organizational world precisely lies in these various attempts to control from a distance and through time what humans and nonhumans are doing in the name of their organization (or at least their supervisor). If we agree that two key phenomena in any collective are teleaction and representation, we then need to show that order is another key phenomenon that should never be approached from a top-down perspective, but from a bottom-up one.

To illustrate this point, let us have a look at the way one form of control is achieved in the real estate agency. As mentioned before, many blue-collar employees work for the agency, which is officially in charge of managing the building. Such an account should no longer be problematic, given that we now understand how many shortcuts have just been taken to produce it. Managing the building is indeed a responsibility that was literally given to the real estate agency—as a collective body, it is in charge of this (somewhat daunting) task—but this is only possible through the several individual entities who, or that, incarnate and represent it: the building manager, secretaries, electricians, plumbers, carpenters, painters, concierge, security guards, as well as the numerous nonhuman devices (machines, computers, documents, file cabinets, etc.) that compose this collective agency.

In the blue collars' case (i.e., the electricians, plumbers, carpenters, and painters), this incarnation or representation mostly takes the shape of the multiple activities of maintenance they are in charge of throughout the day. It can be a light bulb to be changed in one of the numerous hallways that compose the building, a bathroom to be repainted and redone, or a leak to be taken care of. Each time a job is determined as "having to be done"—whether through a phone call from one of the tenants to the agency's secretary or through the building manager's initiative—one of the blue-collar employees is assigned the job, depending on his or her qualifications. Another way, of course, to account for what is happening is to speak in terms of the real estate agency taking care of these different problems. Given that those blue-collar employees work for the agency, they, of course, represent it (i.e., stand for it).

It is precisely here that control intervenes. Let us look at how the blue-collars' job is taken care of. Each time a tenant calls the real estate agency to warn that some maintenance work needs to be done, the secretary is entitled to directly contact the employee who is qualified for this type of work and tell him or her verbally what to do. So far, nothing is very surprising: What we have here is a classical act of delegation so common in any organizational setting, what Taylor and Van Every (2000) coined under the term imbrication. The secretary is, by contract, under the manager's authority, who is himself, also by contract, representing the real estate agency as far as maintenance and renovation work for the building is concerned. As long as the maintenance job is a matter of daily routine, the secretary is authorized to handle it at her level without having to defer to the building manager. This type of decentralization enables the real estate agency to save some precious time in handling of this daily work.

When the employee does his or her maintenance job, he or she can be said to represent his or her company to the extent that what he or she is doing is under the manager's authority (through the secretary who represents it). In other words, the employee, the secretary, the manager, and the real estate agency technically are the coauthors of this maintenance work. The employee's agency is imbricated in the secretary's agency, which is itself imbricated in the manager's agency, which is itself imbricated in the real estate company's agency. Here again, there is nothing mysterious in this agency attributed to the real estate company, because it can precisely be said to be acting, regarding these matters, through the building manager, who is himself acting through the secretary, who is herself acting through the blue-collar's maintenance work.

What seems more interesting is how control really is achieved; that is, how the building manager and the secretary who represents him can be reasonably sure that the blue-collar is going to do the maintenance job he or she was asked to do. It is here that, I think, our conception of the world as a plenum of agencies takes its full meaning. The secretary does not only verbally tell the employee what he or she has to do, she also generates a work order that will state who was asked to do what for whom, where, and when. In other words, this work order will include the employee's name, a brief description of the task to be completed, for which floor or which tenant it is supposed to be done, and the date this request was made. Once the work order is electronically generated in the secretary's computer, a copy will be printed and put in the employee's tray, located in the real estate agency's office. The employee will pick up this form and mark it "completed" once the job has been done. The secretary will then enter the information into the computer.

As the secretaries told me during the fieldwork I completed in the building, the work orders used to be generated manually instead of electronically, which had one disadvantage for the agency. Some employees who picked up the work orders in their trays did not hesitate to get rid of them when they considered they had too much work to do or simply did not want to do a specific task. When asked about the completion of their maintenance jobs, they could easily claim they never received the work order, a statement that was difficult to invalidate. Given the high level of maintenance work to be done, it was sometimes hard for the secretaries to remember if indeed they had put the work order corresponding to the noncompleted task in the employee's tray.

With the new types of work orders generated electronically, the secretaries' memory can simply be bypassed. Given that an electronic copy of the work order is automatically stored in the computer, they have the proof that the work order was indeed generated, which renders useless any attempt to get rid of it on the employees' part. There is control to the extent that the employees are relatively constrained regarding what they do and what they cannot do with these work orders. However, this control does not come from thin air; it comes from the mobilization of a specific form of agency, the one displayed by the computer. More precisely, it comes from a new form of agency shared by the secretary, the computer, the work order, and the tray. With its capacity to store information, the computer makes a crucial difference regarding the control of the employees' activities. It adds a supplement of memory—a form of organizational memory—that was previously lacking when work orders were manually generated.

What we have here is a nice illustration of the etymology of the word *control*. As Levin (2000) reminded us, control comes from the Middle-French word *contre-rolle,* which literally means counter-roll. The counter-roll was a register that medieval officials meticulously kept to make tax collectors more accountable. In other words, it was a counter-account that could literally tell the officials if there was any discrepancy between their account and the ones produced by their tax collectors. With the computerization of work orders, it is now possible to generate a "counter-work order" each time a job to be done is identified (Cooren, 2004b). Using Latour's (2004) terminology, we see how attachments are created through nonhuman agencies. The electronic copy of the work orders can be said to more firmly and solidly attach the blue-collar employees' will to the real estate agency's objectives. They have become more accountable not because of any structural intervention, but because of a new form of agency, the computer's, which makes their dissociation from the company's responsibility more difficult.

Certainly, like any form of control, it can be denounced and even fought (e.g., we could imagine that the employees could still claim they never got the work order in their tray, even if, to my knowledge, they never do that), but we see here that this phenomenon lies in the chain of agencies, and not in any kind of structure—action dualism or even a duality, as proposed, for instance by Giddens (1984) and his followers (McPhee, 1985, 1989a, 1989b; McPhee & Poole, 2001; McPhee & Zaug, 2000). In other words, order has indeed to be done one agency at a time, but acknowledging that means that we have to widen the concept of agency to include nonhuman ones, as the previous example shows.

The process of organizing, or the process by which collective entities are "put together into an orderly, functional, structured whole" (the American Heritage Dictionary, 2000) can thus be said to be performed one interaction at a time through the mobilization of numerous entities with various ontologies. As specified by Taylor and Van Every (2000), an orderly, functional and structured whole, or an organizational form, can emerge to the extent that an imbrication of agencies takes place. Our reconceptualization of agency helps us understand this phenomenon to the extent that different types of agencies are typically created and mobilized to fulfill organizing. In the last case studied, ordering takes place through the mobilization of the secretary, the computer, the work order, the tray, the blue-collar employee, and whatever tools or resources he or she might use to fulfill the task.

Organizing can thus be understood as a hybrid phenomenon that requires the mobilization of entities with variable ontologies, which contribute to the emergence or enactment of the organized form. It is through the imbrications of these human and nonhuman entities that organizing and ordering can be said to occur. As collective entities, organizations thus not only exist through the human and nonhuman entities that speak and act on their behalf, but also through these effects of imbrication that are so characteristic of organized forms. Of course, we all know of organizations that are completely disorganized, or that are just "on paper," but to the extent that they are minimally organized, organizations require such phenomena of imbrication, which our bottom-up approach can account for.

CONCLUSION

Abstraction is an absolutely essential step in the production of knowledge, but it does not lead to anything of value if it does not help us see or study things that we would not have noticed otherwise. Although it is true that several contributions representing the Montreal school approach have been mainly (but not exclusively) theoretically based (Cooren, 2000b, 2000c, 2001a, 2004b; Taylor, 1993; Taylor & Cooren, 1997; Taylor et al., 1996; Taylor & Lerner, 1996; Taylor & Van Every, 1993, 2000), much work has also been done to illustrate its empirical relevance (Cooren, 2001b; Cooren & Fairhurst, 2002, 2004; Cooren & Taylor, 1998, 2000; Fairhurst & Cooren, 2004; Groleau & Cooren, 1998; Robichaud, 2001, 2002; Taylor, Groleau, Heaton, & Van Every, 2001; Taylor & Robichaud, 2004), a relevance that I hope was illustrated in this chapter. Interestingly enough, it has turned out that in seeking a communicational theory of organization, we have increasingly been led toward a form of radical empiricism, consisting of concentrating much of our energy on the activity of description.

If we must indeed focus on agency and only agency, which is another way of saying that we must start from communication and only communication, it is imperative that we demonstrate how organizing (and all its related phenomena, whether they be control, resistance, power, etc.) emerges from human and nonhuman interactions. Such a demonstration requires extensive and detailed description, as conversation analysts and ethnomethodologists have helped us understand. However, it is not a flat and linear description; on the contrary, it is a jagged one, which accounts for the phenomena of selection and imbrication, so essential to understanding the phenomenon of ordering. In other words, it is a description that does not hesitate to travel in space and time, to bifurcate, to stop anywhere, and to show how organizing and sometimes disorganizing occur, one teleaction at a time.

ACKNOWLEDGMENTS

An earlier version of this chapter was presented as a keynote at the 6th International Conference on Organizational Discourse, organized by Tom Keenoy, Cliff Oswick, Ida Sabelis, Sierk Ybema, Marcel Veenswijk, David Grant, Cynthia Hardy, and Nelson Phillips at The Vrije Universiteit, Amsterdam, July 2004, as well as in lectures presented to the Department of Marketing of the University of Southern Denmark, Odense in August 2004, and the Groupe de Recherche en Communication des Organisations (GREC/O) at the Université de Bordeaux 3–Montaigne in July 2005. Special thanks to Professors Dominique Bouchet, Boris Brummans, Valérie Carayol, Lars Thøger Christensen, Daniel Robichaud, and James R. Taylor for their very helpful comments on earlier versions of this chapter. Finally, my deep gratitude goes to Denis and his employees for giving me access to their real estate agency.

CHAPTER SIX

Steps Toward a Relational View of Agency

Daniel Robichaud
Université de Montréal

My concern in this chapter is to address analytically the role of agency in a communication-based perspective on organizing. Recent debates centering on agency and text in organizing[1] have relied primarily on a notion of agency inherited from social theory, and in particular from interpretive sociologies, and thus, I argue, have been trapped in a logic of discourse or agency, depending on which is accorded analytic priority in accounting for the dynamic of organizing. For the most part, the debates have been limited to exploring the opposition between internalist and externalist notions of agency (or, to caricaturize somewhat, modern vs. postmodern views).

In certain respects, the contemporary debates can be viewed as yet one more installment of the classic debate between free will and determinism. Some would encourage us to remain anchored in the Kantian idealist conception of agent, defending in a humanistic style of argument the uniqueness of its symbolic and rationalist capabilities in a world that is otherwise chaotic and meaningless (Giddens, 1984; McPhee, 2004). Others insist that agency does not account for much once it has been extracted from the structural properties of the social and institutional contexts in which it is inevitably located (Alexander, 1988, 1998; Descombes, 1996). Still others urge us to abandon the metaphysical discourse and acknowledge that current historical conditions and technological developments make the idealist notion of agent at best a very poor conceptual tool to understand the unfolding transformations of social life (Latour, 1993). Fieldwork in the social studies of science and technology, for example, goes so far as to argue for the need to incorporate the notion of material agency in our modes of explanation of human engagement in its surroundings (Cooren, 2004b, chap. 5, this volume; Latour, 1996; Pickering, 1995). At stake, of course, is an issue of definition, that is, how agency is analytically broken down into its basic components by the different traditions. However, there is more to it. I suggest in the following pages that recent developments in social and communication theory, marked in many

---

[1] See the recent special issue of *Organization, 11*(3), 2004.

ways by a rejection of both the modernist and substantialist notions of the individual, the self, and the agent, have still not found the theoretical apparatus that would support a conception of agency congruent with a nonessentialist, or nonsubstantialist, view of human engagement with the material and social worlds. Although a growing number of scholars and theorists have been calling for many years now for a process or relational ontology, and although much analytical territory of the social sciences has been revisited in terms of relationships instead of substances (i.e., notions of power [Clegg, 1994], gender [Burkitt, 1998], identity [Gergen, 2000], and structure [Emirbayer, 1997]), the notion of agency has so far resisted a truly relational reconceptualization (Emirbayer, 1997; Emirbayer & Mische, 1998; Gergen, 2000).

The purpose of this chapter is to explore a conception of agency defined as a relational configuration; that is, a situationally embedded connection of connections between heterogeneous entities. In weighing the pros and cons of this relational conception, I rely heavily on the relational ontology offered by the American philosopher Peirce (1934/1965, 1992; Peirce, Houser, Kloesel, & Pierce Edition Project, 1992). In communication studies, Peirce's concept of relation has usually been associated with his theory of meaning, a detailed analytic description of the multiple signifying processes through which an interpretant makes sense of its surroundings by relating its objects of perception (which he termed representamen) to something else (which he conceived of as the object of the semiosis). The analytical distinctions Peirce developed in his semiotics were, however, derived from his ontology, which takes the form of a logic of relations that he took to be the essence of reality (Peirce, 1992). In the past decade, Peirce's relational ontology and its implications for social philosophy and the philosophy of mind have attracted the attention of numerous philosophers, ironically enough, for the most part (although not exclusively), in France (Chauviré, 1995; Descombes, 1996, 1995/2001; Johansen, 1993; Ketner, 1995; Tiercelin, 1993). The work of Descombes (1996, 1995/2001) and Chauviré (1995) is especially relevant to my purpose, because they highlight Peirce's conception of intentionality in a manner that breaks in a number of ways from the concept of intention inherited from phenomenology and that pervades a significant segment of current social science thinking.

The chapter is organized in two sections. First, I briefly review the so-called internalist and externalist conceptualizations of agency to highlight how they conceive the sources of action. Second I describe the Peircian conception of the structure of intentionality and meaning that I suggest we take as a general relational model of agency. I intend to show how Peirce's conception is of particular relevance to transcending the opposition between internalist and externalist theories of agency. The overcoming of this opposition is the great benefit we gain from a relational (i.e., nonsubstantialist) view of agency. However, the price we pay for the resulting clarification is a thorough change in our view of the agent's engagement in the world.

AGENCY IN ORGANIZING: INTERNAL OR EXTERNAL?

The Internalist View

The basic theoretical tenet of the so-called internalist view of agency is the conflation of agency with the human individual actor. Agency implies a human agent in the sense that its basic properties are thought of as that which differentiate humans from other living beings. Giddens (1993), for instance, stated that "the proper unit of reference for an analysis of action has to be the *person*, the *acting self*" (p. 80, emphasis in original). He defined agency as

> the stream of actual or contemplated causal interventions of corporeal beings in the ongoing process of events-in-the-world. [...] It is analytical to the concept of agency: (1) that a person "could have acted otherwise" and (2) that the world as constituted by a stream of events-in-process independent of the agent does not hold a predetermined future. (p. 81)

The definition of agency as human causal intervention in the constitution of a world must be understood in the context of a human agent endowed with properties of (a) consciousness and purpose, (b) power, and (c) iteration and repetitiveness. Let us examine each briefly.

Agency as Consciousness and Purpose or Intention.   Perhaps the notion most commonly associated with the idea of agency is that of intention. The ability to project oneself into the future and into circumstances that actors have envisioned in advance is considered to be a fundamental aspect of humans' experience. In the phenomenological tradition, intentionality has been conceived as a constitutive feature of human consciousness, and as such has received a great deal of attention. Being intentional, for an agent, means being fundamentally oriented toward objects of the phenomenal world. In Brentano's famous formulation, "All conscience is conscience of something."

The intentional consciousness of an agent is also closely related to his or her knowledgeability. Purpose and intention presuppose knowledge, as Giddens (1993) pointed out: "I shall define as 'intentional' or 'purposive' any act which the agent knows (believes) can be expected to manifest a particular quality or outcome, and in which this knowledge is made use of by the actor in order to produce this quality or outcome" (p. 83). As a reflexive being, an agent is an actor who can thus rationalize his or her own behavior as it unfolds and provide an account of what he or she is doing as well as his or her reasons for doing it (Varey, chap. 10, this volume). Much of the "internality" of agency thus lies in the reflexive character of this self-consciousness.

Agency as Power.   Agency thought of as a capacity to make a difference analytically presupposes the notion of power. Giddens (1984) is again the theoretician who has most closely tied together the notions of power and agency:

To be able to "act otherwise" means being able to intervene in the world, or to refrain from such intervention, with the effect of influencing a specific process or
state of affairs. This presumes that to be an agent is to be able to deploy [...] a
range of causal powers, including that of influencing those deployed by others.
Action depends upon the capability of the individual to "make a difference" to a
pre-existing state of affairs or course of events. An agent ceases to be such if he or
she loses the capability to "make a difference", that is, to exercise some sort of
power. [...] In this sense, the most all-embracing meaning of "power", power is
logically prior to subjectivity, to the constitution of the reflexive monitoring of
conduct. (pp. 14–15)

It is difficult to think of a notion of agency that would be more substantive. Here
agency implies the fundamentally inalienable "transformative capability" of the
agent. Another way to describe this dimension of agency is to think of it as the basis
of the autonomy of the agent. The concept of an autonomous agent, who possesses,
at least in principle, the will and self-determination to act by itself, without any impulse or forces from the outside, is indeed the core of the modern notion of agency
(Emirbayer & Mische, 1998).

Agency as Iteration and Repetitiveness, or Habitual.   Finally, perhaps the
most widely discussed feature of agency in social and organizational theory is its
habitual, repetitive, routinized nature. Giddens once again, but also much of phenomenological sociology, considers the habitual character of human action to be the
very basis of the stability of social systems. In organization theory, for example, the
institutionalist school has insisted on routines as the carrier of structure (Scott,
1995), consistent with the classical thesis of Berger and Luckmann (1966). Certain
sociologists of action who have highlighted this dimension of agency in their analysis have tended to downplay the reflexive and intentional character of agency (i.e.,
Bourdieu, Calhoun, LiPuma, & Postome, 1993). However, much contemporary sociology of action insists that even the most routine courses of action require a degree of effort and manifest an agent's competence in dealing with even
nonproblematical everyday situations. Emirbayer and Mische (1998), for their
part, argued that the iterative dimension of agency manifests its historical dimension, that is, the way in which the past intervenes in the present by activating a pattern acquired as a component of the agent's biography. According to them, the
iterative dimension of agent thus refers to:

the selective reactivation by actors of past patterns of thought and action, as routinely incorporated in practical activity, thereby giving stability and order to social universes and helping to sustain identities, interactions, and institutions over
time. (p. 971)

For the purpose of my argument, let us call this brief characterization of agency an
internalist and substantialist view (McPhee, 2004). I would argue that in such a
view the various dimensions of agency all contribute implicitly to a conflation of

agency with the individual human actor. From this viewpoint, agency cannot be analytically reduced to merely any source of intervention or action, because the concept presupposes a number of attributes or dimensions that are thought to be to a large extent constitutive of humanity. Moreover, such humanity is to be found nowhere else other than in the human individual. Any account of action and organizing thus, sooner or later, falls back on the reflexive individual, his or her intentions, his or her projects, his or her transformative capabilities, and his or her habits and routines.

Agency as a Composition

For a radically different view of agency, let us now turn to what we could call an externalist notion of agency, a conception that simplifies the definition of agency to extend its applicability to a range of entities and phenomena that far transcends the realm of individual human action. In insisting on the relationships humans must enter into to become actors or agent, proponents of this view have depicted a new picture of the way humans are intertwined with the pluralities of social and physical worlds. The most significant contribution to this reconceptualization of agency comes from the social studies of science and technology and in particular the work of Callon (1986), Latour (1993, 1994, 1996), and Pickering (1995). For the purpose of this chapter, I focus primarily on an explicit argument made some years ago by Latour (1994) in discussing the philosophical underpinnings of his view of the actor and the action.

The starting point of Latour's reflection is the idea that even the simplest action is not accomplished merely by an agent who, through his or her actions, manifests an "agency" he or she possesses in essence, but is instead realized through the networking of the actor with other actors, be they humans or nonhumans. To illustrate his point, Latour employed the issue of gun control to analyze the contrasting accounts of the act of killing provided by the opponents and the advocates of gun control. On the one hand, the sociological and humanistic account of the National Rifle Association holds that to achieve his or her goal, the agent arms himself or herself with a gun (i.e., a resource). The gun here is a mere tool, an intermediary that does nothing more than passively translate the intention of the agent into action ("People, not guns, kill people"). Indeed, only the agent really matters, the gun counting for almost nothing in this account. On the other hand, a materialist account would argue that the gun makes a huge difference, because it brings with it its own script, its own potentiality, its own function, its own orientation, turning an angry man into a killer. The gun introduces its own functional identity into the process. As advocates of gun control would have it, AK-47s are not meant for deer hunting, but for killing people.

Latour insisted that both accounts are mistaken, for both reduce the act of firing the gun to essences, either that of the human, or that of the gun. By relying on essences they miss the composition at work here by which a third agent emerges out of the connection of the human with the gun. Such a relational configuration creates an actor network (though a very simple one): a gun-citizen or a citizen-gun. The point is that the intention, the script, the path, the direction, and the program of action of the new "hybrid agent" called an actor-network is neither that of the essentially material gun nor that of the essentially human citizen, but is channeled by a new goal path that redefines the interests, the will, the functions, the roles, and the identities of the two agents involved.

> Essence is existence and existence is action. […] You are different with a gun in hand; the gun is different with you holding it. You are another subject because you hold the gun; the gun is another object because it has entered into a relationship with you. The gun is no longer the gun-in-the-armory or the gun-in-the-drawer or the gun-in-the-pocket, but the gun-in-your-hand aimed at someone who is screaming. What is true of the subject, of the gunman, is as true of the object, of the gun that is held. A good citizen becomes a criminal, a bad guy becomes a worse guy; a silent gun becomes a fired gun, a new gun becomes a used gun, a sporting gun becomes a weapon. The twin mistake of the materialists and the sociologists is to start with essences, those of subjects or those of objects. […] Neither subject nor object (nor their goal) is fixed. (Latour, 1994, p. 33)

This does not mean that humans lack intentions, reflexivity, and power. It implies, however, that all these attributes are constantly shifting, emerging out of the relational contexts in which the human actor finds himself or herself connected to various projects, interests, and sources of transformations. Thus, in Latour's network perspective, any inherent property of an agent, be it intentionality or power, must be described as the result of action, not its source. It should only figure in our explanation as a consequence of the creation and maintenance of reliable relationships with other actants (a skill, a tool, a friend, a boss, etc). As he insisted elsewhere:

> Indeed, action cannot have a point of origin except at the price of stopping the circulation, or the series of transformations whose movement continually traces the social body. The competencies of an actor will be inferred *after* a process of attribution, pause, abutment or focusing. […] we need to consider any point as being mediations, that is to say, as an *event*, which cannot be defined in terms of inputs and outputs, or causes or consequences. The idea of mediation or event enables us to retain the only two characteristics of action that are useful, i.e., the emergence of the novelty together with the impossibility of ex nihilo creation, without in the process conserving anything of the Western anthropological schema that always forces the recognition of a subject and an object, a competence and a performance, and a potentiality and an actuality. (Latour, 1996, p. 237)

Thus in Latour's argument, the internalist view of agency ignores all too easily the way in which an agent intervenes in a relational context where he or she has been anticipated, where other agents are also acting through the delegation of their technologies and texts, each incorporating its own projects. In Latour's interpretation of the causal intervention that Giddens spoke of, the agent does not remain the same throughout, nor do the other actors that are involved. To some degree, all are redefined in the process. Intentions emerge in the flow of action and in the reflexive retrospective accounts of it (Weick, 1995). Translations and movements in time and space occur in the carrying out of projects. Not only discourses and intentions take place, but so do treasons, drifts, and unintended consequences. In a world that humanity has shared with the nonhuman for so long, agency is delegated to texts and technologies that take on a life of their own in the sense that they may surprise their creators. Very little is accounted for when organizing is reduced to the naked body and mind of the individual human actor, whatever its transcendental attributes may have been in the Garden of Eden. Perhaps the internalist view of agent had some analytical power back then, but how can we now account for the engagement of numerous living and nonliving beings that deploy the transformative capabilities in the world we humans inhabit along with them? Maybe we need to return to the drawing board and reconsider our analytical tools.

PEIRCE'S LOGIC OF RELATION AND THE TRIADIC STRUCTURE OF ACTION

So far we have learned from the internalist view, on the one hand, that the capacity to intervene and transform a course of events in one way or another must be brought back analytically to the essential or irreducible components of individual human consciousness, in the form of knowledge, intention, and power. The externalist view, on the other hand, argues that agencies have proliferated in such a way in the genealogy of the world as we know it that we cannot account for any agentic process, or action, by reducing it to the mere intervention of humans, however reflexive and powerful they may be. The identity of the self; its orientation toward the past, the present, or the future; his or her orientations toward nature, institutions, discourses, or machines populating his or her surroundings; these are constantly at stake in the unfolding of action. Identities continuously emerge in fundamentally unpredictable ways. What agency accomplishes in such contexts, according to Latour, is the re-creation of the configurations of the relationships between the entities that are involved.

I think the externalist view expressed by Latour makes a very convincing case in arguing that we indeed have shared agency with so many nonhumans for so long (to act at a distance, among other things) that an account of agency and its role in organizing that would reduce agency to the human individual consciousness is analytically sterile. I would like to suggest, however, that taking intention and knowledge out of the analysis of action, with a view to accounting for our intertwined relationships with nonhumans, amounts to throwing the baby out with the bath water. The picture Latour described, I would argue, invites us instead to radically reconsider the very nature of intention and consciousness, and perhaps to envision that they have always been not so much capabilities of humans, as relational realities emerging out of the connections of humans with their surroundings. What I propose in the rest of this chapter is to assemble a view of intention as connections. It is a view that has been around for a while, but that may not have been considered as heuristically useful as it appears to be once we recognize the heterogeneous nature of action.

Following a number of contemporary philosophers of the mind, and most notably Descombes (1996, 1995/2001), I draw on Peirce's logic of relations to identify elements, or steps, toward a relational view of agency. The major step I mean to accomplish here is to argue for what might look like an externalized view of intentionality, despite the fact that one of the consequences of a relational view is to show the uselessness of the distinction between internal and external. This is in no way the only conceptual step we need to make to fully understand agentic processes in contemporary organizing; far from it, but I see it as an essential preliminary one.

The Triadic Structure of Action

As the foundation of his theory of meaning, Peirce developed an elaborate relational ontology in which he distinguished three kinds of relations that, in his view, amount to three modes of being. He called the first *firstness* and defined it as the mode of being of virtuality, or quality, in that it is grounded in the relationship something has to itself, without anything else being considered. *Secondness* is the second mode of being and is defined as the relation of something with regard to something else. A purely causal relationship, like the impact of a stone on a shattering window, was for Peirce the ideal type of the mode of being of secondness. He also considered it as the mode of being of existence, because in his view something could be said to exist only in so far as it is related to something else. Of course secondness logically presupposes firstness, but the reverse is not true. *Thirdness*, finally, is the mode of being of the relations established between entities by a third, by virtue of intentions, laws, or habits.

As is well known, thirdness was the foundation of Peirce's notion of symbol, where something is related to something else by consensus or regulation. Meaningful action is considered by Peirce to be a fundamental triadic phenomenon, because it involves not only action and reaction (secondness) but the intervention of a mind of some sort, be it a law (or habit), or the intention of the young Palestinian aiming at the window with the stone. To grasp the significance of these distinctions for the problems of action and agency, I use a Peircian analysis of the act of giving provided by Descombes (1996) to illustrate how Peirce conceived of intention and consciousness as the product of a relationship linking the individual's cognition to other entities (like the stone and the window in my preceding example).

Peirce argued that the act of giving cannot be described using a dyadic conception of relations or, if you prefer, by a combination of coupled terms. Take the simple case of *John gives Peter a book*. We may ask ourselves if analyzing this act can be explained by combining the couples donor–object or donee–object, where the act of giving is said to be expressed by saying "John gives a book" and "Peter receives a book." Two events are indeed described, but the act of giving actually appears nowhere. In the statement "John gives a book" the absence of a reference to a donee strips away an essential strand of meaning from the verb *to give*. Tesnière developed this argument by demonstrating that the semantic and syntactical structure of an important set of verbs implies at least three agents, which he designated as *trivalent* verbs. More recently, Taylor and Van Every (2000) relied on the concept of distransitive verbs borrowed from Goldberg (1995) to make a similar argument about the basic construction of a communication event. As well as the subject of the action, the verb *to give* requires not only an object complement (one gives something), but also an agent complement (the book is given to someone). In other words, the absence of a donee, as in "John gives a book," denies to the object (a book) its status as an object of giving. The nature of an object as a given cannot be ensured if this object is given to no one, so to speak. In this example, the statement "Peter receives a book" makes even more uncertain the status of the book as an object of giving.

It might be argued, perhaps, that it is in the addition of both statements that the act of giving will appear reconstituted within language, with all its meaning intact. We would then have:

"John gives a book" + "Peter receives a book"

Yet this formula does not solve our problem whatsoever, because the meaning of giving still does not appear. Although it is easily understood that John is making a gift of a book, we are not being told to whom (and this is enough, Tesnière argued, to denude this formulation of the meaning we usually attribute to giving). We cannot even be sure whether it is the same book. All we learn is that Peter receives a book precisely when John—strange coincidence—has just given one. Can it therefore be concluded that John has given Peter a book? The answer should be obvious: We cannot be certain.

Peirce believes that reducing relations between terms only into couples, and even into couples of couples, is not sufficient to describe an act such as giving. Why is this so? What is lost in our preceding description? The answer lies in the fact that giving is an intentional act, that is to say it is meaningful. The physical transfer of the book is in and of itself of secondary importance. For there to be a gift, John must make Peter the owner of the book. The simple physical transfer of the book lacks the essential intentional element, a "mental element" as Peirce put it.

The mental element is the intentionality constitutive of the act of giving. This intentionality is in and of itself an operating description of the act of giving. In Peirce's logic of relations, the intention is that which establishes a specific set of relationships among the three terms involved in the act. The intention is what imposes a structure on the book, and Peter, being put into a relation with John, and vice versa. The intention holds in that John aimed at Peter when giving the book, and the triadic relation thus achieved fits with the social description of a gift. To put it differently, in this case John gave Peter the book and, by doing so, he accomplished an act that mobilizes the description by which the book becomes an object of giving, Peter becomes the donee of the act, and he himself becomes the donor. All three terms of the act of donating are constitutive of the act, which is how it can be given the description of a gift. For a gift to be consummated there must be an object to be given, a donor, and a donee, barring which John does not fit the description of donor and the book-object does not fit the description of a gift. The problem underlying the description of the gift is not purely logical speculation about the accuracy of our descriptions of act; it rather demonstrates the role these descriptions play in the basic constitution of an act. What is lost in the description

"John gives a book" + "Peter receives a book"

is precisely the core meaning of giving: This is a gift and a gift presupposes x, y, z. Meaning only emerges in the relation among the three terms that go to form the unitary system of a gift. This is the mental element Peirce was referring to and which, he said, cannot be accounted for by using only a two-term relation. A gift is an elementary triadic structure that cannot be broken down into the combination of its components. Donor, object of giving, and donee form a system of complementary positions with its own intrinsic unity. The act of giving can be said to constitute a gift precisely because it implies intention, which is to say a specific relational configuration. This configuration is not simply imposed on the act from the outside (say, e.g., by an observer) but is involved in the accomplishment of the act itself.

The intention referred to here is thus quite far from the conception of a mental state (e.g., that of John). Descombes (1996) described accurately this intentionality in the gift:

> It follows that the description of the act of giving is an intentional description. How should intentionality of the gift be understood here? According to Peirce, what characterizes the mental is not intentionality as expressed in "Brentano's thesis," that is a binary or dyadic relation ("any conscience is conscience of something"). Rather, a triadic formula should be used: *Any intentional conscience is conscience about a final (or intentional) relation of something with regard to something else.* Intentionality is the relation of intention glimpsed or set between something (for instance these flowers) and something else (the person to whom they are destined). (p. 239, italics added, my translation[2])

Despite the connotation of the phrase "mental element," Peirce is quite distant from subjectivism insofar as the notion of intentionality is understood by phenom-

---

[2]In the French original: "Il s'ensuit que la description d'un acte de donner est une description intentionnelle. Que faudra-t-il entendre ici par l'intentionalité du don? Selon Peirce, la marque du mental n'est pas l'intentionalité telle qu'elle est en général exprimée dans la "thèse de Brentano," et donc comme une relation binaire ou dyadique ("toute conscience est conscience de quelque chose"). Il faudrait user plutôt d'une formule triadique: toute conscience intentionnelle est conscience du rapport final (ou intentionnel) de quelque chose à quelque chose. L'intentionalité, c'est le rapport d'intention aperçu ou posé entre quelque chose (par exemple, ces fleurs) et quelque chose (cette personne à qui elles sont destinées)."

enologists. What matters, in other words, is not the mental state of the lover bestowing flowers on his or her loved one, but the recognition of a type of structure in the act. Johansen (1993), in discussing the triadic concept of intention as interpretant, as it is understood in Peircean semiotics, explained:

> Stating the intention or purpose of the text [or the act] does not mean looking inside the head of the utterer but rather determining the kind of deed or act of which the utterance is an instance. [...] In other words, the primary frame of reference is linguistic: rules, rules of social interaction, norms, values, and ideals. (p. 202)

Intention in this case should be understood in the institutional framework (Peirce would have said laws) it presupposes. Descombes (1995/2001) added:

> By attributing an intention to someone, we presuppose an entire context made up of institutions and customs. The intention to play chess is the intention to play a well-defined game, with its own rules. [...] If this institution did not exist, nobody would have the intention to play chess. [...] The impossibility here is not, of course, empirical, as if the claim was simply that nobody would think to play chess, that the idea would not occur to one. The impossibility here is a logical one: no matter what idea occurs to one, it cannot be the idea of playing chess unless chess has an insitutional presence in one's world. (pp. 224–225)

Intention, History, and Narrativity

The intention that gives the donation its triadic structure, or the fact that the act of giving is aimed at someone (a donee) with something (the object of giving), ipso facto embeds the act of giving within a narrative context, that is to say a context presenting a conceivable development. The following example, taken from Wittgenstein (cited by Descombes, 1996), is illustrative. Wittgenstein is after all the author of this principle:

> Why can't my right hand give my left hand money? My right hand can put it into my left hand. My right hand can write a deed of gift and my left hand a receipt. *But the further practical consequences would not be those of a gift.* When the left hand has taken the money from the right, etc., we shall ask: "Well, and what of it?" (Wittgenstein, 1953, §263, cited in Descombes, 1996, p. 242, italics added)

This pseudo-gift imagined by Wittgenstein, similar to the one presented earlier, is neither embedded in a narrative context, nor does it produce one, because there does not exist a conceivable development to provide it with a context. As Wittgenstein says, "Well, and what of it?" Peirce would say that the problem is that the relation of each hand to the money is strictly dyadic. The donation presents no intentional relation, no aim, no eventual narrative development. There is a transfer of money and nothing more.

To further clarify Peirce's position, consider one of his examples that illustrates the same problem, this time showing how the intention itself depends on a conceivable development, an ultimate aim:

> Suppose for example, an officer of a squad or company of infantry gives the word of command, "Ground arms!" This order is, of course, a sign. […] In the present case, the object the command represents is the will of the officer that the butts of the muskets be brought down to the ground. Nevertheless, the action of his will upon the sign is not simply dyadic; for if he thought the soldiers were deaf mutes, or did not know a word of English, or were raw recruits utterly undrilled, or were indisposed to obedience, his will probably would not produce the word of command. (Peirce, 1934/1965, p. 324)

As Peirce expressed it, the officer's subjective desire to see the stock of the rifle rest on the ground is not sufficient, as a cause of the act, to make the command an intentional or meaningful act. Such a causal relationship of officer's subjective state and rifles' objective state is not enough to render the meaning of the words spoken by the officer a command. To be meaningful, a triadic relation must link (a) the officer (or his volition), (b) the sign "Ground arms!", and (c) the recipient of the command. In other words, an act, to be meaningful, cannot rely strictly on the dyadic action model, or even on a chain of acts where the intention (as a mental state of the officer) would be the cause of his utterance, and then the utterance would entail a response from its recipients. As Peirce argued, it would still remain to be seen how it was, in this dualistic scenario, that the officer would not have given a command, or, to be more precise, why is it that the command given would not make sense. Having no meaning implies precisely not having a conceivable development, direction, or text that subsequently serves to interpret it. In short it means not having a narrative context, in the absence of which the command cannot conceivably lead to the accomplishment of any act whatsoever. The absence of a narrative context is the direct result of the missing third term, or connection of connections. Peirce's triadic structure introduces this third term, as an agent that makes this narrative development conceivable; with normal soldiers, the act of lowering the rifle stock to the ground represents a conceivable narrative development of the command as an act. The command, in being potentially meaningful in an intersubjective context, supposes the relationship enacted by the subject between the object and a development (which in semiotic terms is in fact an interpretant of the first).

In Peirce's model, the act draws its meaning from the network of relations connecting the officer's will with lowering the rifle stock. It clearly appears that the intervention of a third term is not reducible to yet another dyad or still more dyadic combinatory possibilities. The nature of the act is totally different. Yet this model also instantiates all the conditions of narrativity defined by Wittgenstein. In fact, with Peirce we discover the analytic foundations of Wittgenstein's intuition. Not only does Peirce say that the meaningful action presupposes a narrative context (he would call it a dynamic interpretant or a consequence of the first act), he also shows how the meaningful action generates all the conditions of the narrative context that Wittgenstein referred to when speaking of "practical consequences." This narrativity of the act of donation, and more generally of communicative acts, emerges specifically with the appearance of a term (e.g., a homeless person) in relation to a second term (a $1 coin) through a third (a passerby), using the second term as a means of reaching the first.

Triadicity and Agency

Through Peirce's triadic notion of intentionality we can now better grasp what is missing in Latour's otherwise insightful perspective: a theory of action that does not reduce a course of action to a series of actions and reactions displaced in time and space. Although Latour rightfully rejected subjectivity as the principle of analysis of an organized network of action, he thereby lost the mental (I would rather call it textual) element that makes his chain of action something other than a more or less predictable chain of reactions. Hence his analysis of the agency of humans and nonhumans is always reduced to dyads, one element delegating his will and power to another to act in his name, without a conceptualization of the connection established between these dyads by texts, institutions, or the collective mind (Weick & Roberts, 1993) of organizing. The triadic conception brings the narrative context (and text) of delegation back into the analysis of agency, operating in the conversation in which the delegation occurs, without reducing agency to the human individual consciousness. Far from it. Organizing is constituted through a plurality of agencies, as Cooren argued earlier in this book, but this plurality, despite its complexity, is nevertheless textualized in an organizing and operative organizational text. Peirce would have no difficulty in talking about the organizational mind nor thinking of it as a pragmatic and empirical reality emerging out of agentic processes.

CONCLUSION: AGENCY AS THE MEDIATION OF THE TEXT AND THE CONVERSATION

In the both/and style that Cooren, Taylor, and Van Every introduced in the first chapter of this volume, I have tried to make the argument that what is typically conceived to be an externalist notion of agency relies significantly on an intentional structure (or text) and, on the other hand, that the internalist model of agency should be thought of in much more externalist terms if it is to make sense at all in an organizational context. To transcend these established dogmas, we need to acknowledge that the very notion of agency is devoid of any useful meaning at all once it has been stripped of the intentional structure of human action. At the same time, however, intentional structure is nothing more than a fundamental structure of connectedness and engagement of humans in the plurality of their surroundings. The intentional structure is what allows the sharing of action with nonhumans, especially with texts and technologies, not what essentially distinguishes us from them. Intentions are not a property of human mental activities, but a property of institutionalized nets of practices emerging out of the conversations in which we constantly redefine our connections to others, to machines, to nature, and to texts (Robichaud et al., 2004). As Peirce taught us, semiosis is a natural as well as a symbolic process, and its triadic structure is not a structure of the human mind, but a fundamental structure of the embeddedness of our mind in the rest of nature.

Consciousness is a heterogeneous reality, at once chemical, biological, discursive, and social. On all these levels of reality the mind is in continuous connection with the outside in numerous ways, as Bateson (1979) in his own way envisioned. We share a large part of who we are with nature, language, and technology. We look at ourselves as the builders of the world we inhabit, exhibiting agency in all imaginable contexts of engagement. In following the lead of Latour, I have tried to show that this traditional (and mostly internal) conception of agency no longer works to anyone interested in understanding the conditions and process of organizing. I do not mean by this that intentions, purposiveness, and power are not relevant, but that we need to reconsider them in a truly relational way if we are to account for organizing in our postmodern (Lyotard, 1984), late modern (Giddens, 1991), or a-modern (Latour, 1993) era.

Peirce offered a language of description of the constitutive relations of entities because of his belief that relations are ontologically primary, and thus should be so analytically. His theory is useful in the sense that it permits a more systematic description of the ways in which the realities of relations generate the entities we take for granted, and the texts in which our complex and continuous conversations with humans and nonhumans still make sense. Only further analysis and theoretical developments will tell us, however, to what extent Peirce's triadic model is really useful. I intended this chapter to be an invitation to tap more systematically into the heuristic potential of Peirce's conception of relations—and especially of triadic relations—in the context where so many current postmodern redefinitions of agency and action in relational terms, although well intended and inspired, remain trapped in conceptual vagueness.

ACKNOWLEDGMENTS

I wish to thank Boris Brummans and François Cooren for their helpful comments on an earlier draft of this chapter. James Taylor and Elizabeth Van Every not only identified some places where my argument needed clarification, but also made sure the English language would not suffer too much in this chapter.

CHAPTER SEVEN

Making Worldview Sense:
And Paying Homage, Retrospectively,
to Algirdas Greimas

James R. Taylor
François Cooren
Université de Montréal

> *Each person is positioned, in a "multiple" way, within social relations conferred by specific social identities; this is the main sphere of application of the concept of social role.*
>
> —Giddens (1984, pp. xxiv–xxv)

The concept of worldview, introduced by Taylor and his associates (Groleau & Taylor, 1996; Taylor, 1993; Taylor & Cooren, 1997; Taylor, Cooren, Giroux, & Robichaud, 1996; Taylor & Gurd, 1996; Taylor, Gurd, & Bardini, 1997), may appear to have two differing interpretations. On the one hand, it has been defined (Taylor, 1993; Taylor, Gurd & Bardini, 1997) as an inversion of perspective separating the sensemaking activities of individuals and groups who are joined by a common focus on a shared object, but asymmetrically, to form a complementary relationship that divides them even as it links them. Examples are easy to educe: seller versus buyer, doctor versus patient, parent versus child, employer versus employee. Their perspectives on the transaction are divergent. The contrasting worldviews thus produced, Taylor et al. argued in these articles, do not always block communication (they may even be its basis), but they do result in noncoincident (and always potentially conflicting) attachments to, and interpretations of, a common object (Güney, chap. 2, this volume, is illustrative).

The same authors (Taylor, 2000a, 2005) also offered, on the other hand, what may seem to be a different explanation of the concept. Here worldview is portrayed as the inversion of perspective that results from understanding communication as, alternatively, (a) people in conversation who use text to mediate their interaction, as opposed to (b) discursive formations based in language that shape the contours of the conversation, channel its interaction, serve to identify its participants, and thereby instantiate ideas of normality, hierarchy, and value.

The purpose of this chapter is to show that these seemingly differing explications of the worldview concept are in fact outcroppings of a single phenomenon, rooted in practices of human sensemaking. We delve into the origin of the worldview distinction in the unique work of a little known (in North America, at least) semiotician, Algirdas Julien Greimas. Greimas was the author of what is far and away the most thoroughly elaborated theory of narrative and narrativity to be found anywhere in the literature, and yet, in spite of a current resurgence of interest in narrative in the literature on organization (Boje, 1991, 1995, 2001; Boje, Alvarez, & Schooling, 2001; Czarniawska, 1997, 1998, 1999; Fairhurst & Putnam, 2004; Gabriel, 1995, 1997; Grant, Keenoy & Oswick, 1998; Putnam & Fairhurst, 2001; Westwood & Linstead, 2001; Zilber, 2002a, 2002b), his work is rarely, if ever, mentioned. A secondary goal of this chapter is thus to explore a theory rich in insights into the bases of communication, in all its manifestations, but of particular significance to students of organization.

The chapter has three parts. In the first, we present in broad outline the general theory of narrativity developed by Greimas. We then, in the second part, demonstrate using data from a field study the potential application of narrative theory in analyzing sequences of organizational communication. Finally, we return to explicate worldview in a new light.

GREIMAS'S THEORY OF NARRATIVE

The late 1950s witnessed an extraordinary renaissance of interest in the analysis of narrative. Vladimir Propp's *Morphology of the Folktale*, written in 1928 in Russian, was finally translated in 1958 (Propp, 1928/1968). In France, Claude Lévi-Strauss, deeply influenced by the work and example of Roman Jakobson, was initiating in the 1950s what would ultimately become an exhaustive investigation of the structuring principles that underlie the myth-making practices of a variety of societies. In 1958 he published in French (translated into English in 1963) the first volume of *Structural Anthropology*, including essays on the myths of the western tribes of North America. The cumulative influence of these investigations into the nature of story and myth was most immediately felt in Paris. In the 1960s Paris was afire with brilliant reflections on the nature of language and its role in the structuring of human affairs. The effervescence was animated by theoreticians and analysts that included not just Lévi-Strauss, but also Michel Foucault, Roland Barthes, Jacques Derrida, Paul Ricoeur, Claude Bremond, Umberto Eco (better known now as a novelist), Christian Metz, Tzvetan Todorov, Jean Baudrillard, Claude Chabrol, Julia Kristeva, Violette Morin, and Algirdas J. Greimas.

Greimas was a native of Lithuania who emigrated to France just before the outbreak of hostilities leading up to World War II. He graduated with a doctorate at the

Sorbonne as a specialist of the history of the French language, but his interest soon turned to the study of semantics. With customary thoroughness, he immersed himself in the writings of authors such as Ferdinand de Saussure, Louis Hjelmslev, and Roman Jakobson. The essays of Lévi-Strauss and the translation of Propp's work served to focus his reflections on the narrative dimension of language. Greimas's first essays are really reanalyses of their earlier papers. Unlike his close friend Barthes, whose interest evolved into the literary implications of the new narratology, Greimas was a logician through and through. His work in the semantic bases of narrative became enormously influential in France, where he was progressively transformed into something close to a cult figure. However, there are few traces of influence outside his adopted country. He tends to be treated as an interesting but relatively minor figure in the development of the field (see, e.g., Herman, 2002). It is partly his own fault. Even in French, Greimas makes for a daunting read, and his numerous neologisms and esoteric language make his text singularly opaque in English. That is a great pity, because in his penetrating analyses of the bases of narrative lies the secret to the meaning of worldview.

In what follows, we offer our own (hopefully more accessible although far from definitive) interpretation of Greimas's theory of narrative, and show why it illuminates the worldview phenomenon.

Tell Me a Story

How do you make a story? Obviously, it only counts as a story if there is a sequence of events: action (and interaction) that unfolds over time. By definition, this extension as a sequence of events unfolding in time excludes single sentences as a candidate for storyhood because sentences describe events one at a time. However, as Bruner (1991) observed, a story is not just a reporting of any old sequence of events, one sentence after the other. Perhaps a linear account of the sort "First I went ..., then I went ..., and then I went ...," might count as a chronicle, or a record, but it is not a story. It is just a conjunction of sentences, held together by a common point of reference, and lacking any more complex supra-sentential development. To be a story, it has to have a story structure. But what is a story structure (or what Greimas calls a "narrative program")?

Well, answered Greimas (1993), a narrative has a "certain economic organization" (p. 22, our translation). What he means by economic organization is that a well-designed narrative "subsumes" two chronicles: two narrative paths, and two actors who follow them in pursuit of an object they value—the same object. Complications arise when the same object is conceptualized and valued in different ways. It is the interplay of the paths—their mutual interference in that each enters the other's practice as a disturbance, however minor—that makes a story a narrative structure with some complexity. In the act of translating experience into an account of it, however, the two paths are not accorded equal status, as one of them is the trajectory followed by a protagonist—the "subject" (from whose perspective the experience is being viewed)—and the other by an antagonist—an "antisubject." As Greimas (1987) put it:

> The story is at the same time a story of victory and defeat. What determines the choice between these two interpretations has to do not with narrative syntax but rather with the axiological articulation of content values. Of the two *conformed spaces*, the investment of one is initially given as being *euphoric* and that of the other as being *dysphoric*. (p. 79, emphasis in original; the jargon is typical of Greimas's writing: "conformed spaces," e.g., points to the formal symmetry of antagonistic paths of action.)

The perspectives, in other words, are not accorded equal weight (think of how differently doctors and patients might relate their experience of diagnosis and treatment of the latter): A story is always told from a point of view. It might, in principle, have been told from the other point of view—the antagonist's—but then it would not have been the same story, and it would not have had the same meaning. (And of course dramatists and novelists have been exploiting these reversals of perspective for a long time: One thinks of Durrell's *Alexandria Quartet*, for example, with its complicated narrative structure, and its intricate counterposing of one perspective against another.)

So storyhood presupposes opposition (literally, a "putting in front of or against"). Greimas sometimes called this the polemic property of narrative (Greimas, 1987), but he also observed that the "confrontation" of subjects, in the narrative context, may be either polemic or transactional, "manifested sometimes by a combat, sometimes by an exchange" (Greimas,1993, p. 11; the word *confrontation* has softer connotations in French, incidentally, than in English). The opposition is thus not necessarily overtly antagonistic, although it is always latently so because "transactional" can so easily degenerate into "polemical," as lawsuits often illustrate. In any case, however amicable the transaction, there are still going to be two activity paths involved, and an intersection between them, to produce a disturbance (in the sense that one actor's actions impinge on the other's and oblige a response from the latter, as illustrated in both Güney's and Saludadez's chapters, this volume).

The interpretation of the intersection of trajectories, to the extent that it is based in narrative and expressed in the form of an account, always comes down, however, to one privileged perspective, that of the protagonist. Stories or accounts are generally about how the protagonist overcame some obstacle, met some challenge, and resolved some situation. If there had been nothing to be resolved, then we would be back to "first I got up, then I had breakfast, then I went to the office, then I broke for coffee, … and so on.")

The chronicle of events thus has to be seen as motivated by something that needs attending to: a break with the routine. However, things that need to be dealt with (Bruner, 1991, called them precipitating events) logically have a cause. The cause of the precipitating event is not necessarily associated with a human antagonist; it could be a cataclysm, an avalanche, or a "perfect storm," although even here two agencies are involved.[1] However, it is more fun if the author of the breach, or violation, or deviation, has a human face because then there is the potential for a contest, and interesting complications may follow. Strategy, guile, strength, and purity of spirit as against cynicism can come into play. There is something to sink your teeth into, narratively speaking, as any TV producer or novelist knows.

A precipitating event need not be dramatic for it to generate a story. Daily life is full of things that have to be attended to and dealt with. Any of them is enough to serve as a pretext for a narrative, or what Varey (chap. 10, this volume), calls an account.[2] However quotidian the pretext, the interpretation you manage to convey—your version of the interaction—is a way of presenting not just your own position (what Greimas called a *positive deixis*), but implying that of another (a *negative deixis*). Positive versus negative are not in and of themselves emotionally loaded terms; in logic, they are what Greimas (1987) called "pure designations implying no value judgment" (p. 108). They merely point to the existence of a bipolarity. In practice, however, he conceded, they easily take on an emotional loading by being "invested" with moral value, and translated into attributions of good and bad, heroism and treachery. The boundary between transactional and polemical is all too easily breached.

This is the first contribution that Greimas made that we want to call attention to: All sensemaking, even in the circumstances of an ordinary transaction, catches us up in a potential confrontational logic. This is where the concept of "worldview" becomes relevant. For every story (and every interpretation) there is an antistory, not just another story. The antistory is the obverse of whatever story is in the figurative foreground. It is the ground that lends the figure of the story in focus its meaning potential. Worldview, like story logic, is dichotomous: two-sided, not multisided, even where the point of reference is the habitual, everyday transactions in which we are usually involved. However low-key and innocuous such intersubjective transactions may seem, they always hold the potential for conflict. They always generate attributions of worldview, from the point of view of the narrator who thus claims the privilege of making an account and, by doing so, occults the ambiguity inherent in worldview (Katambwe & Taylor, chap. 4, this volume).

---

[1]As Greimas (1987) observed:

> The paradigmatic disjunction of actants ... is applicable to even minimal stories with only one actant. This is so to the extent that this one actant, in its doing, meets some obstacle or other, and that obstacle will be interpreted as the metonymic representation of the anti-actant associated with the nonconforming deixis for the manifested activity of the actant. (p. 109)

[2]See, for example, Orr (1996), who described how photocopy repairpeople construct a body of common knowledge by the repeated (and narratively based) accounts they make of unexpected complications and how they dealt with them.

Subjects

Note what Greimas has been doing. He made the notion of subject a relational term: the correlate, as he called it, of antisubject. Each defines the other, reciprocally. This move makes sense within story logic, in that the latter is, as Bruner (1991) observed, generic in kind, not circumstantial. Story logic supplies categories and categories imply relationships, typical of any system of classification. How the individual gets fitted into the category, however, is the explanatory task of discourse, not narrative, theory (Greimas, 1987). Any theatre performer understands the principle. *Hamlet* is eternal; it touches some deep chord within us by its delineation of well-meaning impotence in the face of a great crime. Its narrative appeal is universal, transcending generation and culture. How *Hamlet* is played, however, is circumstantial. Making the play come alive by embodying its anguish in a "real" person (perhaps, e.g., by staging it in modern dress) is the challenge that confronts the actor and the director. That is in the realm of discourse. It is still the same story but it is circumstantially grounded differently, and it takes on new connotations.

We will not have grasped the significance of worldview, however, if we are only to think of it as based on an inversion of perspective characterizing individuals' viewpoints on a communicative exchange. The concept is considerably richer than that, as we now see.

Objects and Actors: Defining a Space

In narrative theory, all the terms are relational (Robichaud, chap. 6, this volume), protagonist–antagonist being a case in point. However, intersubjective relations are only one dimension of identity. There is another: the relationship of subject to object, and object to subject.

The object, in narrative theory, "is no more than the subject's intended project" (Greimas, 1987, p. 87).[3] As he further observed: "no object is knowable in and of itself. Only by its determinations can it be known .... To speak of objects as such does not make any sense" (p. 86). It is (and here we might hear echoes of Weick's (1979) notion of "enactment") "an end term of our relation with the world ... the apprehension of meaning meets, in its process, only values determining the object, not the object itself" (p. 87). This is making sense, in Weick's terminology.

For Greimas the concepts of object and subject are mutually defining. Farmers are farmers because they farm, and farms are transformed from wilderness into farms by being farmed. The same goes for the other "membership categories" that make up the generic framework of society (Sacks, 1992). Object and subject are reciprocally constituted (in narrative logic, of course). Without object, there is no

---

[3]As Groleau (chap. 9, this volume) notes, Engeström (1990) offered a similar delineation of object: He defined object as a "problem space" (p. 79) at which an activity is directed. As he wrote elsewhere, "objects are objects by virtue of being constructed in time by human subjects" (p. 107).

subject. Without subject, there is no object. We are what we do. And we do what we are. As Greimas (1993) put it: "there is no possible definition of subject in the absence of a relation to object, and vice versa" (p. 3, our translation).

The welding together to form an indissoluble unit of subject and object in the realm of semantics produces what Greimas called an *isotope* (*iso* is the Greek word for "same," *topos* for "space"). It is, he was saying, the same conceptual space because each pole of the axis, subject and object, presupposes the other. Like a very different analyst, Weick (1979, 1995), Greimas emphasized the mutuality of actor, acting, and acted-on. Grammatically speaking, even, acting—a verb—instantiates both actor and acted-on (i.e., a subject and an object). On the other hand, the linking of subject and object, to the extent that it describes more than a state of being or having (*être/avoir*), implies a doing (*faire*). The "doing" of an action is in turn associated with a time and a place, and an activity that is typical of it. When we take account of these spatial–temporal circumstances and social embedding, the action of subjects defines a conceptual space—an isotope—that both Weick (1995) and Taylor and Van Every (2000) called a "situation" and Engeström an "activity system": a composite reality with parameters that are identifiable as actor(s), their objects, their technologies, and their spatio-temporal circumstances.[4]

The full meaning of worldview, as an intersection of practices, should now become clearer. Worldview is not primarily an interpersonal phenomenon at all, or merely a divergence of perspective involving two individuals engaged in a transaction. It goes deeper than that. It is made salient because the individuals are themselves embedded in contrasting isotopic activity spaces, each characterized by its respective configuring of subject, object, technologies, siting in a place and a time, and habitual modes of accounting for how it deals with problems. These configurations are what Greimas was referring to when he wrote of "conformed spaces," each being a community patterned by its preoccupation with an object and characterized by its internal interagent relationships.

The intersecting transaction that brings two communities of practice into a common space is effected by individuals, because that is a constraint imposed by human communication, but the relationship is not just interpersonal. The constituent communities are immanent in the exchange; not so much present as represented— "*re*-presented" (Cooren, chap. 5, this volume)—in the discourse of the interlocutors. It is a relationship not just of people but of modes of activity, and it is this that makes it not just an encounter of individuals, but a locus of organizational communication. That the transaction is itself focused on an object of value, either in a context of amicable exchange (value for value) or a contest in which the winner takes all (or at least the lion's share), now implies a background of networks of nodes, configuring their internal patterns through interaction. We are in the domain of or-

---

[4]For a recent sophisticated analysis of the importance of isotopic spaces see Law (2000; Law & Mol, 2001). See also Suchman (1996), for whom "work activities and workspaces are mutually constituted" (p. 35). As she observed, "place is constituted by, rather than the container for, culturally, historically, and locally meaningful forms of lived activity" (p. 35).

ganizing, the largely self-generated shaping of the larger organizational network in a restless search for a common object. Any large contemporary organization, such as Güney (chap. 2, this volume) describes, is replete with instances of the phenomenon to which we are referring.

Actors and Actants

Each of us is probably animated by a deep conviction that, whatever the circumstance, there is a part of our identity as individuals that is constant, no matter how many changes of scene we make, how many relationships we get involved in, and how the objects we pursue evolve. Of course that is right, but it ignores the fact that, as Bruner (1991) pointed out, language has no particulars. It is, by its very nature, generic. It supplies categories, and not just categories, but their semantic and syntactic entanglements as well. A tree (a word in a language) is not a particular tree; it is a generic concept: a "large woody perennial plant with one main trunk which develops many branches," to cite *Webster's* (1964, p. 9). It is a cousin of a bush, and a component element of a forest. It is, as *Webster's* reminds us, a plant. There are things we can do to and with trees (make lumber out of them, carve our names in them), including how we use the word in our talk ("I think I will never see a poem as lovely as a tree"). The meaning of the word tree is inherently relational.

Greimas devoted considerable attention to the distinction we are making, between universal and circumstantial. For him, narrative theory was only half the story of how we make sense of experience: the universalize-it part. The other half is what he called discourse theory. Discourse theory is concerned with what we might call "putting some clothes on" the actions that are the domain of narrative theory by translating them into the ordinary language of situated people: now figurative as opposed to narrative. This distinction led Greimas to discriminate between what he termed actants (a neologism in French, as in English) and actors. *Actants* are abstract potentials, based on two kinds of relationship. The first we have already described: subject–object (S → O), in essence having or being someone in relation to something. The second kind of relationship is one of subject to subject, mediated by the transfer of an object (a "doing") from one subject (a sender) to another (a receiver): S → O → R. It is no longer an object of value that is in primary focus (what one has or is), but a modal object, an "intended project" that, once conveyed from S to R, makes the latter's project congruent with the former's. It is what Austin (1962) thought of as "doing things with words": acting on people rather than on insensible material objects, or exerting influence, in other words.

The concept of actant is thus pitched at a high level of generality, because objects have unlimited variety in everyday affairs, and interpersonal exchanges are similarly infinite in their potentiality. *Actors*, however, unlike actants, are tied to circumstances particular to a context of habitual interaction: the familiar "figures" typical of any domain of practice, from coal miner to politician to movie star. They "are recognizable in the particular discourses in which they are manifested"

(Greimas, 1987, p. 106). As he observed, "actants and actors are not identical (one actant can be manifested by several actors and, conversely, one actor can at the same time represent several actants)" (p. 111).

Why, you may be asking, resort to what at first must seem like an artificial distinction: actor versus actant? Is this merely complication for the sake of complication, trying to make esoteric something that is really not particularly problematical? The answer is that there is a very good reason behind the rationale of narrativity that Greimas develops. It is by isolating the basic logical constructions that underlie human action that we can better understand the surface dynamic of communication: why, for example, conflict is such an all-pervading potential in all organizational communication, as we have systematically found in our own research. Much of Greimas's work is, accordingly, devoted to explicating the notion of actantial roles.

Actantial Roles

First, a basic principle: All the operations composing a narrative grammar are oriented. Consider the notion of precipitating event that we introduced earlier, for example. Implicit in the notion of such an event is the idea of an interference, or a disturbance. There is a loss of something, or a usual expectation has failed to materialize: The product you bought was faulty, the doctor was late or inattentive, or the brakes on the car still squeal. A situation that had previously been satisfactory (let us call it s_1) has been made unsatisfactory (in other words, $s_1 \rightarrow {\sim}s_1$) and it is this transformation that motivates the genesis of a story. However, following the Greimasian "economic" logic of narrative, $s_1 \rightarrow {\sim}s_1$ is correlated with ${\sim}s_2 \rightarrow s_2$, an antagonistic perspective: By implication another subject has benefitted in some way from your discomfiture.

One actant's (s_1's) unsatisfactory situation is thus correlated with the opposing actant's (s_2) satisfactory outcome: positive versus negative, depending on whose point of view you take. A kind of communication has been established, but because its negative polarity is unbalanced the situation is invested with tension. (We may, instinctively, read into this imbalance the inevitability of open conflict, but as we shortly show in an analysis of interaction in the most banal of organizational contexts—a building manager talking to an occupant—even though the antagonism is always latently present in normal interaction, it is normally mitigated by the polite conventions of ordinary conversation.) Making a conversation is an act of creation. It is constructed out of language, but how the narrative structures of language are employed in practice depends on the inventiveness of the people engaged in interaction.

An unsatisfactory situation is one that needs correcting. So now a new object is constituted to repair the tear by reversing the transformation: ${\sim}s_1 \rightarrow s_1$. The new project (or object) is an action (a *faire*, or a "doing"). This object must, by the same principle as before, be associated with a subject, but now it is a "subject of doing" (Greimas, 1993, p. 13): an actor.

It may be useful here to recall briefly one of Greimas's sources, Propp (1968). Propp gathered some 150 Russian folktales and discovered that they all, without exception, exemplified a similar pattern. An initial tort (princess abducted and carried off to a distant land) engenders a quest undertaken by Ivan the hero, at the behest of the king. After many trials Ivan recovers the princess and, returning in triumph, is rewarded (typically by getting to marry the princess). What Greimas extracted from this Proppian account is that there are three kinds of actant in such a tale: the king, who has been deprived of an object of value, the princess, and Ivan, who is the actor responsible for righting the wrong and restoring things to their normal order. The king is defined by his link to a valued object, the princess. Ivan is defined by what he does for the king, rescue the princess: an object (and subject) of state versus an object (and subject) of doing. The core of the story is the performance of Ivan, but in acting for the king (and the society he represents) Ivan is his agent, acting for him. The relationship is that of an *initiator* (an eventual beneficiary, or principal, called by Greimas a *destinateur* or sender) and an *executor* (an agent who acts for, or a *destinataire* or receiver). There exists, whether explicitly or tacitly, a contract linking initiator or beneficiary and executor or agent: a contract sited in communication. The ultimate sanction of Ivan's performance is his being recognized as hero: The contract is fulfilled. The outcome of the story, however, is already prefigured in the initial "contractual structure" (Greimas, 1993, p. 22, our translation), "the remainder of the story appearing to be no more than the carrying through of the provisions of the contract by the respective parties: the achievement of his task by the subject, which constitutes the contribution of the agent ("receiver"), followed by a sanctioning of his performance by the principal ("sender") that is both pragmatic (a recompense) and cognitive (a recognition)."[5]

The executor or agent is defined actantially, but its materialization in the action that is being recounted in a particular narrative may involve either one actor, or several. Ancillary actors, if they are contributors, are called helpers (*adjuvants* in French), or opponents if they create obstacles (Greimas, 1987, p. 112). Sometimes, as in the person of Góllum in *The Lord of the Rings*, they are both. But, whichever, their role is secondary to the principal story protagonist, the main actor.

The performance of the subject is book-ended by two other contractual segments: a commitment to, and a sanctioning by, a superior authority ("une instance actantielle supérieure"). That legitimization is conferred by its grounding in an original authority is thus a basic assumption that underlies the Greimasian (1993) scheme of narrativity. A mission is always animated by an ideology (a preestablished model) of society, and the appropriate means of its governance, and it is evaluated ("judged") by its conformity to the norms of the society. Communication thus ultimately has a moral basis (Brummans, chap. 11, this volume).

---

[5]The formal similarity with Shannon's S–R (sender–receiver) model is almost certainly not accidental. However, Greimas's interpretation of the "transmission" is strongly contrasting with that of Shannon, in that he invested it with organizational significance because communication is seen to orient people's actions and not just inform their knowledge.

Russian folktales may seem very far from contemporary life, but what Greimas was arguing is that—forget the fairy tale trappings—the underlying logic is universally valid. Everybody has a project, and performance is a preoccupation of everyday reality, as much in today's world as in any other. Unsatisfactory situations need dealing with, and someone to deal with them. The validity of an action is measured against the standards we hold to apply in our particular society, as Güney (chap. 2, this volume) again illustrates.

The relationship of an initiator with authority and the agent who undertakes the task of performing the action necessary to restore the situation to its satisfactory conclusion is what Greimas (1987) described as a *"communication schema* or, even more generally, the *structure of exchange"* (p. 77, italics in original). Communication is thus not, as in classic information theory, just messaging. It is the conveyance, or at least establishment in the course of interaction, of a mandate or a mission—a mission that will ultimately be rewarded: a transaction in immanence, in other words. It is this missioning or mandating, and its grounding in legitimate authority, that in turn invests the agent with the authority to act. This is, at a more practical, mundane level, no more than a theory-based restatement of a principle that is tacitly exemplified in all organizational communication where managers and employees alike are empowered to act by their being the legitimate representatives of their organization, and the carriers of its mandate, materialized in their performances.

Communication is at the core of narrativity (and not merely the inverse). There are, however, restrictions on subjecthood in narrative logic as well as in real life. To be accorded the capacity (and the legitimacy) to act, the subject must a priori be (a) motivated by the desire or the duty to act, and (b) in possession of the knowledge and the practical know-how, related to a means, to act. Agents (subjects of doing) must manifest the qualifications that distinguish subjecthood. How the contract between initiator and agent is sealed is itself a phase of narrative unfolding. So all narrative form, stripped to its bare essentials, is punctuated by four phases: establishment, via communication, of a contract linking a subject of state or initiator (an ultimate beneficiary) and a subject of doing or executor (an agent).[6] The qualification of the latter, perhaps through trial and error, is a necessary precondition for the subject to be recognized as an authorized agent. The core performance—that which turns a mere chronicle of events into a story with a meaning—is the act that restores an unsatisfactory state to normalcy. The sanction, or ultimate validation, realized perhaps as a reward, may be both material and symbolic, and may be either positive or negative (if the latter, it is typically the pretext for a new story).

---

[6]The story model just described is formally identical, incidentally, with a scheme used in computer science system design concerned with capturing the pattern of an ordinary commercial transaction involving a principal and a contractee. For discussion, see Taylor and Van Every (2000). The pattern to which Greimas was calling our attention is thus far from esoteric; it is a feature of everyday organizational life.

To Greimas, as we have seen, narratives always unfold against a background of values—social values. Values can range all the way from the great oppositions—freedom versus oppression, integrity versus cheating, family and community versus anomie and criminality, and so on—to more banal polarities, such as promptness, thoroughness, integrity, and cleanliness. The opposed values form the background—the structural scaffolding, if you like—that serves to frame the story and give it meaning. You "make sense" (Weick, 1995) of experience by your choice of framework of value: which contradictions you choose to highlight, which you choose to ignore, and thus which basic background values you evoke and which you do not.

PUTTING THE GREIMAS THEORY OF NARRATIVITY TO WORK: AN ILLUSTRATION

In this section we consider how narratively grounded actantial roles come to inform the ordinary transactions of a large organization. Our data are based on field work conducted in New York (for more extensive analysis, see Cooren, chap. 5, this volume; Cooren, Fox, Robichaud, & Talih, 2005). The setting is a large office building in central Manhattan. Denis is the building manager. Andrea represents a company that is moving into its new quarters in the building Denis is responsible for. The tenant needs to have the office complex reconfigured to fit its particular needs. Denis, as building manager, oversees a permanent staff whose responsibility it is to maintain the building. In addition, he is the one who, acting for the client, subcontracts work to outside contractors who actually do the reconstruction of the office space, according to the specifications of the client. The work is now nearing completion, but there are still details to be taken care of. The day before, Andrea asked Denis to stop by so that they can inspect what Denis's team of contractors has done. She has a number of specific concerns that she wants Denis to be aware of. François is a researcher and cameraman (the second author of this chapter) who is recording on videotape Denis's daily rounds as he carries out his responsibilities. Our analysis begins with Denis introducing François to Andrea.

17 to	Denis:	So listen, I wanted to stop in so that I could uh uh introduce you
18 19 20		François and g- get you on camera. And then uh do you have the key for next door?
21 22	Andrea:	I do have (them)
23 24	Denis:	Do you want to take a walk with me? I want to take a [look=
25 26	Andrea:	[Yes

27	Denis:	=at [it and see if uh if there are things we have to finish up.
28		
29	Andrea:	[Yes definitely we can uh

This minisequence establishes a coorientational basis of interaction, initiated by Denis. Denis preemptively positions himself as "wanting to stop by so that he could introduce" Andrea to François and "get her on camera" (Lines 17–18). He does not mention the fact that Andrea initiated this program of inspection by calling his office the day before. It is as though Denis aims to establish a situation in which he is the one who initiated the whole inspection process, something he does by asking her for the key of the quarters "next door" (Lines 18–19). Although Andrea, as the client spokesperson, might theoretically be supposed to assume the role of initiator or executor of the inspection and Denis, as the building manager who deals with the contractors, that of recipient of the "things to be done," he repositions himself as initiator or executor, and Andrea seems to be relegated to the role of a helper. As Denis says on Line 23, "Do you want to take a walk with me?" He explains that "[he] want[s] to take a look at [the locale] and see if ... there are things we have to finish up" (Lines 23 and 27).

Denis is reconstructing through his discourse an actantial role and an identity for himself (and implicitly for Andrea as well) through expressing what it is he wants to do. It is he, he implies, who is the sender. He is the one who is going to judge and evaluate what needs to be done. Although never explicitly denying Andrea the role of evaluator (as primary inspector), he is certainly not explicitly attributing this identity to her.

Andrea acknowledges without complaint, for the moment, this definition of their respective roles. She replies that she indeed has the keys, she gets them (Line 21), and she agrees to take a walk with Denis (Lines 25 and 29). Coorientation is established but it is a coorientation that is enacted by Denis through his skillful exploitation of the categories of narrative: making himself the subject of the inspection, and Andrea the helper.

Now let us consider the same interaction slightly later, after Denis and Andrea have walked from her office to the new office quarters. They reach the entrance and Andrea opens the door, an action that initiates the actual inspection sequence. As soon as he enters, Denis switches on the light and makes an emphatic "Okay" (Line 105) as if to mark that he is now on the premises and the inspection can begin.

105	Denis:	*Okay:::*
106		
107	Andrea:	So there is uhhh
108		
109	Denis:	We're looking good
110		
111		(0.5)

112
113 Denis: Okay, we've got to do a little clean up
114
115   (2.0)
116
117 Andrea: xx What what What's missing, this, I know that for example. See,
118   there's there's here. There's these pieces
119
120   (0.5)
121
122 Andrea: And I'm not sure
123
124 Denis: The what?
125
126 Andrea: These two pieces
127
128 Denis: Oh They go in the ceiling
129
130 Andrea: I don't know which ones. I kept these two because there is no- no-
131   I didn't find anything like these
132
133 Denis: th' [is fine
134
135 Andrea: [I don't know if this goes here or that one
136
137 Andrea: So [I just left it there
138
139 Denis: [Yeah
140
141 Denis: Leave it there, I will take care of it.
142
143 Andrea: So[oo
144
145 Denis: [I'll just do some cleaning up here
146
147   (1.0)
148
149 Denis: and uhh

Andrea starts to speak just after Denis's "Okay," and we understand that she is about to mention that something is missing or that something has to be done ("So there is uhhh" [Line 107]), but Denis does not let her finish her sentence and interrupts her by making a positive evaluation ("We're looking good" [Line 109]), followed half a second later by the affirmation "Okay, we've got to do a little clean up" (Line 113). Again, as we see, Denis positions himself as the evaluator or inspector; that is, he confirms the role he had implicitly attributed to himself at the beginning of the interaction between Lines 17 and 29.

Andrea, however, does not echo Denis's positive evaluation. If we look at the video image of the sequence, we see Andrea unlocking the door, opening it, and letting Denis enter the locale. Denis then switches on the light and makes his emphatic "Okay" (Line 105). He does not really wait for Andrea and starts to walk around in the suite, his hands in his pockets, as if to mark the relatively mundane, ordinary, uneventful, or routine character of this inspection he is now undertaking. Andrea starts to say, "So there is uhhh" (Line 107), but Denis does not turn back to her to listen to what she has to say. By not letting her finish her sentence he appears not to orient at all to what she is saying. Instead, he says, "We're looking good" (Line 109), followed by "Okay, we've got to do a little clean up" (Line 113).

Andrea is still behind him and he is not looking at her. He is looking at holes in the ceiling of one of the rooms. It is at this point, when she sees Denis scrutinizing the room, that she breaks in to say, "What what What's missing, this, I know that for example. See, there's there's here" (Line 117–118). As she says this, Denis leaves the room he was looking at and enters an adjacent one. Andrea then enters the room Denis has just left (they literally cross each other and Denis does not seem to attend at all to what she is saying) and she then finishes her sentence by saying, "There's these pieces" (Line 118), showing them with her finger (but Denis has left this room and is in the other one). She is alone in the room and she turns her head, saying, "And I'm not sure" (Line 122), as if to see where Denis is.

Denis then returns to the room where she is and he says, "The what?" (Line 124), finally orienting to what she is talking about. Andrea then responds, "These two pieces" (Line 126), pointing to them on the floor. Denis responds, "Oh they go in the ceiling" (Line 128). Again, Denis's response implicitly forestalls (and downplays) Andrea's potential complaint. By informing her where these pieces on the floor will go, he does answer her question, but he does not imply in the least a problem with having them there on the floor. All his interactive work downplays potential sources of disruption or disorder. It is as if, from a Greimasian perspective, Andrea's agenda had been to highlight problems or sources of disruption (and therefore initiate programs of action on Denis's part), whereas his agenda seems to have been to minimize the importance of minor annoyances, and to deflect what Andrea might have to say about potential problems. Each in his or her own way is making an account, reflexively, of this encounter, on the fly.

In her agenda, in Greimasian terms, we may assume that Andrea, as client representative, is the originator or sender (the *destinateur*) and Denis, as manager, is the receiver (the *destinataire/sujet*). In his agenda, on the other hand, he appears to combine in his person the roles of sender and receiver. It is he who both identifies the problems and will do something about them. In his version, Andrea does not really occupy any specific actantial role (except perhaps that of helper, and potentially of course, that of opponent or antisubject, an eventuality he is clearly trying to avoid).

Framed in the language of worldview, there would seem to be two incompatible ways to envisage what is collectively being done. In Andrea's reading of the exchange she is the principal and Denis is the agent, and the object of the inspection is to point out problems that need to be fixed. Denis, on the other hand, appropriates that role to himself. For Andrea, the object is a problem that needs to be fixed, which Denis's response does not imply. He merely informs her where these pieces go, in no way admitting that they were not supposed to be where they are now. These pieces go in the ceiling; that is what they are. Period.

Although Denis's answer might appear to have closed the "pieces-on-the-floor sequence" (closure), we see in Lines 130 and 131 how Andrea opens it up again by saying, "I don't know which ones. I kept these two because there is no- no- I didn't find anything like these," which seems to mark again the problematic or disruptive character of these two pieces on the floor. They are presented by Andrea as unique ("I didn't find anything like these"), a singularity that seems to highlight their eventful character. Again, Denis responds to her concern by downplaying what she says ("Th'is fine" [Line 133]), as if to reassure her, and thus imply that there is nothing needing correction. "Th'is fine" seems meant as a way to say that there is no disruption, no disorder, and nothing there really.

Again, Andrea goes back to her source of puzzlement, marking this time the fact that she does not know where they go ("I don't know if this goes here or that one" [Line 135]), an absence of knowledge that she had already mentioned in Line 130 ("I don't know which ones"). Note that by mentioning this lack of know-how ("I don't know if this goes here or that one"), she implicitly disqualifies herself as a competent evaluator. It is as if (and this pattern is recurrent in the whole sequence) Andrea was positioning herself as an incompetent evaluator who points to potential sources of disruption without truly knowing if these are indeed problems. She presents herself as not having the know-how, but she still points to things that seem disruptive to her.

This form of self-disqualification seems to fit Denis's agenda very well. Given that Andrea positions herself as not qualified to pinpoint which problems are important, it becomes easy for Denis to downplay her concerns. She cannot be a sender because she cannot really tell the receiver-subject what to do. Even worse, she cannot even be sure she is accurately reporting authentic sources of disruption. Denis's agenda is thus confirmed: He is the one who can identify problems, the one who knows what to do about them, and the one who is going to intervene. He therefore once again claims for himself the actantial roles of sender and receiver. Andrea is effectively reduced to the person who happens to accompany him in his inspection. She is an unqualified evaluator who cannot back up what she presents as problems. Denis can then position himself as finding nothing problematical: a sender who evaluates (or in Greimas's terminology, who "sanctions").

In Line 141, we finally see Denis saying, "Leave it there, I will take care of it." Again, the putative positions of client and contractor are reversed, as now it is he who tells her what to do, while informing her as to what he is going to do about it.

Denis then closes the discussion by saying, "I'll just do some cleaning up here" (Line 145). He turns his back to Andrea and starts to leave the room while saying "and uhh" (Line 149). We then see Andrea starting to follow Denis out of the room. While following him, she speaks to him, mentioning a conversation she had with Julie, a member of Denis's staff ("So I did call also Julie, but she- you know there was xxx or something" [Line 153]).

```
153   Andrea:  So I did call also Julie, but she- you know there was xxx or
154            something Ah this is still ((touching the box on the wall))
155
156            ((Denis is looking into a room))
157
158   Andrea:  The box here
159
160            (0.5) ((Denis is coming back to look at the box))
161
162   Andrea:  I don't know if you move it or if you should [leave it
163
164   Denis:                                              [Well no, this is your
165            thermostat
166
167   Andrea:  Yeah so we hav=
168
169   Denis:   =So what I'm gonna do is I am gonna have this move over to
170            [your space
171
172   Andrea:  [uhum uhum
173
174   Denis:   So that you can control the temperature, okay?
175
176   Andrea:  uhum
177
178            (1.0)
179
180   Denis:   We'll put a blank on it
181
182            (1.0)
183
184   Andrea:  And uh then uh=
185
```

186 Denis: =And then I'll put a fake thermostat here and we'll make them
187   feel like they are doing something
188
189 Andrea: That would be the best. [Uh uh uh ((laughs))
190
191 Denis: [Okay? How's that. They'll think that
192   they are controlling it
193
194 Andrea: I have to give you the key for Rosie has the key
195
196 Denis: Well, [I'll send him up and he'll ask for [it
197
198 Andrea: [So   [for Rosie yah (0.3) and
199   uh. (0.3) I think everything is done here there is some lock
200   missing for that door there_
201
202 Denis: Uhum. That I'll- That I'll put a lock on it
203
204 Andrea: Right
205
206 Denis: Okay, we're good

At the beginning of this sequence, Denis again seems to disattend to what Andrea is talking about. He is walking through the room, looking around as to inspect it. As she walks behind him, Andrea suddenly stops and says, "Ah this is still" (Line 154), looking at a box installed on one of the walls. We can imagine that she was about to say "Ah this [box] is still there." Denis still continues to walk (he is now looking into another room). She then touches the box and says "the box here" (Line 158).

Denis then finally seems to pay attention to what Andrea is talking about. He comes and looks at the box, while she is saying, "I don't know if you move it or if you should leave it" (Line 162). Denis does not let her finish her sentence and there is a brief overlap of talk when he starts to speak. Denis says, "Well no, this is your thermostat" (Lines 164–165), a remark that seems to work on several levels. He says, "Well no" while Andrea's previous turn is not a yes–no question. She actually says that she does not know if Denis should move it or leave it. By phrasing his reply as "Well no," he seems to imply "you're mistaken." Again, he is affirming implicitly that "there is no problem, no disruption here." Denis knows that if Andrea points out this box, it is because she thinks that something might have to be done about it; that is, that there is a source of disruption (otherwise why would she bother pinpointing it?). By responding, "Well no" he seems to be rejecting the idea of any possible disruption. His saying "Well no" also tacitly disqualifies Andrea's role. She does not know what needs to be done about this box (as she says it herself in Line

162). She does not even know what it is (i.e., a thermostat). Denis positions her as not knowing, although it was not the point of her question.

Again, Denis thus seems to be doing interactional work that aims to forestall her ever positioning herself as telling him what to do. Such an interpretation would explain his interrupting her, his identifying the box as a thermostat, and his contradiction of her by saying "Well no." His interactive challenge is, on the one hand, to acknowledge at least minimally her interventions (this is, after all, a professional relationship) while through his interactive work, downplaying the authority relationship thus implied. The strategy is always the same: Listen to what Andrea says (orient to her question or concern), then implicitly disqualify the implication that there is an issue, or that she is even competent to point it out if there were (e.g., "Well no, this is a thermostat" [Lines 164–165]), and finally tell her what he is going to do about what she brought to his attention. He thus positions himself as acting on his own behalf and not as doing what she asked him to do, at the same time doing what she asked him to do. The difference is subtle but real.

Interpersonal or Organizational?

The encounter between Denis and Andrea is not simply a dialogue involving two individuals. Business is being done. There are two parties to the transaction, and neither is reducible to the individuals whose interaction our camera captured that day in Manhattan. There are corporate interests involved here. In his managerial domain, after all, Denis *is* the initiator. It is he who established the contracts with the satellite companies who serviced the building, and took on the work of redoing the office suite, and it is he who sanctions their work. When he is interacting with Andrea, this role, which he is regularly called to play in the larger sphere of a high-rise, may be for the moment tacit, but it is nevertheless immanent at every turn. As he walks through the quarters, he is already envisioning the commissions he is going to have to transmit to the subcontractors and to his own staff. If he behaves as if he is in charge it may well be because, in this extended framework, he *is* in charge. He is responsible not only to the clients, but to his own superiors. Andrea, by contrast, may be officially the voice of the client in the recorded interaction but she is speaking for a principal. It is her boss that will have to be satisfied, not she herself. Her authority is conditional. So is his, but it is better grounded.

It is thus not just interpersonal interaction. It is organizational communication. The difference is crucial.

From this enlarged perspective, Denis's actions are eminently sensible. For one thing, as the contractee he must be careful not to promise anything he cannot deliver. To admit that there are still major corrections to be made, at this late stage of the contracting process, is to invite cost overruns. As he observed at one point,

357 Denis: You're you're in Manhattan.
358

359   Andrea: I know.
360
361   Denis: Nothing's cheap.
362
363   Andrea: I know.
364
365   Denis: All- it's all union labor, you know

Also, as himself a sender in his own domain, he must constantly be thinking, as he walks through the suite of rooms, how he is going to deal with things that still need correcting. He is physically present in the office, but mentally he is locating himself in the larger space of his usual activities, centered on an office and connected to a network of clients, employees, and subcontractors. That, in fact, both parties share this sense of being a link between their conversation and the larger transactional universe where they are usually found is illustrated by another exchange, this time on the issue of better lighting in one of the rooms (Michael is Andrea's immediate superior).

422   Denis: Okay. Let me talk to him about [xxx
423
424   Andrea: [You have to give me an estimate
425
426   Denis: But I'll talk to [him first okay
427
428   Andrea: [I'll talk to Michael yah
429
430   Denis: Very good

A central principle of Greimasian narrative theory, as we saw, is that the crucial component in the story is the sender–receiver (*destinateur–destinataire*) contract. That contract is fundamental to the establishment of identities, because it instantiates one actant (the sender) as an ultimate authority, and the other as a competent subject actor (the receiver) to whom a mandate is confided. In narrative theory, the roles are unambiguous, because they are grounded in a quasi-mathematical logic of oppositions and alliances. However, in practice, as Greimas himself insisted, the roles become equivocal as they are realized in the concrete circumstances of actual discourse, such as the New York conversation we dropped in on. To claim the actantial role of sender, for example, one must show oneself to be the source of knowledge that initiates a sequence, an initiator of action. This is the source of your authority. Furthermore, the individual laying claim to this actantial role must have a clear idea of what is to be done (otherwise how will he or she be competent to evaluate a successful performance?). On the other hand, to be acknowledged as authorized agent (receiver) one must demonstrate that he or she is fully qualified to take on the task: be appropriately motivated, have the knowledge, and possess the practical means and know-how to take on the task. This actor takes on authority, pragmatically.

In the sequence of interactions we have been analyzing, Denis had all the advantages. A veteran who has to deal with hundreds of sometimes difficult clients, it is hardly surprising that he might have honed the skills of playing the role of competent agent, at the same time learning how to diminish the probability that the client will insist on micromanaging the project, without understanding all the ramifications of dealing with New York subcontractors. Andrea may understand her client role well enough but, up against a veteran with all the savvy on his side, she lacks the tools to play it with panache.

There is thus, from this perspective, nothing out of the ordinary here, as long as we realize that we are in the realm of organizational communication. That was the whole point of our initial introduction of the idea of worldview: not dialogue, but organizing.

Both Denis and Andrea understand the switch of perspective that goes from interpersonal to interorganizational. They began their encounter this way:

```
1     Denis:    I'm gonna be a grandpa again
2
3     Andrea:   Again?
4
5     Denis:    Again.
6
7     Andrea:   How many do you have
8
9     Denis:    We'll come up on four
10
11    Andrea:   Oh well ((laughing a little))
12
13    Denis:    Alright
```

They ended, again on a friendly, personal note:

```
462   Denis:    [Behave behave yourself now
463
464   Andrea:   Now I'm going to vacation
465
466   Denis:    When?
467
468   Andrea:   Tomorrow
469
470   Denis:    Where=
```

471
472   Andrea: =In Germany
473
474   Denis: Are you? [for-
475
476   Andrea: [See my family, yeah.
477
478   Denis: [Oh wonderful

CONCLUSION

Recall that the literature defines worldview in two different ways: (a) as an inversion of perspective typical of certain classes of transaction, and (b) as an inversion
of perspective based on, alternatively, conversation and text.

If we take a conversational worldview on the interaction we have been analyzing we encounter two people who put their respective skills to work to construct
an interaction, and in the process establish their identities as human actors. They
used language to produce the text of their conversation (that it is a text, although
initially only verbalized, is attested to by the ease we had in recording and tran-
scribing it). In their conversation they exploited the resource of language, drawing on the actantial roles it supplies, but the conversational outcome was not
predetermined. However, if we adopt the alternative text-oriented worldview we
see a rather different perspective. Now it is language that is structuring their world
by imposing on them its values. They, as it were, step into their roles, and by doing
so reinforce them. As Greimas (1993) observed "the actions of people seem, in
this perspective, to make sense only if they are inscribed in a universe of values
that surround them" (p. 22).

The difference between the two interpretations of worldview, we propose, is
more apparent than real providing that we understand the implication of moving
from an interpersonal to an organizational register. One way to illustrate the shift
of level is a simple 2×2 matrix (Fig. 7.1). Take the management of the New York
skyscraper as the point of reference. On one axis we list the clients, namely the
renters of space in the building. On the other axis we list the management and
other services that have to be there to maintain the building. The matrix provides
an overview of the organization that emerges out of this set of transactional arrangements. However, because all communication involves human agents to represent collectives, a single cell in the matrix represents an encounter between
representatives of the two communities of interest. The conversation involves individuals who may or may not speak for their community of interest, but they remain actors whose actions manifest, and reiterate, but are not dictated by, their
actantical roles.

One version of worldview applies to classes of actors—buyer versus seller,
doctor versus patient. The second version describes the difference between spon-

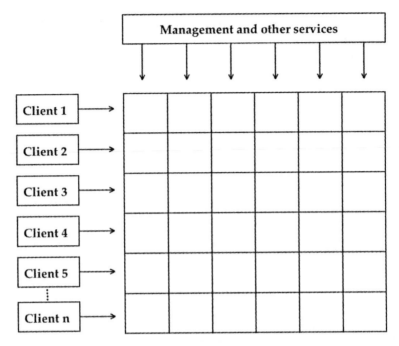

FIG. 7.1.   Matrix of the management of the New York skyscraper.

taneous talk (conversation) involving not actantial classes but real-life actors, and the pattern imposed by narratively structured language, the material of text. We have argued in this chapter that the actions of actors index actantial roles, but creatively. The patterns that are inherent in the basis of sensemaking furnished by language, namely narrative, define what Katambwe and Taylor (chap. 4, this volume) call a subtext. Categories such as buyer, seller, doctor, and patient, already incorporate assumptions that have their grounding in the normative roots of languaging: how buyers and sellers and doctors and patients act. They reveal, as Greimas argued, an ideology that is characteristic of the society in which they exist. So when Denis and Andrea met in the corridor outside the new quarters of Andrea's firm they were simultaneously individuals interacting through conversation (actors) and exemplars of their respective categories of renter and landlord (actants). Their challenge, which each resolved in his or her own way as individual actors, was to enact the transaction in a way that respects the conventions of interactive talk while protecting the interest of their respective principals (their senders), the owners of the building and the tenants. They exemplified how worldview works conversationally, by giving it parameters and creating options.

They exploited the potential inherent in text to generate an interaction in a combination that was unique.

We have tried to show that language, as a narrative grammar, can be used to generate an infinite variety of human transactional encounters, when it is put to work to produce the text of a conversation. Clearly, worldview is a more complex phenomenon than Taylor and his colleagues originally portrayed it.

P A R T III

COORIENTATION

CHAPTER EIGHT

Coorientation: A Conceptual Framework

James R. Taylor
Université de Montréal

A theme that we have seen developed in different ways in this book is the intimate relation between language, on the one hand, and the daily accomplishment of the ordinary activities that give an organization its reason for being, on the other. The emphasis on the discursive basis of organization is not new, of course, but it has not always been the usual entry point even to the study of language, much less to organizational inquiry. For example, Wittgenstein (1953, published posthumously) began his famous set of late philosophical essays by summarizing (and taking his distance from) the traditional view on language that he described as follows:

> It is this: the individual words in language name objects—sentences are combinations of such names—In this picture of language we find the roots of the following idea: Every word has a meaning. This meaning is correlated with the word. It is the object for which the word stands. (p. 2)

According to this view, which Wittgenstein rejected, the meaning of a word can be reduced to the thing that the word stands for; that is, what could be called its ostensive definition. As against this conventional and outmoded idea of how language works, Wittgenstein offered an alternative perspective that focuses on how words are used.

To illustrate, he imagines a builder A and an assistant B. They share a vocabulary of words. Thus when A needs a stone he calls out "stone" and B hands him a stone. For A, it is the saying of the word stone that gets the stone moved. The word is a tool. For B, the word "stone" means, in this context, "Pass him the stone." The meaning of a word can be found in its use. As Kenny (1973), a respected Wittgenstein specialist said:

> the ostensive definition will not suffice by itself because it can always be variously interpreted. For instance, suppose that I explain the word "tove" by pointing to a pencil and saying "this is called 'tove'." The explanation would be quite inadequate, because I may be taken to mean "This is a pencil" or "This is round" or "This is wood" or "This is one" or "This is hard" and so on (PG 60, BB 2). So in the acquisition of the understanding of a word acquaintance with the word's

bearer is not so important as mastery of the *word's general use.* (p. 157, italics added)

The shift of perspective is from what words stand for to what words do, when we use them in practical contexts of accomplishing some activity. For Wittgenstein, language is not only used as a means to represent or picture the world, but also as an agent we proactively put to work in a multitude of different ways to accomplish the things we are engaged in making happen through collaboration with others.[1]

Much the same idea was expressed by another philosopher of language, John Austin. He began his famous William James Lectures at Harvard in 1955, for example, by dryly observing that the phenomenon he was going to be talking about is "widespread and obvious, and it cannot fail to have been already noticed, at least here and there, by others" (Austin, 1962, p. 1). Obvious or not, however, "It was for too long the assumption of philosophers that the business of a 'statement' can only be to 'describe' some state of affairs, or to 'state some fact', which it must do either truly or falsely" (p. 1). Against this impoverished view of language, Austin proposed a quite different image, of language as performing an action. Like Wittgenstein, he would have us concentrate on how to do things with words.

It would be possible to find earlier references to language as instrumental. The original American pragmatist Charles Saunders Peirce (1955) could, for example, be cited as asserting much the same thing: "a conception, that is, the rational purport of a word or other expression, lies exclusively in its conceivable bearing upon the conduct of life" (p. 252). The fact is, though, that, although there are exceptions here and there (for discussion see Cooren, 2000b), philosophers and scientists have, historically, tended to overlook the performative role that language plays in human affairs.

It is a tendency, by the way, that was greatly encouraged in communication studies by Shannon's information-based theory (Shannon & Weaver, 1949). Shannon's mathematically elegant version of how communication works reduces it to senders, messages conveying information over channels, and receivers. However, Shannon's model accomplished its magic by stripping away everything that has any connection to how people who are involved in practical worlds of activity use language to get on with what they are doing—carrying out the many tasks of an organization, for example. Unfortunately Shannon's theory had its greatest impact at a time when behaviorism reigned in psychology and functionalism in sociology. Shannon's seductive source–receiver model could easily be read as a simple variant on the stimu-

---

[1]It is sometimes thought that the "second" Wittgenstein doctrine, traditionally associated with the *Philosophical Investigations* (Wittgenstein, 1953), consisted of rejecting the "first" Wittgenstein doctrine; that is, logical atomism and the picture theory of propositions, as proposed in the *Tractatus Logico-Philosophicus.* However, Kenny (1973, p. 121) argued that although it is true to say that the second Wittgenstein doctrine rejected logical atomism, it is false to say that he also rejected the picture theory of propositions. As Kenny wrote, "the pictorial element of a proposition is separable from its assertoric, or indicative, element. Whatever is pictorial in 'the waters are above the firmament' is equally pictorial in 'Let the waters be above the firmament'."

lus–response formula that dominated, and justified, the individual-centered behaviorism of the 1950s. The concept of communication as information transmission also matched up with ideas about communication as coordination that were prevalent in functionalist writings at the time (Farace, Monge, & Russell, 1977). Neither psychology nor sociology nor management science was focused on the organizing role of language. The study of language was thus relegated to the discipline of linguistics whose practitioners, mesmerized by the brilliant but idiosyncratic ideas of Chomsky (1957, 1965), were all too happy to dispense with the complications that come when we ask how language and organization (indeed, real life) relate to each other.

If you apply these contrasting views of language as merely representations, as opposed to an instrument of action, to an understanding of "organization" you come up with very different views. If language is conceived of as no more than representing or picturing the world then the discipline of organizational communication is an epistemology (a mode of knowing), and organization an object to be known, pictured, or described. Language is thus no more than a privileged window through which to view organization (Fairhurst, in press; Putnam, Phillips, & Chapman, 1996; Smith, 1993; Taylor, 1995). If, on the other hand, language-in-use is how we do organization, organization is no longer independent of communication. On the contrary, it is entirely dependent on it because communication is where the organization gets produced. This is where we enter the domain of ontology: modes of being. This still leaves us with the even more perplexing question of what organization is—and indeed what communication is.

The wheel has finally turned. Language has come back into its own in both sociology and management science—and in communication studies. However, the ontological question remains, and until we have resolved it in our own minds we will have not laid the groundwork for either theory building or empirical research.

CONTRASTING ONTOGENIES

Humberto Maturana is a Chilean biologist who has attained international recognition as the originator of a theory of living beings—the theory of *autopoiesis,* or self-production. The theory assumes that living beings are distinguished from the nonliving by their ability to construct themselves from the inside out, and thus are enabled, in favorable environments, to maintain their organization and their structure, without the intervention of any external maker. His theory is particularly persuasive in its application to the basic cell of the organism, because, in fact, cells really do manufacture themselves, as they house the factories that synthesize the protein on which they (and we, incidentally) depend for their (and our) continued existence. Our internal cells are continually regenerating themselves throughout our lives, until they finally give up or we die. Furthermore, the multiple specialized components within the cell function in a complex pattern of interrelationships to make this self-production possible, and thus display and maintain an internal structure that is the cell's distinguishing characteristic. Cells depend on the environment around them, to be sure, but they remain internally closed in their operational integrity. With the emergence of genetics, it has become obvious how the reproduction of structure from one generation to another is successfully achieved. This self-productive cycle is what Maturana calls an *ontogeny,* or a mode of being.

Maturana and his collaborator Varela soon extended the application of the self-organizing principle into an analysis of cognition. Here too, they proposed, the knowledge we individually generate about the universe around us is also the consequence of internal processes, not merely a passive registering of the patterns that are out there. To the extent that the image of the world that we actively construct works for us we are successfully adapted to the world, and our cognitive universe of understanding is coherent and self-reproducing. When it ceases to be successful, for whatever reason, we become the victim of illusions, coherence is lost, and at the limit we may fall into a kaleidoscopic turmoil of meaningless images, or pure insanity.

This would all be interesting to organizational communication analysts, perhaps, but no more, if Maturana and Varela had not chosen to extend the principle further, into the domain of language and communication. Thus when Maturana looks at conversation, as someone who thinks deeply about the basis of life, what he sees is not merely people talking to each other: interpersonal interaction. He perceives instead what he called "an ontologically established domain of recurrent interactions" (Maturana, 1988, p. 3): "To an observer of the social system, from the outside it will appear as a remarkable congruence of a dance of coordinations" (Maturana & Varela, 1987, p. 209). This ontologically established domain will have a history of previous interactions, typically involving the same people, and will manifest a structural pattern: a way of coordinating actions consensually, to produce what he also called, for reasons we will shortly see, "a linguistic domain" (Maturana, 1988, p. 3).

Each person continues to be, of course, a distinct individual, and each is characterized by his or her own mode of being, or ontogeny, but if they interact together intimately and repeatedly enough, the interactors begin to exhibit the characteristics of a couple, with its own identity. They become a *coontogeny.* A new kind of structural coupling is achieved, beyond the boundaries of the cell or the single organism, one in which words function to produce "ontogenically established coordinations of behavior" (Maturana & Varela, 1987, p. 208). What is uniquely human, compared to other animals, "is that, in their linguistic coordination of actions, they give rise to a new phenomenal domain, viz., the *domain of language*" (Maturana & Varela, 1987, p. 209, italics in original).

Language offers a means for "those who operate in it to *describe themselves* and their circumstances" (Maturana & Varela, 1987, p. 210, italics in original), or picture themselves, for Wittgenstein. The importance of this self-descriptive facility is this: "With language arises also the observer as a languaging entity; by operating in language with other observers, this entity generates the self and its circumstances as linguistic distinctions of its participation in a linguistic domain" (Maturana & Varela, 1987, p. 211). As they went on to say: "All this is what it is to be human. We make descriptions of the descriptions that we make (as this sentence is doing). Indeed, we are observers and exist in a semantic domain created by our operating in language where ontogenic adaptation is conserved" (Maturana & Varela, 1987, p. 211). Language, in other words, is also a locus of being: a different "ontogeny" from the purely physical. As Maturana (1988) put it, "languaging arises, when it arises, as a manner of coexistence of living systems" (p. 4).

It is in this domain of language that we come to exist as human beings, in the full sense of the word. It is all too easy to revert, without thinking (I am not immune from the tendency), to the kind of view of language that Wittgenstein and Austin saw as being incomplete. Language becomes just a way of encoding perceptions, and communication no more than a medium for transmitting them to others. However, as soon as we conceive of language as where we come to exist fully as human beings, in and through interaction with others, a whole different perspective on organization is opened up. For one thing, "objects do not pre-exist language" (Maturana, 1988, p. 4). The reason is clear enough: Objects exist in their contrasting relation to subjects, and we only become subjects who relate to objects through the reflective and retrospective self-consciousness that is enabled, above all, by a description in language (Giddens, 1984; Weick, 1995).

Of course we exist as organisms in the material world of flesh and blood, but as such we have no self-reflective capability, and no apparent-to-ourselves individuality. As Mead (1934) pointed out, whereas the "I" is a spontaneous response of the organism to experience (shared by all forms of life, not just human), the "me" can only come into existence as the result of self-consciousness. Such self-consciousness is only attained in interaction with others, using language (although Mead called language "gestures"). If, as we argue later, "the self and its circumstances" are the product of "linguistic distinctions," then it is not just ourselves as individuals who find our full existence in languaging, it is also our identity as an organization.

What Maturana meant by distinctions is not dissimilar from how Weick (1995) described sensemaking. "Experience," wrote Weick, "as we know it exists in the form of distinct events. But the only way we get this impression is by stepping outside the stream of experience and directing attention to it" (p. 25). Weick emphasized the retrospective, after-the-fact character of sensemaking. Maturana would concur in this view, but he underlined even more strongly than Weick the crucial role that language plays in achieving retrospectivity and sensemaking. Maturana also pointed out that, although we can make distinctions about the world of experience in language, and thus make sense, we can also recursively make distinctions about ourselves making distinctions (Robichaud, Giroux, & Taylor, 2004).

One way to see the relevance of Maturana's theory is to compare it with another framework of ideas that is quite specifically about human organization: Weick's (1979) groundbreaking book *The Social Psychology of Organizing*.

Weick's theoretical treatment of what he called "enactment" also begins with an analogy drawn from biology. He described enactment in this way. People are linked to an environment that is characterized by unpredictable variation and ir-reducible equivocality. To deal with the circumstances in which they find them-selves, people are obliged to make sense of what they are experiencing. They do this by selecting out of all the possible explanations of what they encounter those that seem to work for them. They retain the distinctions that seemed effec-tive, and this becomes part of a stable set of explanations, or what Weick termed a "cause map" (p. 131). Such retained knowledge is not just the end product of sensemaking, however. It proactively enters into any subsequent processes of selection, and directly affects the enactment process itself; that is, how people subsequently act on their environment, and shape it to conform to the expecta-tions of the enactor. Increasingly, as they do, the "environment" to which they are responding is a consequence of their own intervention in it, and may ulti-mately become self-confirming. It is thus not that the people, singly or as an or-ganization, ever objectively know their environment; what they come to know of it is the product of an enactment—a projection of their own sensemaking ac-tivities. Like Maturana's characterization of ontogeny, the organization is in fact a closed system of sensemaking, forever projecting on the world around it its own ways of making distinctions. Even science conforms to this description (Maturana, 1991).

The difference between Weick's concept of organizing, and that of Maturana is thus not in their vision of organizational reality, but in the role they assign to lan-guage. Weick did not much theorize language in his book. His notion of selection and cause maps draws by inference on the way language works to make distinc-tions, but it is Maturana who encouraged us to look at enactment as a complex phe-nomenon in which (a) our experience in living in a hybrid material-social world is transformed, through conversation, into a text-based comprehension of it (what Weick called "selection"); and (b) our frameworks of explanation are transformed, through the same conversation, into object-oriented performances ("enactment").

In the next section, we consider how our reading of Maturana and Weick might be used to encapsulate their perceptions of the complex process of enactment into an effective tool of analysis for those of us who think about organizations.

BUILDING A COORIENTATIONAL MODEL OF ORGANIZATIONAL COMMUNICATION

Like Maturana, we see human communication as embedded in two different envi-ronments, one of which is a hybrid material–social reality to which people respond daily, as actors, and the other of which is language, the medium of sensemaking, and hence of understanding. It is this double embedding that most clearly defines the specific character of the approach we have developed and are defending in this volume.

Because we all find our full existence in a mixture of material–social and linguistic environments, we confront the continual necessity of translating one to the other. This is what communication accomplishes, and modeling the communication process will only be satisfactory if it begins to capture this dynamic of ongoing translation. The mechanism that effects the translation, we propose, is *coorientation*. Coorientation aims to reconcile the contrasting imperatives of material–social and linguistic constraints and enablements. It is through coorientation that the language-based establishing, person to person, and group to group, of compatible beliefs and coordinated responses to events as they occur, is accomplished: how the events are, in fact, enacted (Weick, 1979).

Figure 8.1 is intended to illustrate this process. It shows a core activity that illustrates the idea of a basic conversational interaction with a formal structure that is coorientational, A and B with respect to X. We place no a priori limit on the identities of A or B, either individual or collective, nor on X, which may be concrete (Wittgenstein's stone) or a symbolic abstraction that describes a world (a picture in words of stoneness).

Of course the communication out of which organization emerges is far more complex than this figure suggests. The modern organization is a universe of endless talk, occurring both simultaneously and successively, in many, many places that these days may span the entire world. Boden (1994) thought of this thick overlay of talk as a "lamination" of conversations. We have sometimes conceptualized (Taylor & Van Every, 1993) this thicket of verbal exchanges as a hyperconversation (following the model of hypertext): *hyper,* because each ongoing conversation is in its own way a singular world of text-making,[2] but each also links horizontally and vertically to other conversations through the migrations of people and the texts they produce, as the latter get circulated. Simplifying, as we have done in Fig. 8.1, is justified by a fundamental constraint that applies to all interaction mediated by lan-

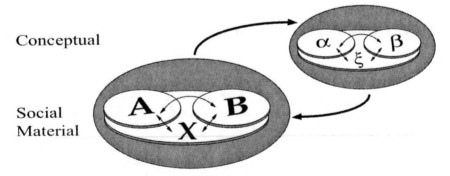

Conceptual

Social
Material

FIG. 8.1.   Coorientation through conversation as the essential unit of organizing.

---

[2]Like Halliday (1985) we take spoken language, such as that which occurs in conversation, to be a form of text.

guage, however cumulatively complex: Someone has to talk, or otherwise initiate an exchange, and someone (or several "ones") has (have) to listen, and respond. Furthermore, they have to talk about something.

These are not invented constraints; they are the way conversation works, as conversation analysts have shown, in their own way, for more than 30 years. If nobody talks (or everybody talks at the same time), and nobody listens, and there is nothing to talk about, there is no conversation. If there is something to talk about, as there must be, it must conform to the basic requirements of language: establish a common topic of talk, something one can orient to. What is said must have, explicitly or implicitly, a subject, (two, if the sentence describes a two-person interaction, as Robichaud shows in chap. 6, this volume), an object, and something to assert about the object and its state, or the events that impinge on it—minimally that it exists; more generally that someone does something to or about it, or it to them. Even when Wittgenstein's builder says "stone," the expression is elliptic: The implicit sentence or subtext (Katambwe & Taylor, chap. 4, this volume) that both builder and assistant understand is "Pass me the stone, please." Without a tacit subtext of this kind he might be able to direct the assistant's attention to a particular stone (especially if he pointed to it as well as saying "stone") but he would not have established the kind of action that leads to doing something about the object. At best, he could only hope the assistant could guess at why he was focusing his or her attention on the stone.

Whatever organization there is, in other words, has to be funneled through a coorientational channel. For just this reason, we can learn a good deal about how organization emerges out of conversation by concentrating first on the elementary communication event: a single moment in an ongoing flow of talk. It is here that reality gets established as a basis of coordinated response; it is here that activity is understood and generated; it is here that the relationships organizational members have with each other are expressed, and sometimes get renegotiated.

The Role of the Object in Coorientation

The reason that the concept of object figures in our model is that we assume people to be caught up in responding to a world. Wittgenstein's example presupposes that his builder and assistant are actually building a wall, not just talking about it. As such, it imposes on the conversation of the people who are acting. If the stone falls on the builder's foot as it is passed, and he sustains a broken bone, there are real consequences, and they will be immediately reflected in the resulting conversation. It will no longer be about passing stones, but about getting medical help, and what to do while the builder is recovering.

On the other hand, the word "stone," once spoken, obliges us to think about the meaning of object in a different way, as an entity of language. Again, we would be mistaken if we thought of language objects as nothing more than how to establish a point of reference in a conversation (Robichaud, chap. 6, this volume). Objects—"mere" words—can become powerful agents in channeling the organizational conversation. The word quality became, for example, a determinant in shaping managerial practice in the 1980s and early 1990s, as did, a bit later, the word reengineering. When these terms—these objects of many conversations— were at the peak of their influence there was not really any shared understanding of what, exactly, they meant (Giroux & Taylor, 2002). But this did not prevent them from dictating the actions of literally thousands of companies and agencies. Linguistic objects, as Foucault (1972) taught us, are potent agents. They too can direct action (Cooren, 2004b, chap. 5, this volume).

A productive way to think about this dialectic of object as real and object as word is Pickering's (1995) notion of a "dance of agency." He had in mind a laboratory of physics, but his concept has much wider application. For him, the scientist acts (makes some kind of manipulation of an experimental nature) and then waits to observe nature's response. How different in kind is this from managers who implement a program in quality control or reengineering and then wait for the payoff? When it does not come as expected (as it did not for either total quality management or reengineering), they start looking for another initiative: knowledge management, for example. It is a dance—a dance of agency. It is how, as Weick (1995) insisted, action gets punctuated: part of what it means to be caught up in a flow of activity. Like canoeists navigating a fast river, they react less to the flow (that is a given) than to things that crop up and have to be responded to ("Look out, a rock!" or "Floating log!"). In the managerial jargon of the 1980s the "rocks" and "logs" had become "Low American productivity!" and "Japanese competition!" We punctuate experience so that it becomes events for us.

The Role of the Subjects in Coorientation

The grounded-in-action model we are proposing has, of course, precedents. As Groleau notes (chap. 10, this volume), Engeström constructed his model of an activity system around a central triplet of actor or subject–tool–object. For him, as for us, an object is a "problem space" (Engeström, 1990, p. 79) at which an activity is directed and that leads to, in turn, an outcome. Tools are the indispensable "mediating instruments and signs" (p. 79) of activity: indispensable because action is always mediated when we pass from the cognitive to the pragmatic world, or from one ontogeny to another. We also, as Engeström did, conceive the subject–tool–object relationship as being embedded within a community, with its own differentiated set of roles and patterned ways of addressing the world (his terms are "division of labor" and "rules").

Where we differ from Engeström (1990) is in our respective conceptions of agency. For him, "the subject refers to the individual or sub-group whose agency is chosen as the point of view in the analysis" (p. 79). Coorientation, however, assumes not one subject, but a minimum of two, caught up in an ongoing interaction: communicating. Furthermore, we assume that agency is not the property of a subject or actor, but is a relationship between individuals. We would, for example, read the "tool" in Engeström's model as itself an agent, in that it is the tool that acts for the subject. It incorporates intentionality (otherwise it is not a tool; Robichaud, chap. 6, this volume). Instrumentality, from our perspective, is an instance of agency: When Wittgenstein's assistant passes a stone to the builder, he is acting as an agent. Agency, from a coorientational point of view, is a concept that takes on meaning only in the context of a communication event.

Consider again the Wittgenstein example from the perspective of agency. If the builder says "stone" it means to pass the stone: an instruction or command. If the assistant says, "stone," however, the implied subtext is "Are you ready for another stone?": a question. The difference between a context-free and a context-sensitive view demarcates schools of linguistics. If we adopt a pragmatic (Halliday, 1985) rather than a cognitive (Chomsky, 1965) view of language we will see the meaning of speech as indexing, and expressing, not just attitudes to the material world of activity but also the social configuration of places that lie behind the talk. This has been called the taxemic dimension of language-in-use because conversations indirectly "tax," or place, the people involved, identifying some of them as agents and others as beneficiaries (Taylor & Cooren, chap. 7, this volume).

Like Giddens (1984), we share a belief in what he called "the monitored character of the ongoing flow of social life" (p. 3). As he put it, "'acts' are constituted only by a discursive moment of attention to the *durée* of lived-through experience" (p. 3). We would agree that the rationalization of action is "a routine characteristic of human conduct" (p. 4). Like Giddens also, we do not see the structure of organization as external to human action: "a source of constraint on the free initiative of the independently constituted subject" (p. 16). We also see structure as "a 'virtual order' of transformative relations" (p. 17). As he wrote, "social systems, as reproduced social practices, do not have 'structures' but rather exhibit 'structural properties'" (p. 17). Structure exists "only in its instantiations in such practices" (p. 17).

Unlike Giddens, however, we do not use the terms "human agents" and "actors" interchangeably (Giddens, 1984, p. xxii). Where he comes closest to our perspective is in his use of the phrase "competent agents of others" (p. 6) but it is clear that what he means by "agent of others" is not what we mean: someone acting for someone or something else. What he means is that actors "will usually be able to explain most of what they do, if asked" (p. 6). They can, as Garfinkel (1967) put it, give an account of their actions. Giddens's focus, unlike ours, is on the actor as individual, not the actors in a communication relationship. He reduced communication to an "interpretative scheme": "signification" (p. 29). In doing so he missed the intrinsic link between communication and the exercise of power. Although Giddens, like Engeström, recognized language as an instrumentality, neither he nor Engeström theorized in any depth its role as shaper of action, or as locus of structure.

Modality

Our approach thus draws on a different tradition, of speech as action. Like Austin (1962), we see speech not primarily as an individual performance but as a tool to be employed in interaction. An utterance in speech is not merely a way to focus inter-subjective attention on some object; it is also a means by which force is applied ("illocutionary force," for Austin). A relationship of agency is thus negotiated, in the sense that one outcome of a successful interaction is a differentiated set of roles.

There is nothing mysterious about this force. Language, competently used, always accomplishes a double outcome. On the one hand, it establishes an object (Engeström's problem space). On the other hand, it is an instrument for the conveyance of speaker attitude (and listener attitude, depending on the latter's response). The aligning of attitude to attitude and both to object is the essence of coorientation. Wittgenstein, as well as Austin (1962) and Searle (1969), clearly distinguished between what he called "proposition radicals" and the force (which Wittgenstein calls "mood") the utterance conveys.

The linguistic property that expresses attitude or force, we call *modality*. It sometimes gets expressed quite explicitly by phrases such as "I think that ... " or "I wish that ... " However, language furnishes a multitude of subtle ways to express attitude. In addition, supralinguistic features of speech (e.g., tone of voice) and non-verbal expressions (e.g., shrug of the shoulder, raised eyebrows, gesture of the hands) enrich even further the repertoire of ways to convey one's attitude to an interlocutor.

That such modes of expression work to create a relationship of coorientation (or coontogeny) is because people are motivated to find ways to collaborate with each other and in doing so take on an identity within a coorientational relationship. They are also motivated, of course, to preserve their independence of action and their autonomy. The result is that coorientation is often ambiguous, even contradictory (Katambwe & Taylor, chap. 4, this volume), what Giddens (1984) called a *dialectic of control* (p. 16; see also Güney, chap. 2, this volume).

This is another aspect of the dance of agency to which we referred earlier. People must simultaneously compute their interest as it intersects with that of the object they orient to, in the context of the relationship they are involving themselves in with others who share their object orientation but not necessarily their view of the appropriate orientation to it. The originator of the concept of coorientation we have borrowed from (Newcomb, 1953) assumed such a relationship might be positive or negative in polarity; as we have seen (Katambwe & Taylor, chap. 4, this volume), we think of it as often simultaneously positive and negative, or "equivocal," to use Weick's (1979) term.

The Recursivity and Reflexivity of Language-Enriched Communication

People are involved in activities that frequently require interaction with others for entirely practical reasons. Activities, however, are typically ongoing affairs, and communication is as well, as it involves recurring interaction with many of the same people, often on a day-to-day basis. Thus people quickly become embedded in more or less extensive networks of activity, talk, and relationships. Each particular communication event is, however, an instance of coorientation, involving some people whose attention is focused for the moment on one or a few specific objects that reflect their activities but must also be established in language. The objects get established in language intersubjectively, however, by people displaying an attitude to each other, using the facility of language that we have identified as modality (as well as other indexes such as nonverbal signing). Adding speaker and listener attitude to the simple drawing of attention to an object—picturing it—gives spoken (and written) communication a "force" that it would not otherwise have, if only because the expression of attitude imposes a response on the part of the other: to agree or not to agree; to do or not to do (Taylor & Van Every, 2000).

Attitudes are, modally speaking, of two kinds, which Searle (1969) called their "direction of fit." Fitting the word to the world is equivalent to expressing a belief in the reality of a given state of affairs, what is termed, technically, *epistemic* modality (or what Wittgenstein [1953] would call the "indicative mood"). Fitting the world to the word, however, amounts to expressing an attitude about what is to be done about some state of affairs, an ought to do: *deontic* modality (or what Wittgenstein would call an imperative mood).

These are well-established conventional categories but they are not yet explicitly organizational. What makes an act of speech inherently organizational had already been identified by Austin (1962) in his original formulation of the theory: *"the particular persons and circumstances in a given case must be appropriate for the invocation of the particular procedure involved"* (p. 15, italics added). Generals give orders; umpires call strikes; delinquents give excuses. Searle (1969) called these "institutional facts" (p. 51), but they actually figured very little in his original treatment.[3]

They are critically important in the study of organizational communication, however. Although we agree with Giddens (1984) that "the structural properties of social systems are both medium and outcome of the practices they recursively organize" (p. 25) we do not see the locus of structure as internal to actors: mere "memory traces" (p. 25). To us this explanation sounds suspiciously like a medieval logic of "iron is hard because it has an innate hardness": not really an expla-

---

[3]Searle (1989) somewhat belatedly seems to have become aware of the importance of institutional embedding. In his later article he emphasized the critical importance of extralinguistic institutions, and the special position of the speaker (and the hearer) within the institution, at least for the performance of certain kinds of speech acts. We believe it is a characteristic of all performances using language.

nation at all. We prefer the reasoning of Latour (1987, 1993, 1994), because it locates the structuring effect in the construction of agency, and thus makes it fundamentally communicational. For Latour and his colleague Callon, human action always reflects the mobilization and organizing of agents (including Engeström's "tools"). Agents, however, come with their own built-in purposes, like guns, for example, which are made for killing (Robichaud, chap. 6, this volume). Even tools incorporate the intentionality of their makers. Agents thus quite normally reflect the purposes of actors who are not physically present in the situation: As Hutchins (1995) observed, the navigational charts that every sailor now routinely uses incorporate the purposes and experience of navigators who lived many centuries ago.

It is the same for organization. To support their own purposes, today's Washington, DC legislators, executives, and justices recruit the actions and thoughts of the original Founding Fathers and the many others who have since established the traditions of American government. It is the same for all organizations. The structure is in the construction, not in someone's memory traces. How we construct an interaction to produce directed activity is part of how we have learned to use the principal tool of communication: language. The structuring property of language is fundamental to how organizational form is sustained over space and time (Cooren & Fairhurst, 2004; Taylor & Giroux, 2005).

The Recursivity and Reflexivity of Conversation in Language

The concept of object is not limited to a world outside the conversation. In chapter 4, focused on the integrating processes of organization, we saw instances of a different phenomenon, where the conversation cycles back, recursively and reflexively, to become its own object. What starts as a CEO who criticizes a subordinate is transformed into a critique of a president who is failing to act like a real president because he is not performing his role correctly, as his own intervention has just illustrated. Or it is a mayor responding to the critique of citizens by incorporating them and himself into a collective actor whose well-being is threatened by another actor that they had not even mentioned: the union (Robichaud, Giroux, & Taylor, 2004). Or it is an ex post facto reconstruction of the experience of working in interdisciplinary teams (Saludadez & Taylor, chap. 3, this volume).

This latter feature illustrates a critical further principle: how organization takes on reality as a collective actor. In the coontogenic processes of the domain of language-mediated cognition, there is no syntactic discrimination between individual and collective actors: Bill "decides," but so does Microsoft. I "believe," but so does the faculty, or the police, or just "they." In the coontogeny that is created by communication there are no restrictions on who may be counted as actor, or subject (or indeed object), other than those that are part of the conventions of language.

INTEGRATION IN THE CONTEXT OF COORIENTATION

In a differentiated "multiverse" (Maturana, 1997) or "pluriverse" (Latour, 2004) of many communities of practice and their corresponding cognitive domains, each characterized by its own rationality (management included), the attainment of what Lawrence and Lorsch (1969) called "integration" is not self-evident. Coorientation at this level is no longer seen to be merely an interpersonal accomplishment (although it always comes down to that in the end because even communities of practice get represented by spokespersons); now it is entire communities of practice, as Güney's chapter illustrates, whose attitudes are being expressed, and whose collaboration is to be established.

To become a distinct practice, and an associated domain of language and cognition, the community in question had to have attained a measure of autonomy, what Lawrence and Lorsch (1969) thought of as "differentiation" (Katambwe & Taylor, chap. 4, this volume). However, it is that very autonomy that now becomes the impediment to integration. The medical staff of the hospital, embedded in practices and modes of reasoning that are tied to the care of patients, are unlikely to see eye to eye with the bean-counting accountants who have to deal with the budget and pacify the board. The design communities of a technology firm, as Güney's (chap. 2, this volume) work illustrates, find themselves in opposing camps, and their conversation founders. Much the same tension is found in the university, or the police force, or a design company. The dilemma this presents is how to construct a kind of metatext that justifies the translation of the diverse interests of the different communities into a common purpose and a collective identity: coorientation in the large.

Consider the basic unit of coorientation from a slightly different perspective: how it unfolds in time. The finality of all coorientation is dealing with an X: a performance. Let us adopt the convention that it is B who deals with X: acts, in other words. Then A is a beneficiary and perhaps a moral justification for action. Going upstream (*en amont*) from the B performance to the coorienting of A-B that must have preceded it, A and B must have negotiated a commonality of attitude, including an alignment of belief and intention (the so-called epistemic and deontic modalities of speech). They must, in other words, have come to a discursively grounded accommodation, perhaps even to the point of generating a text that materializes their joint understanding. Let us call this the *cognitive* dimension of coorientation because it is enfolded by a linguistic environment and depends on sensemaking (Weick, 1995).

The performance accomplishes a translation from sensemaking to action, in what we might call the *pragmatic* dimension of coorientation, as B's acts take place in the material and social environment concretized in an object X. Once accomplished, the performance must be in turn translated back into an interpretation, and in this way it reenters the domain of language as a part of the ongoing sensemaking that is characteristic of the A-B community. This is the downstream side of coorientation (*en aval*). Its effect is double. On the one hand it closes the sequence and turns the latter into the kind of discrete event that both Weick and Giddens saw as the indispensable basis of sensemaking. On the other hand it confirms a relationship of agency: a relationship of actor(s) to beneficiary or beneficiaries. An actor is being mobilized. This is closure in a different sense, as the cementing of a relationship or relationships through its or their expression in action.

In the arena of organizational negotiation, the notion of mobilizing actors applies not just to individuals but to entire communities of practice: distinct systems of activity. However, the principles of coorientation still apply: The communities will continue to find their identities in the way they relate to each other, as agents or beneficiaries whose respective roles are discovered in an ongoing conversation centered on common objects of concern. Wittgenstein's masons form a (temporary) system of activity, which must itself be imbricated into another system of activity, the construction site, which must itself be imbricated into another system, the building company. The two masons (agents) ultimately work for the building company (beneficiary), but between them, a chain of agencies must be taken into account, each having its own interests, constraints, and objectives: the site foreman who needs to strictly follow his day schedule, the architect who wants to make sure that all his indications are properly followed, and the CEO of the building company who needs to make sure her organization is profitable.

CONCLUSION

So what is an organization? What is its ontogeny?

On the one hand, it is in the nature of activities to generate their own coorientational structure. The food chain that stretches from farmer to consumer only works because the different phases articulate one with the other: from producer to processor to distributor to merchandiser. We have described this interconnected and overlapping set of activities, each linked to the next by coorientation, as imbricated (Taylor, 2001b). In this sense, organization is real, whatever we call it.

The problem is that this is not what we call an organization. The chain we have described is sustained by many different organizations: from agribusiness to packing houses to supermarkets. As Cooren and Fairhurst (in press) pointed out, a group of friends who organize to move one of them to a new apartment, or organize a Saturday afternoon football game, are certainly organizing and indeed organized, but we would not normally think of them as an organization.

On the other hand, it might seem that we could argue that an organization is whatever we call an organization. We would then have to assume that organization comes into existence when the name is established, declaratively, by, for example, registering the company and having its charter approved. However, this way of answering the ontogenic question is also flawed, because if what we call the organization corresponds to nothing but a name, it is a fraud: a so-called dummy company, or a front.

The answer to what an organization is thus reduces to this: an organization emerges in the intersection of (a) an ongoing object-oriented conversation specific to a community of practice, and (b) the text that names, represents, or pictures it. Nowhere else. Maturana's coordinating through language is a necessary but not sufficient condition. Constituting the organization as a cognitive entity in language is a necessary but not sufficient condition for its existence. The organization, it follows, is always in the communication. Its reality must forever be reconstituted by filtering it through the sieve of an ongoing conversation, mediated by language, and focused on coorientation in a mixed social and material world of experience.

ACKNOWLEDGMENTS

I want to thank François Cooren for the several suggestions he offered that contributed substantially to the writing of this chapter, and aided materially in clarifying the expression of my ideas.

CHAPTER NINE

One Phenomenon, Two Lenses: Understanding Collective Action From the Perspectives of Coorientation and Activity Theories

Carole Groleau
Université de Montréal

Over the years Taylor (Taylor & Van Every, 2000) and his colleagues have situated their work in organizational communication with respect to several different theoretical frameworks ranging from structuration (Giddens, 1984) to sensemaking (Weick, 1995) to actor-network theory (Latour, 1987). Six years ago, a dialogue among researchers working within the coorientation perspective and activity theory was initiated.[1] In those exchanges, the themes of community, subject, language, and transforming human practices have come up for discussion. In this chapter we propose to add our voice to that conversation by means of an in-depth analysis and comparison of the two frameworks.

Originally, activity theory surfaced in the 1920s among a group of Russian psychologists. Its founder, Vygotsky, whose conceptual framework gradually evolved over the following decades, was a source of inspiration for numerous researchers. Our analysis focuses primarily on the work of Engeström and the Finnish branch of activity theorists, who are the third generation of the theoretical tradition established by Vygotsky and his student Leont'ev (Engeström, 2000). Engeström's work has been influential in various fields, including organizational studies. With the propagation of his ideas by a range of authors such as Blackler (1995), Blackler, Crump, and McDonald (1999, 2000), the activity framework has inspired numerous studies of organizational phenomena (Artemeva & Freedman, 2001; Hasan & Gould, 2001; Jarzabkowski, 2003).

The theory of coorientation and activity theory share a preoccupation with object-oriented human practices and their social dynamics. To explore more fully the

---

[1] Recently, panels bringing together researchers from both approaches were organized at the 1999 and 2000 International Communication Association yearly conferences and a special issue of *Communication Review* (1999, Vol. 3, No. 1–2) was devoted to the work of Taylor, Engeström, and their colleagues.

similarities and differences between the two perspectives, we begin the chapter with a brief description of their common orientation. We then set out the main concepts of activity theory, which we subsequently compare with the coorientational perspective. In the sections that follow we discuss selected studies from each that highlight their differences and commonalities with respect to two questions: the language–action articulation and the place of materiality in collective action. In our conclusion, based on our identification of both the contributions and limitations of the frameworks, we propose several avenues of research that, we suggest, can contribute to deepening our understanding and appreciation of the language–action articulation and of materiality.

THE COMMON THREADS OF THE THEORIES OF COORIENTATION AND ACTIVITY

Activity theory, like the theory of coorientation, explores the conduct of collective human practices. Even if this broadly defined research interest is also shared by numerous other frameworks such as structuration, actor-network theory, situated action, and distributed cognition, we have selected these two frameworks in particular because they appear to converge along several dimensions.

To begin with, our interest in comparing the activity and coorientational perspectives lies in seeing how their shared conception of human practice as object-oriented activity actualized through language and material entities, plays out in their respective theories and analyses. Both Engeström and Taylor emphasized the concept of object, which is central in their depictions of the orientation of collective action toward an outcome. Like a project under construction, the object unfolds as individuals interact with tools and other human beings over time. It cannot be reduced to goals or rational motives; rather, "the object is both something given and something anticipated, projected, transformed and achieved" (Engeström, 1990, p. 181).

Beyond this common orientation, which distinguishes them from Suchman (1987) and others, the two perspectives are characterized by their shared belief that human practice takes form through language and materiality. Within activity theory, activities are defined as object-oriented collective actions undertaken by subjects through the mediation of tools, community, rules, and division of labor. Activity theory contends that, "[t]he tool's function is to serve as the conductor of human influence on the object of activity" (Engeström, 1987, p. 59). This broad definition of tools includes psychological tools (a category that includes signs, language, and codes) as well as the category of technical tools, under which we find material entities such as a hammer, or a computer.

> Both technical tools and psychological tools mediate activity ... the essence of psychological tools is that they are originally instruments for co-operative, communicative and self-conscious shaping and controlling of the procedures of

using and making technical tools (including the human hand). (Engeström, 1987, pp. 60–61)

The central place of coordination and communication through language and material entities in the conduct of activities was echoed by Taylor and his colleagues. These features become particularly apparent in the following excerpts in which Taylor and Robichaud (2004) defined conversation, one of the main concepts of the coorientation perspective:

> We contend that conversation is where organizing occurs. Its finality is the co-orientation of organizational members in relating to each other through some common object of concern (Taylor & Van Every, 2000; Taylor 2001). The practical effect of the conversation is to establish a basis of action, and to maintain the coordination of members of the organization in responding to a mixed material and social environment. (Taylor & Robichaud, 2004, p. 397)

Furthermore, in both frameworks the action phenomenon is investigated within extended temporal and spatial frames that bring together multiple actors:

> An activity system is always a community of multiple points of view, traditions and interests. The division of labor in an activity creates different positions for the participants, the participants carry their own diverse histories and, the activity system itself carries multiple layers and strands of history engraved in its artifacts, rules and conventions. (Engeström, 2001, p. 136)

> Co-orientation occurs simultaneously in the short and long term, and involves many people, not just two. On the one hand, communication is consequential in the short term (Sigman, 1995). On the other hand, the relationship is never just an effect of the moment .... Thus, coorientation occurs within the constraints imposed by a common object and a membership in an extended community. (Taylor & Robichaud, 2004, pp. 403–404)

The common ground they share in their conceptualization of collective human practice, in our view, provides an interesting starting point for the comparative analysis that follows. In the next section we briefly set out the main concepts and premises of first, activity theory, and then, of the theory of coorientation.

THE ABCs OF ACTIVITY THEORY

Our presentation of this framework, as we have noted, centers on the third generation of activity theorists, largely represented by Engeström and his Finnish colleagues. Before presenting the revised activity model proposed by Engeström (1987), however, we first outline the key concepts as developed by Vygotsky (1978) and his student Leont'ev (1978), whose influence continues in the work of the Finnish scholars.

The concept of mediation, which is central to activity theory, was developed by its founder Vygotsky (1978). He argued that childhood psychological development is related to the human use and manipulation of words and tools that enable children to solve problems and perform difficult tasks as well as to control their impulses and behaviors (cf. pp. 28–29). Moreover, according to Vygotsky, it also favors the transmission of social-historical means and methods. When children interact with other humans they internalize cultural forms of behavior that are socially rooted in activities that have developed over time:

> The internalization of cultural forms of behavior involves the reconstruction of psychological activity on the basis of sign operations. The internalization of socially rooted and historically developed activities is the distinguishing feature of human psychology, the basis of the qualitative leap from animal to human psychology. (p. 57)

Mediation thus links situated activities with their larger historical and cultural frames. This concept has been transmitted across the different generations of activity theory researchers.

Although Vygotsky's work is largely centered on interindividual communication in the child development context, Leont'ev (1978), one of his students, offered conceptual tools to link the individual to the collective in human activities. Here is how he explained the relation between actions and activities:

> The appearance of goal-directed processes or actions in activity came about historically as the result of the transition of man to life in society. The activity of participators in common work is evoked by its product, which initially directly answers the need of each of them. The development, however, of even the simplest technical division of work necessarily leads to isolation of, as it were, intermediate partial results, which are achieved by separate participators of collective work activity, but which in themselves cannot satisfy the workers' needs. Their needs are satisfied not by these 'intermediate' results but by a share of the product of their collective activity, obtained by each of them through forms of the relationships binding them one to another, which develop in the process of work, that is, social relationships. (p. 63)

Leont'ev defended the premise that activities are constituted through a chain of actions. Actions are performed by purposeful individual subjects who come together to fashion an object-oriented activity.

Different activities can therefore be distinguished from one another by their objects. As Engeström (1999) noted:

> Objects should not be confused with goals. Goals are primarily conscious, relatively short-lived and finite aims of individual actions. The object is an enduring, constantly reproduced purpose of a collective activity system that motivates and defends the horizon of possible goals and actions. (p. 170)

Actions are subordinate to activities although their orientation, on the surface, may appear to diverge at times. For example, in an activity geared to people's need to eat, one subject might perform the action of preparing the fishing equipment. The action is not identical to the activity because the individual preparing the equipment might not use it himself to catch the fish. Nonetheless, setting up the fishing gear occurs in a chain of action leading to the object defined as feeding the collective (Leont'ev, 1978, p. 63).

Leont'ev (1978) rejected additive explanations of how actions constitute activities, According to him, activities are accomplished instead through what he calls a "certain complex of actions" (p. 64). Engeström (1987) reiterated Leont'ev's argument when noting that, "human practice is not just a series or a sum of actions. In other words, 'activity is a molar, not an additive unit' (Leont'ev, 1978, p. 50)" (p. 67).

Engeström also employed Leont'ev's distinction between actions and activities to explore human practices. He used the two concepts in his analysis of a baseball game (Engeström, 2000), for example, where he broke the activity system of a team playing a game into a series of actions involving the pitcher, the hitter, and the umpire. More specifically, his investigation was guided by the following sequence of actions: pitching, hitting, and calling the ball. His analysis is organized along the series of actions constituting the activity. For each one of the actions, Engeström identified the subject, the purpose of the action, and the tools and signs that mediate or support it.

Leont'ev's conceptualization of activity rests on a chain of actions. In addition to the subjects directly engaged in the various actions, however, Engeström extended the analysis to include coaches, the audience, the national baseball association, and the Finnish state betting company (with whom people place their bets on the outcome of baseball games). This broadened collection of actors was conceptualized by Engeström as the community, which brings together all actors involved in the activity. The members of the community are characterized by a willingness to attain a common object.

The total activity system was depicted by Engeström (1987) as shown in Fig. 9.1.

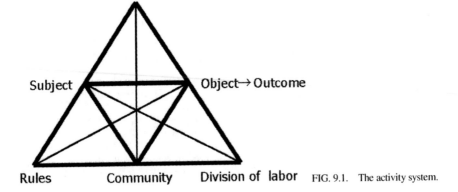

FIG. 9.1. The activity system.

Engeström extended the triangle made up of subject, object, and tool that was the model proposed by activity theorists in the past, to integrate community, rules, and division of labor. The *community* comprises multiple individuals and groups striving to attain the object that characterizes the activity. It groups together individuals with differing points of view and interests: As such, activity theory describes a multivoiced system. Furthermore, the concept allows him to formally recognize both the fact that activities unfold in a situated context with a variety of actors who are copresent, as well the fact that individuals, although perhaps spatially distant from the immediate context, contribute to its accomplishment. The concept of community thus enables him to highlight in a unique way the interactive dimensions of activity.

As shown in Fig. 9.1, Engeström (1987) introduced two intermediary concepts, *rules* and *division of labor*, into the activity triangle to refine the newly developed activity system integrating community. Rules link subjects to the community and describe how individuals interact with others involved in the activity. They govern being together and may be explicit or not. Similarly, the object and the community meet through the division of labor that organizes their doing together. The concept of division of labor, which Leont'ev had already raised with respect to the action-activity articulation discussed earlier, was integrated by Engeström into the activity triangle, giving it formal recognition as a component of the activity system.

The concept of the subject in the activity system was defined by Engeström as the point of view through which the activity system is examined. For example, the baseball players are the subjects of the activity system we referred to earlier. The subject distinguishes itself from the audience, the coaches, and the national baseball association by being directly involved in game playing, although the other actors may influence how the activity takes shape.

As others have noted, Engeström's extended activity theory framework shares many similarities with other social approaches such as Weick's (1979) and Giddens's (1984).[2] Even though his model may at times be associated with constructivist frameworks, Engeström (2000) distanced himself from them in two ways. First, unlike many of the authors under the constructivist label, he refused to define the constitution of social reality exclusively through sign-mediated actions. Following Vygotsky (1978), he argued that mediation has to be understood through the use of technical tools as well as through signs.

---

[2]Blackler, Crump, and McDonald (2000) drew a series of analogies between activity theory and other frameworks. As they say:

It has similarities with Goffman's (1974) notion of "frames", Schank and Abelson's (1977) notion of scripts, Strauss's (1978) "social worlds" and Bourdieu's (1977) habitus. Unlike these approaches, however, activity theory features the intimate relations between the factors that mediate activity and the activities themselves. Like Weick's enactment theory and Giddens' structuration theory and Unger's notion of formative context, activity theory interprets social structures as both the production of human activities and the context for them. (p. 297)

Furthermore, Engeström (2000) asserted that he differed from constructivists in his belief that social reality is created historically. In so doing, he refuted the ahistorical type of argument proposed by some authors that explains social reality as a local and situated phenomenon where individual subjects create their own world in the here and now. His unit of analysis, he maintained throughout, is not the individual but an activity system. As Star (1996) noted, "In exploding individualist explanations for activities ... both interactionists and activity theorists created new units of analysis powerful enough to explicate how we are coimplicated in each others' action" (p. 308).

To these specifics characterizing activity theory, we would add the transformative logic that underlies this framework's explanation of how activity systems evolve over time. The transformation of an activity system, its theorists claim, follows from tensions experienced due to the coexistence of conflicting points of view.

Engeström (1987) saw contradiction as being an inescapable dimension of human activities (cf. p. 82). Contradictions surface among the connections within and between activity systems, bringing together partially autonomous contexts to constitute larger wholes. These partially autonomous local contexts can be defined as actions constituting an activity system or, at a broader level of analysis, as activity systems shaping the whole of societal production. Each of the contexts constituting the totality has its own logic and its own social arrangements, which may or may not be compatible with others or with the whole system. The autonomy of these contexts creates discontinuities, which lead to contradictions whenever they become imbricated in a single endeavor.

Activity theorists contend that it is the contradictions experienced by individuals taking part in a collective production that trigger change. As the tensions associated with a contradiction heighten, people start to question the way activities are being conducted. They may also begin to reconsider what they are doing or raise questions about the logic of the activity system itself. As individuals attempt to reorganize and transform their context to ease their discomfort, the resolution of the contradictions may take various forms such as organizational change or change brought about by researcher intervention (Engeström, 2000). It is through such changes that activity systems are reorganized, redefined, or expanded (Groleau & Engeström 2002). Later in the chapter we explore activity theory further, but first, let us take a look at coorientation.

THE ABCs OF THE THEORY OF COORIENTATION

Like activity theory, the coorientation approach focuses on activities that orient around an object. As such, coorientation analysis explores the communicational means by which individuals or groups of individuals strive to organize to accomplish an object. The link between individuals and their object is represented in Fig. 9.2.

Figure 9.2 is a model of the core unit of coorientation (Taylor, Groleau, Heaton, & Van Every, 2001). A and B can be either individuals or groups of individuals

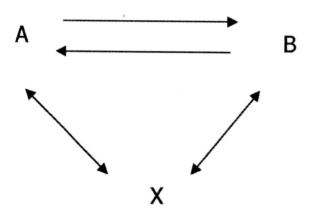

FIG. 9.2. ABX coorientation system.

linked to each other through their relation to an object X. For Taylor, as for Engeström (1990), the object is understood as a problem space. Consequently, X is inherently negotiable and is established through the interactions in which A and B engage to align their knowledge, intentions, and feelings. These interactions that link individuals and their object constitute the heart, communicationally speaking, of the organizing process. Thus, collectivities such as large organizations are understood from this perspective as being composed of multitudes of these imbricated coorientational units in which individuals strive to align themselves with others to construct a variety of objects.

For coorientationists, individuals not only engage in talk in their verbal exchanges but, more important, in action. Taylor and his colleagues, it must be noted, have differentiated themselves from the influential body of research that equates language meaning with what it represents. Instead, taking up the premises of the later Wittgenstein and Austin, they have insisted on the assumption that language is action. Consequently, conversation, one of the main concepts of this perspective, is understood as an instrument of organizational action:

> The "organizing-ness" of conversation is *fundamental*. It is only when we can identify a form of coordination of actions accomplished through the medium of language that we distinguish it *as* a conversation: "What we, as observers, call conversation is a flow of coordination of actions and emotions that we perceive as occurring, involving human beings who are interacting recurrently in language (Maturana, 1997, pp. 58–59, our translation)." (Taylor & Robichaud, 2004, p. 400, italics in original)

In other words, conversation is the medium of coorientation. Practically speaking, it is through conversation that individuals, engaged in the material and social world of ordinary activities, come together to organize themselves.

However, conversation alone does not fully capture coorientation. What these researchers call text also serves action. Texts are discursively based interpretations of situation, past and present, which also support collectivities in action:

> Sensemaking ... invokes language as members call forth knowledge of previous events through recollections and understandings of an appropriate response, given the situation. They use language to name events and to influence each other as they act: but they also use it to stand back from it and understand it. They construct *texts* in other words, and these *texts*, in turn, become an environment for future conversation. (Taylor & Robichaud, 2004, p. 397, italics added)

It therefore is in conversations that texts are generated and, in turn, texts are used to create further conversations. Text and conversation, in other words, are mutually constituted. To recapitulate, the coorientational process is aligned through conversation and text, to produce coordination of action around a commonly determined object.

The way in which sensemaking through language is linked to the material–social environment is another important dimension that characterizes this approach:

> We see human communication as embedded in two different environments, one of which is a hybrid material–social reality to which people respond daily, as actors and the other of which is language, the medium of sensemaking and hence of understanding. It is this double embedding that most clearly defines the specific character of the approach we have developed. (Taylor, chap. 8, this volume, p. 147)

This final characterization of language allows Taylor to claim that "coorientation aims to reconcile the contrasting imperatives of material–social and linguistic constraints and enablements" (Taylor, chap. 8, this volume, p. 147).

CONCEPTUALIZATIONS OF LANGUAGE AND MATERIAL ENTITIES IN THE CONDUCT OF ACTIVITIES

One of the commonalities that drew us to compare coorientation and activity theories was their definition of human activities as object-oriented practices involving language and material entities. In this section we examine more thoroughly how each approach conceptualizes language and material entities in relation to human action. Our goal is not to present an exhaustive exploration of the work of these prolific authors, but to compare, with reference to several recent examples of their research, how they have approached and investigated two themes: the language–action articulation and the place of materiality.

The Language–Action Articulation in Both Frameworks

Our discussion of the tenets of coorientation and activity theories has already provided some insight into the ways they interpret the role of language within human practice. Both approaches claim that human practice is born out of language. Furthermore, they both claim that language bridges the gap between situated practice and wider historical and spatial frames. Now, let us look at each in turn.

Activity Theory.   Within the Finnish branch of activity theory, there have been only a few studies that actually conceptualized discourse.[3] Here, we center our analysis on one of them, conducted by Engeström, Engeström, & Kerosuo (2003) in which they argued that utterances exchanged between members of collectivities constitute a site of emerging spaces of transformation or what Engeström (1987), following Vygotsky (1978), labeled zones of proximal development. Within these spaces of transformation, changes unfold to alleviate tensions within or between activity systems. Engeström et al. (2003) were particularly interested in actions and how they are "fundamentally future-oriented in that they contain an aspect of imagining what might be possible. This means that history is made in future-oriented situated actions" (p. 287). The focus of their study is to see how this horizon is created in discourse, produced in the conduct of practical activities.

To explore this process the authors borrowed the concept of history-making (Spinosa, Flores, & Dreyfus, 1997), which they applied in their analysis of the types of discourse obtained during a research intervention in a hospital where health professionals and a patient were asked to reflect jointly on their common practice. History-making, according to Spinosa et al.'s conceptualization, is a process that can be broken down into three modes: articulation, cross-appropriation, and reconfiguration. *Articulation* is the mode through which coherence is created from the various aspects of the basic patterns of an activity. In *cross-appropriation* "practices, ideas, or tools are taken over from other activities or social worlds" (Engeström et al., 2003, p. 294). Each participant draws on his or her own personal experience, thereby contributing dimensions unknown to the others, to make sense of the activity in which they are all involved. Finally, *reconfiguration* alters the whole activity as one of its formerly marginal parts becomes dominant. This last process opens up new horizons that allow transformations to take shape.

Within the history-making sequence Engeström and his colleagues identified forms of discourse that they labeled joint decision-making, modeling, co-narrating, and gaining a voice. These discursive types characterize the process through which verbal exchanges constitute the means by which courses of action take shape, become aligned, make sense, and are questioned and transformed through confrontations between alternative models of organized action. Engeström and his colleagues used Spinosa's modes to explain how the participants in an activity system not only make sense of their experience through various types of discourses but also reflect together on their practice. This is not merely an occasion for mutual ad-

---

[3]We invite readers interested in the conceptualization of language within this framework to consult the work of R. Engeström (1995), who has coupled Leont'ev's activity–action–operation hierarchy with Bahktin's conceptualizations of social language, voice, and speech genre.

justment, they maintained, but a way to redefine the practice and open up new spaces in which it is possible to evolve.

Coorientation Theory.   As we know, the language–action articulation constitutes the main research object of coorientationists, who have been greatly influenced by scholars such as Austin (1962) and Greimas (1987), among others. We briefly illustrate how they interpret those two influences by reference to recent research conducted by Katambwe (2004), Taylor and Van Every (2000), and Katambwe and Taylor (chap. 4, this volume).

Following the seminal work of Austin (1962), Taylor and his colleagues move away from a vision of words as representations of reality to focus on what words actually "do." Katambwe's (2004; see also Katambwe & Taylor chap. 4, this volume) work offers an interesting example of this type of research. He analyzed an episode of discourse taken from a 1969 Canadian National Film Board documentary that covered a strategy meeting of top managers gathered in a lodge for a weekend to discuss the future directions of their chain of retail food stores.[4] Focusing on the propositional content and the illocutionary force of speech acts he examined two different types of articulation: first, the process of appropriation of the organizational text by managers participating at the meetings, second, the way in which they used these texts in interaction to institute roles and status. Greatly influenced by Taylor's work, Katambwe's research enriches and expands that framework by exploring, for example, the use of ambiguity and contradictions in the discourse of the company's president in his attempts to align managerial decisions with his own interests.

Another important body of research within the coorientational perspective that explores the language–action connection has been based on narrative theory. Instead of adopting the more traditional definition of narrative as storytelling, this stream of research employs the conceptual framework of the theoretician Greimas (1987) to focus on the canonical types of action and roles that can be found in the narrative forms that people use to make sense of their experience. Taylor and Van Every (2000) and Taylor and Cooren (chap. 7, this volume) maintain that it is through narrative (language) that we instantiate and negotiate a world of meaning. Following Greimas, they distinguished between the circumstantial and generic nature of narratives:

> Greimas reserves the word *actor* for the figurative or purely circumstantial level of narrative and invents a neologism, *actant*, for the generic or structural. The same bivalence applies to the objects of a story on which attention is focused. They, too, are both specific to a time and place, and generic—conceptual, not circumstantial. At the generic or structural level, subject and object are mutually defining, in the sense that their meaning is not reducible to circumstances, either

---

[4]This discursive empirical material is the same as that referred to in Taylor and Robichaud (2004).

psychic or physical, because they are components in a logical structure of relationships that not only has no expression other than in the form of narrative but
also is what gives meaning to happenings in a purely circumstantial world. (Taylor & Van Every, 2000, p. 43)

The coorientational locus of analysis, whether based on speech acts or narrative, is
not the immediate circumstances in which verbal exchanges are produced. Actually, Taylor and his colleagues made little mention of the local conditions under
which these exchanges are formulated, except for the necessary rules that make it
possible to perform them successfully.

The context, as they saw it, is not tied to the enunciating subject but to the performing subject that comes into being through discourse. Through language-
instantiated exchanges, the intentions, actions, and a whole world of organizational
members is produced. Reality is not reinvented each time a conversation takes place
but is constructed by reference to a body of discourse, which they called text, which
is both the starting point and the outcome of each conversation.

Comparing the Language–Action Articulation in the Two Frameworks.

Before we begin our comparison of how these frameworks explain the relation between language and action, it is important to note that their starting points with respect to action are very different. Activity theory can be characterized as a
framework preoccupied with acting out, in which discourse becomes one of the
means to access the process by which human practice unfolds and evolves. We find
only a few conceptual propositions that explain the role of discourse. Coorientation
theory, developed within the field of organizational communication, is, on the other
hand, focused on talking out, which is equated with action. The main research focus
has thus been to identify the various manifestations of agency in discourse and their
potential for explaining the organizing of human activities. Consequently, although
these authors have developed a rich conceptual tool to characterize discourse they
remain fairly silent regarding other manifestations of human activity. Although
both frameworks propose a connection between language and action, they appear
to favor opposite sides of the equation.

Nonetheless, despite their dissimilar starting points, the authors within these
two frameworks share some points of view. For example, on a number of occasions,
Engeström recognized that actors take action through their discourse. For example,
he argued, "There are instances where practical activity and discourse seem to
merge almost completely: preachers, auctioneers and talk show hosts would be examples of that" (Engeström, 1999, p. 171).

However, rather than adopting this as a principle, like Taylor, he subsumed these
examples under a category of the ways in which language can be linked to practical
action. In other categories he included different types of situations like metal-work-
ing, where the role of language is downplayed in favor of the use of technical tools
(Engeström, 1999). Consequently, he saw variation in how language can serve

practical activity rather than framing the two together unilaterally. The study of discourse, in his view, is particularly pertinent to the understanding of both the relation linking actions to activity and to the transformative process of the activity system. In the balance of our analysis we focus on the latter link.

Although our examination of the conceptualization of language in the activity and coorientational perspectives reveals that both make use of the concept of narrative, this apparent similarity masks differences in the way each defines narrative. Engeström et al. (2003) used the term to refer to a collective sensemaking process in which individuals intersubjectively construct an interpretation of their present and future experience. Yet it is just this type of definition that Taylor and his colleagues attempt to redefine. In their case, narratives are seen as both generic and circumstantial, bringing together a basic generic structure and the local circumstances of individuals, their objects, and their activity. Similarly, the status of narratives and the roles played by organizational members within them are different, depending on the framework. Coorientationists focus on subjects as they perform and evolve within structures that are isomorphic to the ones we find in narrative. For activity theorists, narratives are used to explore the subject's experience of reality through the story they tell as well as through the context in which the narrative is enunciated and unfolds.

Nor is the difference between the two approaches merely in how they define and use narrative. It also becomes strikingly apparent in the way they connect discourse and action. In the Engeström et al. (2003) study, discourse is considered to be a sensemaking process that renders new forms of activity possible. It offers a space through which activities can be imagined and projected. In contrast, the primary focus of Taylor et al.'s conceptualization is how individuals create their roles, status, and relationships through discourse. Acting here is a synonym for organizing. Their emphasis on organizing, and more specifically, on how individuals act on each other and in the name of one another, is, interestingly enough, reflected in their choice of empirical setting where they opt to conduct their research. Their privileged field of study is managerial practice.

In both frameworks, language is conceptualized as a means through which actual contexts for action are linked to more temporally distant environments. Activity and coorientation theories maintain that humans are able to bring temporally distant models of organized human practice into their interactions through language. For coorientationists, past practices, conceptualized as texts, are brought to bear in the actual context of action, through conversation. Engeström et al. (2003), in this particular study, also examined how actual models of organized actions constitute future models of human practice. Coorientation theory, from the examples we selected, explains present models of action by resorting to the past, whereas activity theory seems to draw on the present to explain future models of actions. It must be said that many studies inspired by activity theory, including several conducted by Engeström, are similarly preoccupied with the connection linking past and present human practices.

In the studies we selected for this chapter, both sets of authors argued that their interest in studying the language–action connection lies in the social dynamics it reveals. This is understood in the Engeström et al. (2003) study as the tensions and contradictions that lead individuals to undertake the necessary means to transform activity systems. On the other hand, inspired by Austin and Greimas, coorientational analysts, quoted in this section,[5] interpret social dynamics as the means by which humans act on and on behalf each other. We suggest therefore, in summary, that the divergences we have observed lie in how they define social dynamics as well as the other aspects of their scientific inquiry we have discussed. Their definitions of their respective research objects and concepts are anchored in dissimilar sets of premises. In the end, they offer two very distinct readings of the language–action articulation to explore object-oriented activities.

The Place of Materiality

Materiality is a dimension of collective human practice discussed in both perspectives. Each explores materiality in some form in their study of object-oriented activities. Engeström (2000), abiding by Vygotsky's (1978) vision of mediation through and intertwining of signs and technical tools, differentiated his framework from those more communicationally based that focus primarily on language to explain human action. Although within the coorientationist perspective, the material dimension may not have been frequently problematized, we find Cooren's (2004b) work to be of particular interest to explore this dimension of collective human practice. Let us now look at how materiality is conceptualized within both frameworks.

Activity Theory.   As observed earlier, Vygotsky's (1978) legacy has allowed activity theorists to distinguish themselves from numerous other social constructionist approaches by their emphasis on tools. Over the years, they have come to focus on various technical tools to problematize the negotiation process leading to their development and use. One of the most interesting cases within that literature has been a study conducted by Hasu and Engeström (2000) describing the transfer of a neuromagnetical measurement system (MEG) from designers to users. Their research illustrates the difficulties encountered by technology users and developers when a new technology designed for medical scientific research is utilized for clinical purposes.

Initially, it was expected that MEG would be used for clinical readings in the same way as for scientific experiments. Problems arose, however, when users realized that readings from patients were unsatisfactory. Activity theory explains the problem associated with this new usage as being a conflict between research

---

[5]Within the coorientationist family, the work of Searle has also been an important source of inspiration. Among them, Cooren (2000a) used Searle as a basis to reconsider speech act theory and propose his own model of organizational processes.

and clinical logics, each of which possesses its own specificity of distinct rules, division of labor, and setting requirements. The contradiction created by the confrontation of the research logic for machine use with its use for clinical purposes forced the laboratory workers to reconsider their way of doing things. They had to create a new routine that was more adapted to the use of the machine for clinical readings.

Engeström and his colleagues also conducted a research project, again in the Finnish health care system, in which they intervened to identify and resolve tensions through the creation of a new tool, the care agreement. This agreement is a written document devised to coordinate the care of chronically ill patients who are being treated by numerous different health care providers. The agreement and its implementation within the health care system offered fertile ground in which to investigate how newly created tools become part of the daily work practice of individuals within an activity system. Kerosuo and Engeström (2003) argued that the integration of any new tool in an activity system often requires the participants to rethink and re-create their routines. They followed the process through which the tool evolved to eventually find its place within the collective activity. The use of this newly created document requires health providers to rethink how they collectively dispense care and coordinate their efforts to heal patients. Through this dynamic process, the tool, as well as the activity, is questioned and constantly redefined.

Although until this point we have equated materiality with tool, material entities can be explored within activity theory through alternative concepts. One of the most enlightening contributions of Hasu and Engeström's (2000) study is to conceptualize the MEG technology at one and the same time as an object and a tool within different activity systems. More specifically, they integrated the same technology in the activity system of the users as a tool and in the system of the designers as an object. Making a similar argument, Kuutti (1996) explored the conceptual ramifications of categorizing technology as an object, a tool, or rules. Although it has opened up various possibilities, this is a research avenue that remains to be explored.

Coorientation Theory. Although the material dimension has always been present in Taylor's work, it has seldom been investigated to explore fully its connection to collective human practices. Among Taylor's close collaborators, Cooren (2004b), however, recently addressed the agency role of textual agents like memos and reports and in doing so contributed to clarify the place of materiality in the organizing process sustaining coorientation.

In the first article we selected, Cooren (2004b, chap. 5, this volume) defended the notion that memos and reports "do things" in organizational settings. Citing Latour's (1996) work, he argued that written organizational documents—texts—perform actions and consequently participate actively in the organizational process. To illustrate the power of material entities to perform action he used the ex-

ample of a sign that reads, "All visitors must sign in. This building is under TV surveillance" (p. 379). Cooren characterized this sign, which is located in the entrance
of an apartment building as follows:

> The sign in this situation displays agency in that it *invites* the visitor to check in
> and it *indicates* to them that the building is under video surveillance. By implica-
> tion, the *organization* that manages the building can also be said to perform the
> acts of *inviting* and *indicating*. (p. 379, italics in original)

Textual agents are seen as part of a chain of hybrid associations in which humans
also participate: "Recognizing nonhuman agency does not reduce human agency to
an empirical artifact. On the contrary, it shows how a hybrid association between
human and nonhumans enables people to do things that they could not do otherwise" (p. 377).

This same example is also used in an article by Cooren and Fairhurst (in press)
to illustrate how nonhuman entities "tend to not only dislocate interactions, but
also stabilize them." Dislocation refers to the process by which nonhuman agents
can bring together various entities that are "put out of place" to serve the conduct
of operations within a specific local context. For example, the sign brings into the
immediate context of its reading the building manager and the tenants who organized a series of meetings to discuss the purpose of the sign, and its production. Its
installation is thus the outcome of a string of associations: Humans like the tenants and the owner come together with nonhumans like the procedure and the sign
to serve a common cause in a local and specific situation. Consequently, the actual local interaction of a visitor to the building with the sign rests on a series of
past interactions among humans and nonhumans, which occurred in various
times and places.

Cooren and Fairhurst also employed the concept of *stabilization*, which refers to the transcendence of persisting roles, rights, and duties. This same sign,
they pointed out, over and over again has the capacity to invite people to register
themselves. It has a lasting quality that continues to make a difference through
time. In other words, as a nonhuman agent, its capacity to trigger human action
transcends time.

Reconsidering Materiality in the Two Frameworks.   In both the perspectives we have been comparing, the authors recognize materiality as transcending
time and space. Cooren, for example, was very explicit about the capacity of textual
agents, through stabilization and dislocation, to extend the actual temporal and spatial frames of local actions. Within activity theory, this argument is implicit but omnipresent as well. The empirical settings in which material entities such as MEG
and the care agreement are introduced bring together both design and use. Each of
these tools carries a cultural legacy that is integrated in the design and surfaces in
the course of its use. This cultural legacy may take the form of how researchers ma-

nipulate scientific instruments in the case of MEG, or how care is given by various health specialists in the case of the care agreement. As argued in the previous section devoted to language, textual agents as well as material entities like tools in an activity system become the mediators through which past human practices become part of the actual setting in which actions unfold.

In both approaches, language is strongly associated with materiality. Most of the material entities that are explored in the two frameworks are text supported. Cooren investigated written documents such as memos, signs, and reports, and Engeström devoted an entire research project to the care agreement. In addition, however, activity theorists, through the study of various technologies (MEG among them), also consider the potential of the material characteristics of tools to support activities. Here activity theory distinguishes itself from the coorientational perspective.

In line with the coorientational focus on organizing and agency, Cooren questioned the capacity of material entities to support the "organizing process" through language. Even though he defined acting as making a difference, not as attributing roles and statuses among collectivities (Cooren, 2004b; Cooren & Fairhurst, in press), Cooren remains preoccupied by the capacity of material entities such as a printed sign to act on behalf of someone. This potential of "acting for" recalls other analyses through which authors like Katambwe (2004) used conversation to investigate how power is conveyed through language. Furthermore, Cooren's use of speech act theory to make sense of the discourse on the sign is somewhat similar to previous analyses in which the organizing dimension of speech in face-to-face interactions is the object of study.

As in the case of conversation analysis, which tends to underplay the context of enunciation, in our view, Cooren's analysis of textual agents overlooks important contextual considerations associated with the production of these material entities. For instance, a series of unanswered questions surface about the sign in the lobby of the apartment building: Is it a handwritten sign produced by a janitor? Or an official-looking sign associated with an important institutional actor? In the same way, the discourse produced in memos and letters may have different repercussions depending on the paper on which it is printed, whether it is on letterhead or not, or bears the signature or the department from which it is issued. In our view, the varying institutional and circumstantial conditions that frame textual agencies may very well contribute to their power to organize.[6] Like Austin's proposed felicity conditions under which speech can be equated with action, we suggest that the analysis of textual agents needs to take account of certain elements of the context in which they appear. Just as Austin identified respect for conventional procedures such as the use of certain words, the setting, the role, and involvement of the participants as a necessary condition for a successful speech act, we too suggest that, to do things with words, textual agency must be similarly examined in light of a set of contextual conditions.

---

[6]We are thankful to Nicole Giroux for this interesting reading of Cooren's work.

For Engeström and his research group, in contrast, reflecting on materiality becomes another occasion to investigate further the social dynamics within and between activity systems. Many of their studies examine the association between the production and use of tools and tensions and contradictions at different levels. In the Hasu and Engeström (2000) study, cited earlier, we find an interesting example of this type of investigation. Activity theorists make the assumption that material entities such as tools are created and manipulated by reflexive agents who use them to support their activities. Material entities and humans are understood as occupying two different orders of reality, having each its own form of participation in activities (Hasu & Engeström, 2000; Kerosuo & Engeström, 2003). Here they differ from Cooren who, following Latour, treated human and nonhuman contributions to action as being symmetrical; that is, as contributing equally to a long chain of associations supporting action.

DIFFERENT LENSES LEADING TO DIFFERENT READINGS OF A PHENOMENON

Our comparative analysis of activity and coorientation theories was motivated by their common interest in the study of object-oriented action. We have found, however, that they approach that issue using very different assumptions regarding the place of human subjects, language, and material entities. Even if we can identify a certain common ground in our understanding of how organized actions transcend time and space through language and material entities such as mediation, text, and textual agents, we note important differences with respect to the language–action articulation as well as in the way the two approaches frame materiality in relation to human activity. The different postulates on which each is founded in fact seem to render any reconciliation or unification unlikely.

Yet, can they still benefit from each other?

In our view, even though each approaches the phenomenon in its own way, it may be possible to build on their common concern for understanding object-oriented practice. For example, the transformation of activity systems, although highlighted in Engeström's work, is recognized but not problematized in the coorientational approach: "Thus, organizational patterns of interaction replicate themselves with considerable reliability, but they also evolve as people engage in practical activity and develop innovations" (Taylor & Robichaud, 2004, p. 409).

Without necessarily adopting the assumptions on which activity theory rests, namely the omnipresent tensions that characterize human activity, such themes as diverging logics, the evolution of interactional patterns, and the emergence of innovation, could be promising research themes to pursue within the coorientational perspective as well.

Similarly, activity theorists might take a closer look at organizing in their research. The organizing process is often part of activity theory analysis, but it is rarely problematized as it is in the coorientational perspective. More specifically, we would suggest that activity theorists pay attention to the dynamic process through which the activity is progressively constituted in time and space. As we noted earlier, because an activity system is historically grounded, analysts often compare a system's state at two different times in its evolution. Only rarely do they investigate its dynamic constitution over time. We also suggest that to examine some of the system articulations can be an interesting research avenue. Engeström's distinctive model opens the door to the study of numerous articulations among system elements. For example, studies could attempt to elucidate the constitution and propagation of modes of being together and doing together through mediation. The analysis of material and linguistic mediations could be used to explore a series of connections within Engeström's (1987) activity system such as subject–rule, object–division of labor, division of labor–community, and rule–division of labor. Researchers could attempt to answer questions such as these: How are rules formed, produced, and reproduced through interactions with material and linguistic mediations? Aside from being an interesting area to explore, these questions could allow us to shed new light on the concepts of contradiction and transformation, by exploring the dual dynamic that simultaneously constitutes both the system and its contradictions.

In the course of our comparative analysis we observe that, in their respective research agendas, both perspectives underplay the place of materiality. In the coorientation perspective, materiality is not directly problematized even though the material dimension is discussed in three different instances in the writings on coorientation we selected. Taylor suggested that text occurs in various forms, including the material. Unfortunately this promising incursion into the world of materiality appears not to have been pursued. We suggest that the implications of text supported by a durable and shareable medium deserve exploration within the coorientation perspective. Furthermore, although the organizing process in which people transform their social and material reality into discourse is at the heart of coorientation, and this group of researchers has succeeded in explaining the mutual constitution of social dynamics and language, they remain almost silent on the materiality–discourse connection with regard to human action.

Finally, without directly problematizing materiality, Cooren's work on textual agents opens up an interesting possibility to extend the logic of coorientation into exchanges involving discourse made accessible through material entities such as signs, memos, and reports. However, as we argued in the previous section, this type of analysis could benefit from being framed in the larger context of the conditions under which the textual agent takes form, to fully appreciate its power.

In the case of activity theory, we have noted that materiality, and more specifically technology, is conceptualized both as tool and object (Hasu & Engeström, 2000). Our suggestion here is that they also examine the mediating effect of material entities in the constitution and propagation of rules and division of labor. This extension could open new avenues that, we suspect, would enrich considerably their conceptualization of materiality.

In our overall view, there are numerous questions still outstanding concerning the place of materiality in practical action that neither perspective explores fully. As an example of what such exploration might potentially consist of, we conclude by referring to the socioethnographic research of Grosjean and Lacoste (1999; Lacoste, 2000) carried out in hospital settings in France.

Their analysis focused on the production of written documents constituting a hospital patient profile. The written documents they examined contained information such as measurements of vital signs as well as notes and comments on patient progress, his or her psychological state, and other types of nontechnical description. They saw this information tool as a collective production because doctors, nurses, and other health care providers on various shifts all participate in its creation. It is what they call *polygraphic* because multiple individuals produce its written traces. In addition to being a descriptive tool, the documents it contains also juxtapose and superimpose different discourses. Grosjean and Lacoste (1999) observed, for example, that in some cases the writings of one person may reply to the questions of another. Furthermore, the same document may contain requests for an examination of a patient, or information that has been scratched out when found to be false. Grosjean and Lacoste observed a discourse in these writings that reveals both the dependencies and authority status of the different contributors. For example, nurses were enrolling the document in a social power game of asserting their independence. They did so by making their workplace knowledge explicit in this written form.

These written texts are, in a way, similar to the conversational exchanges used to negotiate status and roles analyzed by Taylor and his colleagues. The written documents become organizing tools in which both the tasks and the place of each one of the participants in the process is negotiated and distributed. This type of document, which offers an alternative to Cooren's example of a printed sign, opens a door to another way of learning how writings on a durable medium contribute to the organizing process.

Although this hospital document may appear similar in many ways to the care agreement in Engeström's research, Grosjean and Lacoste's (1999) approach differs from his in their emphasis on the organizing function of the tool, or more specifically, the dynamic constitution of rules and division of labor produced through the writings collected in the file. Through their empirical work, they traced who wrote what, at what time, and in response to what observation, to learn how this particular collectivity of health care providers actually shares a common way of being and doing. Rules and division of labor are both negotiated and reproduced through the detailed recorded writings. Their analysis illustrates the interest of examining how rules and division of labor take form in tools. More specifically, we can see from Grosjean and Lacoste's work the prominent role tools are called on to play in the constitution and propagation of the organizing process of an activity system. The patient file and the organization of work through division of labor and rules become mutually constituted.

To conclude, we submit that the pertinence of the Grosjean and Lacoste (1999) study for activity theorists is dual. First, it illustrates the dynamic process of mutual constitution of tool and rules or division of labor. Second, the patient file is simultaneously used as a functional and legal document, two dimensions that are bound to create tensions leading to contradictions. Viewing the patient file as both a dynamic source for organizing as well as a potential source of contradiction allows us to capture the simultaneous evolution of the activity system, through the constitution of its rules as well as its division of labor and the inherent tensions leading to a contradiction.

Grosjean and Lacoste's (1999) work forces us to rethink how in the workplace, organizational members are brought together as a collectivity through materiality. This is useful because it allows us to formulate pertinent research avenues for activity theory as well as for coorientation theory. Still, it is clear that more work needs to be done to fully appreciate the organizing properties of material entities. We suggest that, beyond written documents, there are numerous material artifacts that deserve our attention if we are to develop a richer understanding of collectivities in action (Groleau, 1995, 2002; Groleau & Taylor, 1996).

ACKNOWLEDGMENTS

I would like to express my gratitude to James Taylor and Yrjo Engeström for their inspiration, their encouragement, and their fruitful comments on my work over the years. I am also grateful to Christiane Demers, François Cooren, and Elizabeth Van Every for their generous feedback on previous versions of this chapter. Finally, I would like to thank the Social Science and Humanities Research Council of Canada for its financial support (CRSH 410-2004-1091).

P A R T IV

SOME IMPLICATIONS

CHAPTER TEN

Accounts in Interactions: Implications of Accounting Practices for Managing

Richard J. Varey
Waikato University, New Zealand

In this chapter, from the managerial point of view, I reflect back on the proposals made in this book for an alternative conceptual framework. What are the implications of this distinctly different communicational theory of organization for management studies and managing practice? How are the concepts of communication, organization, and interaction used in management theory? How does orthodox management science rely on the transmission of information conception of communication? If the way of explaining language use proposed by the authors of the preceding chapters of this volume is accepted, how must we reexplain management? Language in use is not a way of expressing social reality to make it available to others, but rather the manner in which we ordinarily make the reality for ourselves during our dealings with others—accomplished in our acts of accounting. Descriptions of what is and what was are thus not just reports of potentially objective facts, but also (inter-)personal, motivated depictions for a purpose. Such descriptive accountings are practical actions in the organization and management of social situations.

I examine the notion of accountings as constitutive of organization—people's reasonings and choices of courses of action are connected through their conversations—and reexamine the orthodox explanations of management, drawing on the preceding chapters. I conclude with some thoughts on implications for managing.

MANAGERS IN DISCOURSE

We might study the impact of forms of interaction in work settings as joint action, that is (at least potentially) inherently and fundamentally organizing in nature. This stems from a reading of Cooren's (2000b) recent review of the semiotic analysis of language in use, and the earlier chapters of this volume.

My interest in language use among comanagers was provoked by Johnson and Duberley's (2000) suggestion that "a management discipline [is seen from the postmodern stance] as a particular historical and social mode of engagement that restricts what is thinkable, knowable and doable within its disciplinary domain," and "through their education and training, managers learn to speak [this] discourse and the discourse speaks to them by structuring their experiences and definitions of who they are" (p. 102).

The new approach proposed in this volume has some obvious antecedents. For example, one way of investigating this idea of language use is through the adoption of ethnography, including critical ethnography (Forester, 1993). This has been forwarded as a method for concrete social and political investigation of actual communicative practices that shape relationships. I am especially interested by Weber's (1949/1962) methodological suggestion that subjective understanding is required before causal connections are pursued, but that both are necessary conditions of academic knowledge production and must be combined for an adequate explanation of social phenomena to emerge.

CRITICAL ETHNOGRAPHY

In proposing the deployment of critical social theory, Forester (1993) was concerned with the benefits of understanding social interaction as a practical matter of making sense together in a politically complex world. This is exactly the theme taken up in each of the chapters of this volume. This is not a typical approach to understanding communicative action, in that managers' everyday talk in negotiations, staff meetings, personal accounts, and profiles of practice is more usually explained (by microeconomics) as a resource exchange or (through social psychology) as strategic behavior. Forester's interest is in the politics and ethics of dialogue and social interaction. This goes beyond Schön's (1983) studies of the individual practitioner, to examine the political (i.e., social) significance of managers' actions. Katambwe and Taylor analyze managers' talk in a staff meeting (chap. 4, this volume), and Güney (chap. 2, this volume) ethnographically analyzes managerial negotiations in a large high-tech company.

Forester (1993) recognized communicative action as both intentional and purposive and his proposed analysis reveals the how and what of practice—the communicative organizing of others' attention to what matters. This agenda-setting form of influence and power can be revealed by the analysis of social and political relations within a group setting. Forester viewed management and communication as inherently political, but also as critical, because it focuses on relations of power and hegemony and their contingencies.

Seen from this perspective, communicative interaction has a double structure. This recognition makes the new approach quite distinctive. Speaking is not the transmission of messages from a human sender to a human receiver, but the performance of speech acts in socially structured contexts to make meaning (see Cooren, 2000b; Katambwe & Taylor, chap. 4, this volume; and Taylor & Robichaud, 2004). Thus, research carried out from a critical perspective should pay attention not only to what is said but also to the political messages produced (sometimes unintentionally), and to the impact of what is said on the group's dynamic. This is done by Katambwe and Taylor in their study (chap. 4, this volume), although Forester's idea of what constitutes "political" may differ from theirs.

This approach to uncovering social and political relations within a group is based on Habermas's sociological analysis of communicative action, in which he suggested that social actors make pragmatic validity claims on listeners (Habermas, 1984). Typically, speakers make truth claims that may influence the listeners' mental images of what may truly, or falsely, exist (knowledge). Speakers also invoke contextual norms that legitimize any proposed action to which listeners may consent or may challenge (consent). We may attempt to show how we feel about an issue and express these feelings to influence the group; listeners' reactions to our expressions of our inner state may accept them as true or feigned (trust). Speakers also select language forms and terminology that may be acceptable or incomprehensible to listeners but nonetheless have an impact on how listeners feel and react (attention). Thus, in Forester's (1993) analysis, we can assess how in speaking, managers can shape the way others learn (or fail to learn) and therefore, whether or not managers change their behavior as a result of what has been said. Habermas (1971) argued that learning can be either technical-instrumental (productive, concerned with ends) or moral-practical (reproductive, concerned with means). This kind of categorical systematization is rather different from the more pragmatic view offered here (e.g., in Brummans, chap. 11, this volume).

We can also examine the uncertainties raised from the doubts of participants about truth, and the ambiguities that arise from doubts about legitimacy and trustworthiness of expression. Uncertainty can be dealt with by gathering information, whereas ambiguity requires practical, authoritative judgment. Questions of ambiguity are often cast as questions of uncertainty, and calls for more information may obscure the political and social judgments made. This is nicely illustrated by Katambwe and Taylor (chap. 4, this volume).

Forester (1993), like the authors in this volume, also pointed out that this double structure of speaking can be uncovered in the working of the group as a whole. Members of a social unit act purposively to accomplish goals and in so doing reproduce the very social relationships that sustain the corporation.[1] Work is done toward reputation and identity even as members concern themselves with getting things done. This critical account of organizing leads to a view of power as a social relationship reproduced in concrete actions—as power in action.

MANAGEMENT COMMUNICATION: CORPORATE CONVERSATION

The human species has developed communication as an adaptive mechanism that we can each use to recognize and respond to threats to our well-being by cooperat-

---

[1]Here I have chosen this term to mean a purposive social collectivity, and carefully avoided the term organization as is typically used entitively in such discussions.

ing. Conflict, competition, and cooperation are three modes of human interaction that are mediated, in differing degrees, by communication. However, in an age of management aided by mediating technologies, we have become deluded into thinking that communication is merely about making and sending messages and moving information as a copyable, distributable resource. In everyday life, we have almost universally succumbed to a simplistic ideology that is convenient for the technological handling of information for control and decision processes. Often when we talk about communication, it is not the wider and subtle communicative interaction that we talk of, but the transmission of signals along copper wires.

We really need to popularize a more sophisticated and relevant explanation. A variety of viewpoints on communication have been developed in a number of fields of study—political science, economics, sociology, psychology, social psychology, management science, anthropology, linguistics, cybernetics (the science of control), biology, philosophy, and government. All have conceived of communication differently. Today, we should recognize that we need a conception of communication that allows people an active contributive role in a cooperative coalescent world (Salk, 1973).

Drucker (1973) pointed out some time ago that communication is not the means of conducting business but the mode. Contemporarily, communication is no longer universally seen as relatively peripheral, but as the principal constitutive element in the process of organizing (Mumby & Stohl, 1996). The model of communication as a linear transmission of information and reproduction of intended meaning is outmoded and dehumanizing, and a more realistic model envisions an interactive process of meaning formation. Mantovani (1996), among others, saw this to be essential as "new media" and new technologies of human communication are developed and adopted at an accelerating pace.

The conception of communication is critical to communicative practice, but also to the methodological foundation of the communication research conducted by scholars who try to aid understanding and to guide practices. More on this later. In making a comparison between German and Nordic traditions in communication scholarship, Langer (1999) aptly concluded from his "stocktaking" work that a state of "wretchedness" prevails in communication research. I conclude that this is true in British, North American, and Australasian studies also. This is partly because scholars and students continue to read and use the same books that reinforce and recycle the orthodoxy without questioning the appropriateness of their theoretical basis or the reasoning for "management." Communication, in management thinking, is generally treated as merely a tool; there has been little attention paid to developments in communication theory from other disciplines. This wretchedness is illustrated here, first in an examination of marketing communication thinking, and then the review is widened to general management thinking.

Buttle's (1995) review of the treatment of marketing communications in marketing textbooks showed that very few marketing specialists have attempted to produce or apply comprehensive, integrative theory for marketing communication at both the interpersonal and mediated levels. He found that although all of the "101" introductory texts he surveyed tried to provide some theoretical basis for the development of managerial strategies, many did so only implicitly and did not explicitly recognize the theoretical origins or grounds of their discussion. Buttle showed that the work of Schramm (1948) has been by far the most widely adopted in promoting a set of communication practices designed to produce cognitive, affective, or behavioral outcomes among a specified target audience through expressive performances. This can be applied to the portrayal of communication in management generally.

Telephone engineer Shannon also provided a theory of communication in which "The fundamental problem of communication is that of reproducing at one point either exactly or approximately a message selected at another point" (Shannon & Weaver, 1949/1963, p. 31). Weaver, in the same book, defined communication as "all of the procedures by which one mind may affect another" (p. 3).

The work of Shannon and Weaver and of Schramm became popular, remains disproportionately influential, and is still the main basis of the prevailing orthodoxy in the consideration of the communication aspects of marketing and management. Although Schramm (1971) did update his thinking some years later to spell the demise of the earlier bullet theory of communication, he still retained the encoder–message–decoder model, and this has become firmly entrenched in management and marketing texts. In fairness, Schramm's thinking did shift to communication as "a relationship, an act of sharing, rather than something which someone does to someone else" (p. 8), although this has yet to be commonly recognized. This was a considerable development from the earlier view that communication was a magic bullet (the term *hypodermic effect* also became popular in mass communication studies; Klapper, 1960) that "transferred ideas or feelings or knowledge or motivations from one mind to another" (Schramm, 1971, p. 8). Communication came to be seen, at least by some, as the study of people in relationship. Indeed, Schramm claimed that all communication necessarily functions within a broader framework of social relations: the physical or spatial relationship between sender and receiver, the situational context, role expectations, and social norms. Yet, this conclusion and essential orientation has not yet percolated into business and management texts. Another problem remaining is that some texts have taken either an interpersonal or mediated communication perspective, thus failing, one way or the other, to cope with the diversity of activities that fall within the field of managed communication.

Buttle (1995) highlighted the problem that the very themes and assumptions on which marketing and marketing communication textbooks are designed (he termed this *normal marketing communication theory*) have been questioned by contemporary communication theorists, including those advocating the kind of approach set out in this volume. The wider communication literature can better deal with the weaknesses and omissions of popular (textbook versions of) marketing communication theory. What resides in most marketing textbooks is outdated, ill informed, and in need of revision.

In the wider field of management, most writers treat communication as informational. For example, in a case study that examines the relation among culture, communication, and information (Brown & Starkey, 1994), the investigators see the organization as a "meanings system" and "information processor." Following the information tradition, Daft and Weick (1984) conceived of organizations as complex interpretive systems that transform environmental information into strategic business decisions. But, pointed out Deetz (1995), when communication is confused with information processing, sensitivity to political issues is left out. This perspective disregards the manner by which data and information are socially constructed, taking the environment as objective and objectifying communication content. The small number of texts that deal specifically with corporate communication are also, mostly, trapped in an informational perspective. For example, van Riel (1995) suggested that information [is] transmitted during the process of communication, whereas Horton (1995) took an economic approach to the management of communication that is necessarily premised on packages of information that he termed "messages." Argenti (1997) saw no need to raise any question over the nature of human communication—it is to be taken for granted. Heath and Deetz are the exceptions, each providing a critique on what is to be taken as communication and the consequences of this selection (Deetz, 1992, 1995; Heath, 1994).[2] Both Mantovani (1996) and Krugman (1965, 1977) eschewed the notion of transportation in favor of transformation as a model of the process of communication. Deetz (1992) warned us of the consequences of conceiving communicating as the transportation of knowledge and information and not as participation in constructing identity, meaning, and knowledge. When meaning is strategically reproduced outside of awareness and not participatorily produced, the one-sidedness precludes the opening of representations to consideration of alternatives in pursuit of common understanding.

ACCOUNTINGS

I now discuss the concept of accounts, to show the formative power of accountings. This is consistent with the central idea of the organizing property of communicating (Cooren, 2000b). In our everyday behavior, with and among others, we need to know what we are doing, and to be able to give an account of our behavior to others, if called on to do so. We also need to be able to explain situations to ourselves as we ponder possible and desirable courses of action. Activity is seen as consciously chosen from among available alternatives, not as mindless doings. Practical accounting is the construction of worlds of meaning in the course of social interaction. This doing determines the form of our consciousness, our categories of thought, perception, feeling, action, and expression. Thus, we determine, through our language use, our own modes of being in the world in which we apply these cat-

---

[2]Neither book could be claimed as a mainstream management textbook!

egories. In the process of accounting, we make our actions seem appropriate by explaining our situation, meanings, purposes, beliefs, and reasonings. The authors in this volume use the term sensemaking for this practice, and, elsewhere Taylor and Van Every raised this as the theme for their analysis of a communication technology system implementation (in an unpublished report on the INCIS research project conducted at The Waikato Management School, New Zealand).

Despite our tendency to ascribe to accounting a rather technical role in financial management, it is an everyday activity. Several day-to-day uses of the term are readily found:

- To "call to account" is to challenge or contest, hold answerable for, request an accounting.
- To "give an account of " is to formulate and tell a story—a justified and justifiable[3] intelligible formulation, to narrate, explain, recite a record of events, make known to another, provide relevant information, describe, state reasons/causes/grounds in explanation to vindicate one's conduct with reference to a judgment. To make a situation accountable to each other is to give comprehensible descriptions and explanations of a situation. Accounts, to be comprehensible, require a situation—and the situation is constituted by the accounts that occur in it. In such conversations commitments are generated for the speaker and the hearer, leading to the possibility of certain actions. People can manipulate each other's behavior by establishing conditions necessary (but not always sufficient) for desired outcomes (goals) to occur.
- To "account for" is to explain why, to provide a view of a situation for an outsider.
- To "take account of/into account" is to consider, or allow for, accounts of our own or others' actions.
- "On account of" is an explanation—because of, for the sake of.
- To "be held accountable for" is to be deemed responsible for one's acts, to be expected to be able to account for your actions—to explain and justify them.

An account is a story told about organizational life—an organization is a sea of accounting as coworkers go about their day-to-day activities of explaining and justifying their decisions and actions. Yet, "accounts are not just in and about the situation; they are it" (Taylor & Van Every 2000, p. 11). This, then, is a self-organizing (human) system.

Organization is the product of the accounting process—the making of accounts is a social achievement of talk in interaction. An account is itself a social activity. An account is addressed to second persons who monitor, understand, receive, and so on, and who are involved in a situation with a first person actor or performer.

---

[3] A justification is the expression of some fact or circumstance that shows an action to be reasonable or necessary, or reasoning in defense or explanation.

Such an account is context-dependent and personal. Participants are personified, related as persons, and present to one another in a situation. They talk about an action or activity to render it rational and reportable for practical purposes for those who confront it or are involved in it.

The making of accounts of one's own and others' activities and decisions is organization in action—accounting is not a personal accomplishment—it is interactionally accomplished. Our experience of other agencies arises in the relation between them and us—both contribute to the outcome of a situation. Of a second person, we would ask "What are you doing?'. Of a third person (in a triadic social grouping), the query would be "What is she or it doing?" In each case, we seek meaning for the situation. Thus, accounting (verb) is done as a first person within the action, for a second person, by further action. Alternatively, an account is given as a third-person outsider who breaks off from the action to observe, judge, or critique. Beyond the scientific notion of objectivity, the first person has the right to tell and to be taken seriously as meaning what is intended. What matters is how the account of the situation is used: as a first-person, present-tense, self-descriptive statement (a confessional telling), as a reporting of fact, as an expectation, or as an appraisal.

Conversational analysis reveals the strong tendency for conversations to proceed in ordered pairs or adjacency pairs (Sacks, 1992). The action of the first person speaking calls forth a particular kind of response from the follower. Typical conversation pairings are greeting–greeting, question–answer, invitation–acceptance or rejection, request–compliance or refusal, and so on. Social accounts may be the first or second component in the pairing. When it is the first entry in a conversation pairing, an account serves the purpose of scene setting for pursuit of a goal. When it is the second entry in a pairing, an account is a response to an act of blame or accusation, and will take the form of excuses, justifications, reparation, and so on.

The concept of accounts, accountings, and accountability has been explored in a number of studies (Garfinkel, 1967; Harre, 1979; Harre & Secord, 1972; McHugh, Raffel, Foss, & Blum, 1974; Mills, 1940; Scott & Lyman, 1968; Shotter, 1984; Tompkins & Cheney, 1983). We can find discussion in the communication sciences, sociology, and psychology of coping mechanisms deployed in instances where social norms are violated by personal behavior to result in disapproval or sanctions. In this sense, accounts are "statements made to explain untoward behavior and bridge the gap between actions and expectations" (Scott & Lyman, 1968, p. 46). Accounts are called for because we need to understand each other's actions by linking unusual, unanticipated, special, puzzling, untoward, suspicious, or enigmatic behavior to a more familiar, intelligible everyday pattern of behavior, with reference to people's intuitive knowledge of the normative structure of everyday social life. Benoit's (1995) study of image restoration in situations of attack-defense also draws on this form of account, as well as the notion of apologia, as does other recent work on impression management and crisis management (Bromley, 1993; Giacalone & Rosenfeld, 1989; Schlenker, 1980).

Schonbach's (1990) taxonomy of accounts, in this sense, is probably the most widely known scheme. This provides a classification into four types of account: concessions, excuses, justifications, and refusals. These are of the "how do you account for your actions" type. A person making a *concession* acknowledges a problematic action, accepts responsibility, and expresses remorse for his or her action, offers compensation, or, promises prospective different behavior in accordance with the others' normative expectations. People using *excuses* attempt to reduce responsibility for their actions by claiming external cause or absence of intention. In giving a *justification,* an actor attempts to alter others' interpretations of his or her actions by minimizing the importance of violated standards or by advocating alternate standards that show his or her behavior to be good. The *refusal* form of account is a denial of the occurrence of an untoward event, denial of involvement, or stated inability to give the reasons for the action.

In the other sense, making an account—a definition and explanation of the situation—is what people do together with a purpose. This is the sense of account that is of interest here, and it is distinct from concessions, excuses, and refusals. In this form of accounting, a situation is constructed by those who attempt to explain and characterize their circumstances to choose, or justify, a course of action. Our speech reflects and creates our experience of reality, and the process of accounting (account-making) is central to this (Shotter, 1984). In conversation we make demands on one another in regard to how to behave, and what to think. We can recognize this when observing the rise of accountability and responsibility in the management field. We assign meaning to and make sense of our experiences, and this is determined, at least in part, by the language we use to account for, as participants, the events.

As participants, or observers, we have an interest in controlling the meaning of events. Accounts are a way of accomplishing goals, reframing events by creating a context in which to interpret them. Accounts of states of affairs are a common feature of human behavior toward others—defining a situation, before, during, or after the event, as the basis for justifying a personally desirable course of action; for example, "It is an exceptionally large class this semester, so I need tutor support if the students are to have a high-quality educational experience," or "We marked the selling price down because we had too much stock on the shelf." By giving an account, a participant attempts to control the meaning of a situation. Goal-directed accounts are particular portrayals of an actual or possible situation in support of, or counter to, the preferred anticipated outcomes of the accounters. They are goal-setting proposals that are used to make sensible and desirable the accounter's preferred goals: "To preserve their autonomy, people must be able to account, not only for their actions, but also for themselves, i.e. who and what they are" (Shotter, 1984, p. 5).

Accounts refer to beliefs, motives, desires, imaginings, and so on, to discover what can be done by their use. To account, in this sense, is not to illustrate, depict, or represent—to reproduce one's behavior—but to communicate something about what one's behavior was, is, or might be. Such talk is an explicit description of what the action is (to distinguish it from what it is not), rather than a causal theory that explains the behavior in terms of events or objects existing prior to it. The speech act describes the behavior as something explainable in the familiar everyday language and experience of the social group.

Potential accounts are what we would say if we had to explain our actions to others. These shape our actions before we do them. We believe we have the power to act, by complying with or breaking social rules (norms), and we expect to have to explain our actions, done or planned, on the basis of these rules or exceptions to them.

People give accounts of their own actions as well as those of others. These may be anticipatory (prospective), retrospective, or contemporaneous with events and objects (Harre & Secord, 1972). Each may be an indicator of future action, by describing the goal sought through current or past action, or by explicating criteria or standards applied as the grounds for action as acceptable, legitimate, appropriate, and so on. For example:

- "We/You should do A, because B ..."
- "I did C, because the situation was D."
- "I have to do this because ..."

Consider, for example, an annual budget review that shows that during a period of widely recognized growth in activities and resources, the expenditures of the central services group of a large institution have grown much more rapidly than those of the other constituent groups. Group managers speculate in discussions about how the accounts that they can suggest for this situation might be different from or similar to an account that is likely to be given on request by the chief officer. This theme of developing a common account can be found in Güney's study (chap. 2, this volume).

Accounts are descriptions and explanations of a situation using ordinary language—personal and collective or official versions of an intelligible environment that makes sense—saying what is happening. However, the sense is not carried by the events, rather it is constructed in the communicative interaction[4] of the participants—in their talking—in their sensemaking. Accounts can be evaluated as right–wrong, accurate–inaccurate, adequate–inadequate, true–false, good–bad, and so on. We can evaluate each others' accounts as satisfactory, inspirational, helpful, or misguided, ill informed, sense or nonsense, unprofessional, incomplete, risky, and so on—to serve a purpose.

Talking and making accounts determines how reality is experienced, and the experience of reality affects communication. Shotter (1984) drew on Giambattista

---

[4]Reason-giving in interaction, or reasoning together, can be thought of as dialogue (dialogical interaction). Such accounting together produces coaccountings: alignment, common understandings, and potential commitment to coact further.

Vico's work in showing that human phenomena are understandable in a way that natural phenomena are not, and that this requires precise historical detail of how particular knowledge came about and why it came to be accorded a place in human affairs. Accordingly, Shotter showed that forms of life provide grounds for ways of speaking, which provide grounds for theories that we deploy in structuring common accounting practices that work to structure our everyday activities. The process turns full circle. Account analysis has been proposed as a research strategy for the study of decision making and identification (Tompkins & Cheney, 1983). In asking social actors to account for their actions, researchers can invoke the realization of anticipated actions (plans), commentaries on action in process, and accounts in retrospect. Otherwise, all that exists is the readiness to account (Harre & Secord, 1972).

Accountable (i.e., explainable) social actions are, and have to be, observable and reportable, as a precondition for action. Further, the accounting is part of the activities described in the accounting. This form of accounting is understood in the field of ethnomethodology, drawing on the pioneering work of Garfinkel on language use in constituting social relations and social reality (Garfinkel, 1967; Heritage, 1984; Sharrock & Anderson, 1986). Here it is not the descriptive accounts of states of affairs (or accountings, to use Garfinkel's preferred term) per se, but the accounting practices that are of interest. It seems to me that managing is an accounting practice, with a central concern for adequate description, and that several specific forms of, or purposes of, accounting have become more prominent in recent times in discussions of corporate social responsibility and relationship management.

Socially constructed institutions are reproduced and transformed by the accountable activities of people in interdependent (joint) action as they make sense of what they do together. Common sense is made through accounting practices. In conversation we make demands on one another in regard to how to behave, and what to think. What we can talk about, and how, bears on how we relate socially with one another. Note how relate in this sense has a similar meaning to account or tell.

IMPLICATIONS FOR MANAGING

What do we see if we approach management from the perspective of organizational communication to find communication practices of humans engaged in collective, coordinated, and goal-oriented behavior mediated by accounts?

Management is commonly understood as disciplined decision making, planning, organizing, leading, and controlling. Management, through command and control of resources, mediates evolving wants and evolving capabilities to deal with change. This is accomplished through goal-directed productive enterprise: action to accomplish desired results, the allocation of resources, and the organization of people and work. The self-image of the effective manager is as decision maker, strategist, planner, initiator, and chooser.

Yet if language use (speech), as a tool of interaction, is not only representative (saying, expressive, locution), but also performative (doing, instrumental, illocution), that is, consequential action—doing by and in saying, then managing is a communicative act, and not merely action, optionally with the use of communication tools. This was elaborated by Taylor and Van Every (2000). The commonplace explanation of management, however, is not at the level of purposeful interaction—mostly, the transmission of information is assumed.

However, different people have different points of view on the world. Accounts, thus, may be contradictory, conflicting, and inconsistent, as we see in Güney's study (chap. 2, this volume). The transmissive conception of communication (noun) helps to explain expression of a point of view in pursuit of a predetermined outcome (goal). In following Dewey (1910), Penman (2000) promoted the alternative of communicating (verb) as a way of proceeding.

Earlier chapters in this volume have applied the communicational theory of organizing to cases to show that the essence of being organized is teleacting, knowing, and integrating or differentiating; that is, doing, with knowledge, together. Several implications arise from this. To do is to cause to do—there is appropriation[5] of the actions of others. Knowledge is a resource for, and a product of, situated interactions. Ambiguity is an inevitable consequence of being simultaneously different and unified, and is valuable as an integrative mode of organizing (see Katambwe & Taylor's study in chap. 4, this volume). Action, knowledge, and integration are communicative achievements or enactments, rather than tools or techniques used through the means of effective communication in organizations. Communication and organization are not separate, but rather the latter arises in the former.

We can better understand the process of managing as a way of proceeding, rather than the object management (again after Dewey). People manage in talking. For example, knowledge is never transmitted, but rather knowing is done communicatively. With this understanding of information, knowledge, and communication, ICT (Information and Communication Technologies) is not a repository and carrier of information—knowing is the product of interaction for directed activity. Management knowledge is constructed (done) in translating the material, social, and linguistic aspects of a situation in coorientation—a particular rationality of the community of practice that we term management.

Talk is the work of managers. Account-ability is the social competence of being able to provide plausible or credible explanations of what they do (accountings) together with reasonableness in terms of compliance and cooperation. Accounts are used to construct positions to realize action and outcome agendas. They are explanations of actions that lead to consequences, and explanations of situations that legitimize preferred actions.

As Boden (1994) pointed out, accounts (in the form of reports, summaries, position statements, etc.) are central to processes of coalescing the differing goals and

---

[5]Take possession of, or devote to special purposes.

agendas of specific actors in particular action settings into "what happens" in the organized whole of action together. Situational interpretations and accounts are "not simply post hoc rationalizations of action but are continuously updated, revised, redefined and realigned ... reflexively" (p. 180).

Actions are observable and accountable as actors make sense of their shared activities, as knowledgeable agents in the production and reproduction of their lives together in their intersubjectively accomplished social order. It is in making their activities accountable that they produce and reproduce self-organizing social structure in their interaction.

LIFE BEYOND THE CONDUIT

In adopting the conduit metaphor for communication, management is taken to be a control mechanism located in a fixed structure. This is an instrumental model that treats communication as a means to a predetermined end, that of control of the receiver by the sender. This is fundamental to the rhetoric of science and alien to that of art.

The traditional communication studies field (on which the management studies field uncritically draws) has grown from the seed of Shannon and Weaver's transmissive model of communication, and should now be abandoned. No serious communication theorist would still accept this model uncritically, but it has been the most influential and reflects common sense, yet is misleading. The endurance of the informational model of communication in popular discussion is a liability. In reflecting the naive realist notion of meanings as preexistent and to be discovered so that we can transmit our thoughts to each other, this model fundamentally devalues the creativity of the act of appreciation in which sensing, meaning, valuing, judging, and selecting is crucial (Vickers, 1983). We should abandon unreflective (managerialistic) accounts of communication management, and turn more attention to reflective (managerial) approaches.

The alternative participatory conception of communication promotes organization as patterned social interactions in structured human relationships (mutual, but not necessarily shared, expectations), but does not inherently and covertly support the deployment of power over others. In a turbulent social milieu, the manager role makes more sense as that of steward of a responsive and responsible productive community. As router and filter in the shunting of information between isolates, the manager has no value-creating role.

Most of us are still operating in outmoded instrumental-technical modes in pursuit of control—communication is seen as a conduit for the transmission or transportation of expressions of self-interest (i.e., informational for understanding)—but these no longer suffice. Information conceptions of communication only work in situations in which consensus on meaning, identities, construction of knowledge, and basic values can be taken for granted. This is no longer a realistic view of our world. If we control through information systems, we are in danger of nonresponsive self-referentiality—what Hayek (1990) called the fatal conceit—we do not ask questions because we think we have the answers. Some crucial questions are never asked. Imaginary worlds are misrecognized as real. Management practice distorts, manufactures (artificial) consent, excludes, and suppresses differences—asymmetrical power relations suppress natural conflicts. Social divisions are assumed to be fixed and in need of promotion. Consensus over problems, personal identities, knowledge claims, norms of interaction, and policies for directing joint action are assumed as the basis for interaction, when they need to be negotiated through interaction for creativity and to meet diverse stakeholder interests. When the corporation is taken to be the senior management team, all other stakeholders are externalized as costs to be contained. Then, stakeholders are managed for the managers' benefit. Such a biased or particular (even peculiar) view is, of course, to be expected in a field of strategic endeavor, it can be argued. And that is true. It is also true that management is so pervasive a way of thinking—it has been used to colonize so much of our life experience—that we generally talk in managerial terms.

We must shift from our general belief in liberal quasi-democracy and its adversarial expression of self-interest, opinion advocacy, and persuasion, to a constitutive real participatory democracy of negotiated codetermination through interaction ("It's good to talk" is a moral stance). We need to move from controlling to stewardship, but this requires a mind shift from self-interest to service, from patriarchy to partnership, from consent to coordination, from dependency to empowerment, and from involvement to participation.

Communications are best understood as interaction acts, not as objects and artefacts. We communicate in some of our interaction. Communication is best understood as constitutive—interests should be understood as social products, often produced by decisions and opportunities. The moral question is this: Are all positions granted an equal right of codetermination? Morally, psychology pursues reflective autonomy (of the person), sociology pursues legitimate social order (of the collective), and communication pursues equal participation (in the social system). We need a communicational theory of managing—this is largely a personal value decision—about why, rather than about how.

We no longer have a universal sense of total cosmos (an ordered, predictable structure)—the (post)modern world is at least partially chaotic (largely formless, highly ambiguous flow). There is no longer fundamental consensus on what things mean; interaction has become about values and differing meanings. We no longer have a stable, homogenous society. The problem of inadequate communication is not merely one of divergent understandings but one of divergent interests. We need real communication, not more or better communication. Interaction can no longer be the expression and transmission of meaning (an information process). It has to be about the construction and negotiation of meaning (a communication process). Communication is a regulator, bringing balance in the middle ground between pathological order and self-defeating chaos. Communicating is negotiating between both too much order and too little order. This new approach set out in this volume emphasizes text that structures by reinstating the past order of things, and conversation that evolves and restlessly searches for accommodations that become, in their turn, tomorrow's frameworks for action (see Taylor & Robichaud, 2004).

Practice and theory, of course, can diverge. For example, marketing is theorized as participative (i.e., voluntary exchange or a negotiative constitution), but is mostly practiced as strategic or consensual (a dominant constitution supported by systematic distortions). For example, advertising is almost always the dominant expression and is selected as the means of communication because it is so. Yet, goals cannot be preconceived, but are codeterminate. In selecting a course of action, each participant considers "If I did that, they would/might do that ...." Each takes into account the other. Everyone can give an account, and takes into account the others' accounts, toward coorientation.

Organizing can be explained as a dialectic of conversation and spoken or written text—shifting, temporarily stable contingent discursive practices and constructions—rather than as a continuously stable, physical or material site of purposeful action. This is precisely what is specific to the approach developed in this book, and it is this feature that differentiates this approach from other contemporary communication theories. Managing is a form of authoring (Weick, 1995)—of the network of accumulated (sedimented) texts that constitute the state of organization. Managing is the authoring of a conversation in which the task is not choosing solutions to a self-serving, self-evident problem, but the generating of a shareable linguistic formulation of current actualities and further possible actions. Thus the managerial text is a string of statements focused on a topic or expressing a point of view. Management is a community of practice in which certain forms of account are institutionalized. To be organizational, each has to be part of a larger corpus of texts of members. Each text is made jointly accessible by interactors through their speech together. Such collective narratives are contested and negotiated accounts.

Corporative relationships make possible a wider range of collective responses for and by a working society, but physical and organic models of such systems are inadequate when they fail to account for the frame of mutual expectation within which human communication takes place. Communicating can be conceived of as information transmission between stable entities, or as the interactional coproduction of knowledge, meaning, and identity—and organization as a complex, living (self-organizing) human system (Vickers, 1983).

Perhaps it is time to replace the term *corporate communications* with *corporative communication* and *relationship management* with *interaction management*. Management educators and researchers must stop promoting convenient, simplistic conceptions of communication if this is to come about. That will require much greater reflection on the nature and purpose of models of communication. Social constructionists may even deny the appropriateness of modeling communication at all, although the authors in this volume, collectively, do suggest a direction for such modeling.

The accounting concept has profound implications for the practice of research on the social phenomenon of management. Reports "that it is ..." from third-person scientist-observers do not provide the explanations of why it is as it is that the first-person accounter of managing can provide as a person-author.

CHAPTER ELEVEN

The Montréal School
and the Question of Agency[1]

Boris H. J. M. Brummans
Université de Montréal

> *An alignment of the universe along moral lines, not intellectual ones.*
>
> —Martel (2001, p. 70)

Almost a century ago, Dewey (1922) noted that people are inclined to regard those who ask questions about morality or ethics[2] with suspicion for they could be moralists. Raising these questions is still a risky business, especially in academic fields where scholars tend to abstract spectator-theories of human behavior by taking bird's-eye views on objects of knowledge and distancing themselves from the world of human infightings about conflicting moralities (Deetz, 1992; Dewey, 1939).

We may discern a similar inclination in organizational communication studies when it comes to addressing the question of agency and structure. Indeed, scholars in this field may ask what it means to act, how it is that action means something, and, more exactly, how organization is possible through communicative action. However, although there are exceptions, it seems that organizational communication scholars interested in this question generally stay away from bringing ethics to the forefront of their work. Through this chapter, I hope to contribute to the language game (Wittgenstein, 1953) about the relation between communication, agency, and organization by centralizing ethics and suggesting how the ideas presented in this volume can benefit from such a focus. To develop this perspective, I begin with clarifying the motivations behind my writing.

---

[1] I wrote this chapter, having just arrived at the Université de Montréal. Possible misunderstandings, misreadings, overinterpretations, or underinterpretations of the works of my new colleagues are mine. I kindly thank James Taylor in particular for his open participation in conversations about the school which provided this text with its footing.

[2] Ethics, I argue, are ground rules for moral conduct constituted in, rather than applied to, communication. Accordingly, I agree with Evens (1999), who defined ethics as "the creative and paradoxically natural *conduct* whereby humans together inform themselves and their world, both wittingly and not, with second-nature or value" (p. 7, italics added).

THE CONCEPTUALIZATION, ATTRIBUTION, AND APPROPRIATION OF AGENCY

People give different meanings to the terms *agency* and *action*. Peeking in *Merriam-Webster's Collegiate Dictionary* (1998) is more bewildering than enlightening. We find that agency denotes the "office or function of an agent," the "capacity, condition, or state of acting or of exerting power," or the "person or thing through which power is exerted or an end is achieved." Thus, the term may signify a function or capacity attributed to an agent as well as the agent itself. Looking up *action* is just as mystifying. It denotes "the bringing about of an alteration by force or through a natural agency," "an act of will," "a thing done," "the manner in which [something] operates," "the movement of incidents in a plot," or "the most vigorous, productive, or exciting activity in a particular field, area, or group." Hence, action might refer to (intentionally or unintentionally) doing something, that which has been (or is) done, or the way something has been (or is) done.

Although I lean toward a pragmatist view of action in that I see life as a stream of interconnecting actions with mutually impinging consequences,[3] I do not seek to resolve this unresolvable language game. Rather, I hope to propel this game by asking how the act of conceptualizing, attributing, and appropriating agency produces consequences for individual and collective, human and nonhuman agents (e.g., trade unionists, journalists, scholars, world leaders, grizzly bears, satellites, iPods, Greenpeace, Apple, the University of Cambridge, national parks, or nations, and, not to forget, ourselves). Wrestling with this question creates an opportune moment for discussing ethics because the conceptualization, attribution, and appropriation of agency implies the enactment of principles of conduct that are developed through processes of valuation (Dewey, 1939). To illustrate the relation between agency and ethics, let us look at the domestication of scallops in the Saint Brieuc Bay on the Atlantic coast of France, which Callon (1986) used to explain actor network theory.

Having discovered an artificial way to cultivate scallops, Japanese scientists joined with representatives of the Saint Brieuc Bay fishery to counter the declining scallop catches in this region. All seemed well, other than that the scallops "refused to 'collaborate'" (Cooren & Taylor, 1997, p. 241) by attaching themselves to the installed breeding collectors. The conceptualization, attribution, and appropriation of agency is important in this instance. It is possible, for example, to attribute agency to the Japanese scientists and French fishery representatives by abstracting them as agents from an ongoing stream of activities and imbuing them with different kinds of agency. However, this would leave out some crucial nonhuman agents,

---

[3]To act is to participate in this stream. "Things" (human beings, animals, machines, texts, organizations) act, even if they are "lying around doing nothing." While acting, things are acted on; they interact. Accordingly, and in line with Dewey's thinking (see Cronen & Chetro-Szivos, 2001), the cause of a consequence does not differ in character from the consequence itself, even if human beings employ words such as cause and consequence to order their existence. What causes and is caused are matters of perspective—or, as I argue, a matter of conceptualizing, attributing, and appropriating agency.

the scallops. We might think of other human and nonhuman agents as well, in addition to the ones mentioned. The sea, subjected to experimentation, could be an important agent, for example, or the French government, which allowed and encouraged this experimentation. The act of adding, subtracting, or simply leaving out agents has thus important bearings on who and what participates—and is allowed to participate—in collective activities, whether involving the artificial cultivation of scallops, a demonstration against the "war on terror," or the publication of an edited volume on communication as organizing.

In line with this reasoning, I argue that the act of conceptualizing, attributing, and appropriating agency, whoever performs it, implicates the practice of ethics, because such an act affects who or what is given the agency to produce consequences that might be considered right, wrong, aesthetically pleasing, important, insignificant, cool, and so on. To develop this argument in the context of the Montréal school (hereafter, mostly referred to as the school), I start in the next section by locating the school in the agency and structure language game of organizational communication studies. Patently, the school also positions itself—and is positioned—in other fields, such as linguistics (pragmatics in particular; see Taylor & Cooren, 1996; Xie, 2002), psychology (see Weick, 2001a), informatics (see Van Every & Taylor, 1998), semiotics (see Cooren, 1999), and organization and management studies (see Glynn, 2002). However, I do not investigate the school's positioning within these other social spaces. Then, I explain how the school's presuppositions bear a resemblance to the presuppositions which drove early pragmatists like Dewey to fuse questions of ethics and action or agency. Subsequently, I capitalize on this resemblance to suggest how the ideas presented in this volume can provide us with excellent springboards for lifting the agency and structure language game to a new level that confronts the question of agency from an ethical point of view. In closing, I briefly consider the research implications of my argument.

LOCATING THE MONTRÉAL SCHOOL IN ORGANIZATIONAL COMMUNICATION STUDIES

Locating a school in academic social space is in itself an act of conceptualizing and attributing agency. Through my actions, I abstract a set of agents who operate from a more or less similar set of presuppositions out of a stream of interconnecting actions, club them together, and call them "a school." I do not deny that individual agents within the Montréal school take more or less diverging perspectives on, and employ more or less divergent methodologies to study the equivalence between organizing and communicating; this volume, in fact, demonstrates this plurality. However, most of the scholars associated with this school do operate from relatively similar presuppositions. For example, they share a common belief in the importance of studying action, have been strongly influenced by the writings—and in many cases teachings—of Taylor, are familiar with a more or less similar body of literature, and, perhaps most important, conceive of communication as organizing. In this chapter, I prioritize this commonality rather than the school's plurivocality.

Based on another delineation, we can situate the school in the field of scholars who constitute organizational communication studies as a social space. As I have pointed out elsewhere (Brummans, 2004), organizational communication studies, as any academic field of study or school of thought within a field, is enacted through various language games that revolve around antinomies (fundamental intellectual contradictions or conflicts) (see also Bourdieu, 2000; Bourdieu & Wacquant, 1992). As Collins (2000) has suggested, conflicting ideas chauffeur intellectual life:

> To deny the point is to exemplify it. Yet, there is no intellectual war of all against all. Not warring individuals but a small number of warring camps is the pattern of intellectual history. Intellectual conflict is structured by the focus of attention on a few topics by alliances within factions. Conflict is the energy source of intellectual life, and conflict is limited by itself. (p. 158)

We find, then, that a field of study or a school enacts or organizes itself by distinguishing itself in relation to other fields or schools. Antinomic language games, in turn, enable and constrain this organizing. This notion suits the argument made by the Montréal school that organization and communication are intimately linked through conversation and text (Cooren, 2000a, 2004b; Cooren & Taylor, 1997; Robichaud, 1999; Taylor, 1993, 1999; Taylor, Cooren, Giroux, & Robichaud, 1996; Taylor & Robichaud, 2004; Taylor & Van Every, 2000). In other words, a field or school organizes itself in communication by ordering social action in conversation mediated by texts. In case of academic organizations like a field or school, this theory seems unusually applicable because "textwork" (Van Maanen, 1996) quite literally instates these social entities. Textwork denotes all those practices performed to produce a publication, such as note taking, reading, outlining, conversing and corresponding with colleagues, or drafting. Textwork "does things." That is, through these more or less regulated activities, an agent (individual or collective) makes himself, herself, or itself public and "officializes," ratifies, or legitimizes a positioning in social space (see Bourdieu, 1990; see also Latour & Woolgar, 1986).

Of course, we can take this volume in itself as an example of this principle, for it shows how a text enacts a school as a school.[4] That is, although the exact inception of the Montréal school is difficult to determine, it is a fact that the school was instated, and is reinstated, through its writings. Many of these writings directly or indirectly contribute to the agency and structure language game that constitutes an important part of the field of organizational communication studies. As Conrad and Haynes (2001) have argued, scholars position themselves in different, more or less

---

[4]Other publications (e.g., Cooren, 2000b; Robichaud, 2000; Taylor, 2000) corroborate this observation as well.

opposing, ways in this game. Some scholars, for example, cluster in a faction that privileges structure over action by foregrounding the idea that organizations are constituted as relatively objective social systems that circumscribe agents' actions. A second faction privileges social action over structure by highlighting the idea that autonomous agents enact organizations. Finally, other scholars attempt to integrate agency and structure by utilizing, for example, structuration theory, the theory of unobtrusive control and identification, or critical theory.

It is surprising that Conrad and Haynes's (2001) text does not refer to the role of the Montréal school in this language game, especially because this school expressly sets out to develop a reformulation of this antinomic conundrum by arguing that texts mediate the conversation between agents, but that conversations also produce texts. Thus, organizational structuring occurs because human interactions are mediated by nonhuman agents (including "objects" like texts or language more generally) that constrain and enable these interactions, give them a relatively lasting character in time and space, and allow the translation of individual into collective action (Cooren & Taylor, 1997; Taylor & Giroux, 2005). The school therefore refuses to locate agency in a subject or object, maintaining that agency emanates in networks of interacting human and nonhuman agents. Hence, unlike the aforementioned structurationist, unobtrusive control and identification, or critical approaches, the Montréal school contends that organizational life is "spatially and temporally ordered." This is not "because of a sui generis entity called 'the organization,' which would structure its own activities a priori, but by the human and nonhuman (including textual) interactants who not only contribute to its orderly emergence but also re-present it" (Cooren & Fairhurst, 2004, p. 819).

Unlike Conrad and Haynes, Fairhurst and Putnam (1999, 2004; see also Putnam & Fairhurst, 2001) foreground the ideas of the Montréal school. In their most recent effort, for instance, Fairhurst and Putnam (2004) developed a typology of orientations underpinning the study of organizations as discursive constructions. The first interpretation of the relation between discourse and organization assumes that the organization is an object formed prior to discourse, although this object's features and outcomes are reflected in discourse. In the second interpretation, an organization is in an unremitting state of becoming through discourse; in this case, discourse exists prior to organization. Fairhurst and Putnam mainly situated the Montréal school in their last category, which grounds organization in communicative action and presumes that an organization does not take its form outside such action. Nonetheless, the authors argued, a book like *The Emergent Organization* (Taylor & Van Every, 2000) is not to be pigeonholed, because it invokes each of these orientations. That is, it invokes

> the object orientation by arguing that organizations, once they are constructed as texts, become objects with real material constraints around which actors must orient. [It invokes] the becoming orientation when [examining] the formative power of conversational sentence structures and story grammars that grow out of texts. Finally, [it invokes] the grounded in action approach by arguing that the or-

ganization exists at the intersection between text and conversation. (Fairhurst & Putnam, 2004, pp. 21–22)

I believe that Fairhurst and Putnam's texts that discuss and appropriate the ideas of the Montréal school provide fitting examples of how the uptake of scholarly texts helps to instate and reinstate a school of thought and give it prevalence in a field. In other words, their appropriations of texts produced by the Montréal school contribute to the enactment of the school, as well as its social recognition in organizational communication studies. It is through this intertextualization, then, that the school has become a macro-agent (Callon & Latour, 1981) in itself, constituting a collective voice that speaks on behalf of its individual agents within the field.

Interestingly, this example also illustrates that attributing agency to a collective agent involves valuation (Dewey, 1939). Fairhurst and Putnam could have appropriated other scholars' texts and thereby furthered the institution of another school of thought, yet they chose to bring the texts of the Montréal school to the fore. This choice involves the practice of ethics, because it implies the enactment of principles that determine what texts are compelling and convincing. As Collins (1998, 2000) has noted, academic eminence is a function of the actor network density between scholarly agents. My example suggests that this is also true for the Montréal school. That is, like any school of thought, this school exists in the communication that constitutes "a community of speech making before assembled audiences and of focused discussion and argument [which] records its judgments in a cross-referenced chain of words and texts that are given the status of 'knowledge' or 'truth'" (pp. 159–160).

However, the notion that textual agency (Cooren, 2004b) plays an important role in the institution of a school can also be demonstrated by taking the textwork of scholars who criticize the Montréal school into account, because such disagreement inspires an academic language game and legitimates its continued enactment. The work of organizational communication scholar McPhee (2004) offers perhaps the best example here.

Contrary to the Montréal school's positioning, we see that McPhee's view of organizing foregrounds a structurationist conception of human agency, based on the idea that agents reflexively monitor the flow of their social life and can account for the reasons behind their actions in language (Giddens, 1984). This view implies an "internalist" view of agency, centering organization in the social capabilities and powers of specifically human agents (see Robichaud, chap. 6, this volume). Moreover, while discussing *The Emergent Organization*, McPhee critiques Taylor and Van Every's (2000) conception of a text, suggesting that they do not sufficiently emphasize "the durability of the material medium" on which a text is written, "or the special technologies of production and processing of texts such as personnel records and financial data as texts that have important organizational consequences" (McPhee, 2004, p. 368). McPhee stated, in turn:

> Although I concur that collective memory of meaning and relational implica-
> tions of linguistic and narrative grammars are important in the constitution of or-
> ganizations, I think that the specific contribution of structured, inscribed
> symbolic formulations has distinctive importance that Taylor and Van Every
> elide in developing their broad sense of the term *text.* (p. 368)

By generally positioning himself in opposition to the Montréal school in texts,
McPhee reinforces the polemic of the agency and structure language game of organizational communication studies. In so doing, he, like Fairhurst and Putnam,
helped to instate and reinstate the Montréal school as a macro-agent in the field by
attributing agency to the school's ideas. However, his own textualizations also reinforce the structurationist school, which identifies his own positioning in the field
(see McPhee, 1985). Hence, through his textwork, McPhee appropriates agency as
well. The constitutive effect of this kind of "textual rivalry" is best exemplified
when McPhee and Trethewey (2000) charged Taylor and Van Every with an "un-
characteristically demeaning reading given to Anthony Giddens' (1981) work."
That is, in their text, McPhee and Trethewey argued that Taylor and Van Every un-
duly critiqued Giddens for omitting Latour's concept of mediation, because they
ignored Giddens's "mediational analysis of capital, cities, the clock, and so on in
his most organizationally relevant work, published in 1981." In turn, McPhee and
Trethewey noted, their "theory could have profited from the attention to time and
space, as well as to power and large-scale social reality, that structuration theory
provides (McPhee, 1985)" (pp. 333–334).

Having located the Montréal school in one of the principal language games of
organizational communication studies, I now take the situating of the school in social space one step further by arguing that its fundamental presuppositions parallel
those of early American pragmatism, in particular Dewey's kind (for discussions
on this pragmatism, see, e.g., Diggins, 1994; Lewis & Smith, 1980; Menand, 1997;
Perry, 2001).

A COINCIDENCE OF PRAGMATIST PRESUPPOSITIONS

It is interesting to notice that the Montréal school interlinks American pragmatism
with "European pragmatism" by appropriating texts from both sides of the Atlantic
Ocean that centralize the consequentiality of action in a world of interactivity. Pragmatism is often mistakenly thought to be distinctly American (Simonson, 2001)—
perhaps partly due to the simplistic notion that Americans are essentially "pragmatic." Nevertheless, European and American scholars, each with their own orientations toward action, have influenced each other for years. Illustrations abound.
Bourdieu's work resonates with Dewey's and Goffman's ideas—Goffman being a
graduate of the Chicago school founded by people like Cooley, Mead, and Dewey.
Rorty has evidenced links between Nietzsche's ideas and those of pragmatists.
Moreover, currently, there is a revival of Peirce's theory of signs and signification in
France (see Robichaud, chap. 6, this volume) and the effect of Dewey's ideas about

the intimate connection between communication and democracy on a critical theorist like Habermas is evident as well.

In developing its perspectives on communication as organizing, the Montréal school frequently draws on works from scholars on both sides of the Atlantic with explicit or implicit pragmatist underpinnings (e.g., the works of Peirce, Dewey, Wittgenstein, or Latour). Indubitably, the coincidence of "pragmatisms" on which the school draws results in part from the school's location in Montréal, Québec, for this geographical intersection facilitates the import and export of ideas across the oceanic divide. The effect of location on the development of ideas is not to be trivialized. Certain texts, authors, or even complete literatures produced on one side of the ocean sometimes never see the light of day on the other side due to poor translation, lack of recognition, or sheer unawareness (e.g., see Wacquant, 1993). Hence, through its simultaneous interaction with European and American scholars, the school frequently bridges this divide and introduces new texts, authors, and literatures to audiences relatively unfamiliar with them.

In the next section, I emphasize the connection between the school and early American pragmatism, because this latter kind of pragmatism systematically centralized the relation between ethics and action or agency. Drawing this connection subsequently enables me to consider how the school's work might be appropriated to confront the question of agency from an ethical point of view.

Presuppositional Coincidences

From the beginning (e.g., see Taylor, 1993, 1995), the Montréal school has focused on developing an actional theory of organizational communication. In line with Peirce's ideas (e.g., see Cooren, 2001b), the school has consistently argued against the notion that organizing occurs monologistically by grounding organization in communicative action and suggesting that signification involves socially developed, organized habits of action, especially those of language. In line with what Dewey suggested more generally, the school postulates, in turn, that organizations exist in communication, not by it. This echoes Wittgenstein's (1953) writings that suggest that language exists in activity and "has no single essence, but is a vast collection of different practices each with its own logic" (Grayling, 1988, p. 67). Correspondingly, the school sees organizations as "life forms" established in language games (see Taylor, 2001b, chap. 8, this volume): Communication (involving the practice of language) enables individuals to express and constitute themselves as agents, yet communication also helps agents to transcend themselves as individuals and to establish social order, for example through teleaction (Cooren, chap. 5, this volume) and coorientation[5] (Taylor &

---

[5]Woodward (2001) placed Newcomb's (1953) coorientation theory, which Taylor and others extend to develop a theory of communicative organizing, at the center of a pragmatist, transactional approach to communication research. This is understandable, because the theory presumes that "it is an almost constant human necessity to orient oneself toward objects in the environment and also toward

Robichaud, 2004; Taylor & Van Every, 2000). Organization is thus not so much an individual, "mentalistic" accomplishment, but a collective one, involving distributed rationalities enacted in conversation between agents (Taylor, 2001b). Organizational knowledge is accordingly a communal affair, circumstantially and situationally achieved through the practice of language (Heaton & Taylor, 2002; Taylor, 2001b). Like many other scholars with a pragmatist inclination (Elias, 1991, 2000; Mead, 1934), then, the school circumvents atomism and encourages "connectionism" (McPhee & Trethewey, 2000, p. 331).

McPhee and Trethewey's label is appropriate, because connectivity forms the nucleus of pragmatist thinking. In line with this presupposition, the Montréal school operates from the idea that there is no clear division between the social and material world: Organization occurs when human agents mobilize other human or nonhuman agents through conversations. In so doing, the subject–object duality becomes foggy and untenable, suggesting that a "'thing' is in action, and 'action' is observable as a thing" (Dewey & Bentley, 1949, p. 123; cited in Woodward, 2001, p. 73). In turn, "language is made up of physical existences [b]ut these do not operate or function as mere physical things when they are the *media* of communication" (Dewey, 1938, p. 46, italics added).

The resemblance between Dewey's words and those of the Montréal school is striking here. As Cooren and Taylor (1997) have explained, for example, it is through *mediation*, that is, through the mobilization of mostly material nonhuman agents (language, texts, fax machines, computers, Palm Pilots, cellular telephones) that the complex of a great many individual voices can be translated into the voice of a macro-agent. For instance, a collectivity of agents may enroll a nonhuman agent by documenting an organizational ethical code. By deferring to this nonhuman agent, agents create possibilities for disciplining each other on behalf of "the organization," that is, without having to rely on their own individual agency. As Cooren and Taylor have pointed out, a text like this might be an artifact, but the consequences of its use are factually experienced—an agent might be fired for ignoring what the text signifies. In this case, the symbolic produces real, material consequences that affect future signification.

Diffusing dualities like the ones between materiality and sociality or subjectivity and objectivity is one of the key characteristics of the Montréal school's textualizations. Pragmatists work from a similar agenda, assuming that life is a stream of interconnected activities, involving a social world that is seamlessly continuous with the natural one (Cronen & Chetro-Szivos, 2001). As this volume shows, the school also aims to explode other dualities, for example, between micro- and

---

other persons oriented toward those same objects" (Newcomb, 1953, p. 395). Woodward also demonstrated the centrality of Bruner's work, known especially for its emphasis on the narrative construction of reality, to pragmatist transactionalism. Montréal school scholars like Taylor, Van Every, Cooren, and Robichaud often rely on Bruner's (as well as Greimas's) writings on narrativity, suggesting yet another link between the school and American pragmatism.

macro-action (Cooren, chap. 5, this volume; Groleau, chap. 9, this volume) or integration and differentiation (Katambwe & Taylor, chap. 4, this volume).

In summary, the coincidence of presuppositions between the Montréal school and early pragmatism is strong, particularly in terms of their emphasis on action as interactivity and connectivity, the habitual nature of human life in relation to non-humans, the formation of all meaning in communication, and the detonation of dualisms. Nonetheless, we can also observe one important difference. Whereas early pragmatists like Mead and Dewey, and Habermas (1984) and Deetz (1992) more recently, have underlined communication as "the stuff of *morally authentic* communities pursuing common ends and cognizant of themselves as a collective" (Simonson, 2001, p. 9, italics added), the school does not centralize questions of morality and ethics in their studies of communication as organizing. For pragmatists, Dewey especially, communication is a way to democracy, to a more pluralistic universe (see Shepherd, 2001).

Thinking about organizational communication necessitates thought about the question of valuation, then, as well as about the responsibility which the heightened consciousness gained through this contemplation induces. As Saussure (1974) and Cassirer (1942) suggested, it is through the linguistic practice of valuation (implying matters of classification) that things become differentiated (Deetz, 1992). Within language games, that is, agents constitute the world in terms of categories (teacher–apprentice, lord–serf, master–slave, man–nature, man–woman, friend–fiend, citizen–alien). Through valuation in communication, in other words, agents regulate and control participation in the construction and reconstruction of social life.

In what follows, I suggest that valuation is inseparably tied to the conceptualization, attribution, and appropriation of agency. In so doing, I indicate how the ideas offered in this volume (and, without too great a stretch, many of the school's other writings) present springboards for investigating the relation between these two activities as an integral part of communicative organizing. It is through such investigation in particular, I believe, that the organizational communication language game about the duality between agency and structure, in which the Montréal school plays an important role, can continue to make a difference.

SPRINGBOARDS FOR ETHICALLY CONFRONTING THE QUESTION OF AGENCY

According to a pragmatist like Dewey, to act is to produce consequences based on a particular kind of valuation. Action implies to act on ideas about what it means to be right, wrong, righteous, wicked, scientific, pseudoscientific, empirical, metaphysical, and so on. Values are the "aims or purposes governing action," which "become more concretely specified as possible courses of action are considered in reflection" (Craig, 2001, p. 137). They guide interaction while interacting, rather than being applied to it. Valuation, then, is part of action and, as such, involves linguistic differentiation. The idea that valuation is inseparable from other kinds of action is important, because life would not be possible otherwise. As Schumacher (1995) noted,

> Ortega y Gasset once remarked that "life is fired at us point-blank." We cannot say: "Hold it! I am not quite ready. Wait until I have sorted things out." Decisions have to be taken that we are not ready for; aims have to be chosen that we cannot see clearly. (p. 15)

For instance, the separation of valuation from other actions would be quite detrimental for a hunting lioness:

> Imagine that she first observed the prey, then observed the position of the other lionesses, then selected a moment to move, and then responded to each of the prey's moves one by one. If so, she, her cubs, and the rest of the pride would starve. The lioness' way of observing is an aspect of an integrated pattern of coordinations. She observes the way she does because she runs and leaps the way she does. She anticipates how the prey will move and acts in response to the anticipations. (Cronen & Chetro-Szivos, 2001, p. 34)

It is not any different for human agents; human life or human organization would not be possible without the continuity or fluidity of action. As the Montréal school has pointed out, organizing is part of this continuity and involves in particular the habit of language that allows agents to punctuate, classify, and order the stream of actions that constitutes their existence.

Because valuation is such an integral part of human behavior, it tends to slip beneath the surface of everyday activities. This is partly so, because people often consider reflection on valuation to be an "act of inaction," so to speak—that is, something separated from other activities like valuation itself. As the lioness example illustrates, though, reflection occurs as part of other activities, as does valuation. Even if it does not seem so, people reflect and valuate while acting (e.g., while giving a speech, riding a bicycle, or writing a book chapter). In so doing, they conceptualize, attribute, and appropriate agency (e.g., President Bush should not be allowed to speak in public, I can ride a bicycle, this book chapter wrote itself).

The same can be said for the relation between valuation and organization: Organization, involving communication, implies valuation. More precisely, it implies the act of conceptualizing, attributing, and appropriating agency according to values enacted within the language games in which a set of agents are involved. We can illustrate the relation between valuation and agency by extending Cooren's (chap. 5, this volume) interpretation of the sexual abuse case in Newfoundland—I repeat the newspaper text here for the sake of clarity and convenience:

> A Roman Catholic diocese in Newfoundland is liable for hundreds of sexual assaults committed against young boys over a 30-year period by one of its priests, the Supreme Court of Canada ruled yesterday [March 25, 2004]. A 9-0 majority said a diocese is much more than a faceless, landholding entity. It is instead a cen-

tral authority intimately linked to the lives of parishioners, especially in isolated areas where its priests enjoy godlike status. The court concluded that the Roman Catholic Episcopal Corp. of St. George's is both directly and vicariously liable for the failure of two successive bishops "to properly direct and discipline" Rev. Kevin Bennett during his prolonged sexual rampage. "All temporal or secular actions of the bishop are those of the corporation," Madame Justice Beverly McLachlin wrote. "This includes the direction, control, and discipline of priests, which are the responsibility of the bishop."

As Cooren has explained, the chain or *plenum* of agencies in this example includes the Supreme Court (Agent 1), Madame Justice Beverly McLachlin (Agent 2), the Roman Catholic diocese (Agent 3), Rev. Bennett (Agent 4), and the community of parishioners (Agent 5). As Cooren says, important, in this respect, is where we *end* (or start) the chain of agents. For example, the chain could have been extended by including the Catholic Church with its center in Rome as a macro-agent (Agent 6), the Pope (Agent 7), the Canadian province of Newfoundland (Agent 8), the group of young boys who were assaulted (Agent 9), the newspaper that published the article that Cooren and I analyzed (Agent 10), or the law book (Agent 11) used by Madame Justice Beverly McLachlin to arrive at a verdict. Conversely, the chain could have been considerably shortened, as would perhaps have happened if the parishioners, Rev. Bennett, and the diocese had managed to keep a closed lid on the affair.

Although Cooren has suggested that where the chain of agencies is interrupted determines which agent is taken to be the author (or the authored), I think that locating this break implies an act that is even more rudimentary than the social enactment of authority or power. As Evens (1999) has indicated, human practice is a question of "value *qua* value" (p. 4), that is, of ethics, "before" it is a matter of authority—power, then, is a form or modality of a particular practice of ethics. That is to say, although the conceptualization, appropriation, and attribution of agency is not often taken into account when thinking about communication as organizing, contemplation on the valuation or ethical decision making that directs this conceptualization, appropriation, and attribution occurs even less frequently. Let me suggest the implications of taking a larger, ethical point of view on the question of agency with regard to the discussed example.

In the first place, we might consider how agency is conceptualized; that is, what does it mean to be an agent or to "have" agency and how do different valuations lead to different conceptions of what is going on in the "same" situation? In the example, agency denotes responsibility for an act already committed (rather than a potential to act) that Canadian society (Agent 12), as well as numerous other societies, denounces. Hence, in case agency is judged negatively, being attributed agency is something an agent will avoid by denying such attribution (i.e., by denying agency). If, for example, Rev. Bennett had saved a group of boys from being sexually abused, he, as well as the entire diocese, would have probably wanted to appropriate this agency, this responsibility for an act already committed.

Furthermore, as I have hinted already, the elaborateness of the actor network or chain of agencies, and variations in attributing micro- or macro-agency, is part of the conceptualization of agency. Consequently, this involves valuation as well. For instance, as Cooren has indicated, the situation could have been *framed*—to use Goffman's (1986) term—without attributing macro-agency to the diocese if the Supreme Court had simply ended the chain of agencies at Rev. Bennett as an individual agent. In other words, enacting an individualistic sense of human action, the court could have held him responsible as the sole agent for this whole affair. Moreover, we might ask whether the abused boys are to be seen as a collectivity with one voice (as one macro-agent) or as individual "cases" (as different micro-agents)? How is agency to be conceptualized in this particular instance? Are the boys to be seen as victims of the actions of an individual adult or did they play a part in their own destiny?

These are indeed ethical questions and "I," the author or conceptualizer, play a central role in their formulation. For example, you might ask: How dare I, the author, question whether these innocent (lack of agency?) boys participated in the unfolding of these grisly circumstances? This illustrates, once again, that the act of conceptualizing agency, implying the attribution and appropriation of agency (or agencies), involves an act of valuation. In any such instance, then, it is important to ask who conceptualizes, attributes, and appropriates. Additionally, it is important to ask how an agent is able to appropriate the agency that allows him, her, or it to be in a position to determine what agency is, who or what it is attributed to, and so forth. In other words, conceptualizing, attributing, and appropriating agency entails social rather than individual acts of valuation. Hence, agents engage as a sociality in such acts by participating in language games with their own logic and, within these games, they grant one or more individual agents conceptualizing power.

For instance, in the example, the newspaper might have attributed conceptualizing agency to the journalist of the article in question. Although the journalist wrote as an individual, however, he or she wrote on behalf of the entire newspaper, *repre*senting (Cooren, chap. 5, this volume) the organization as a macro-agent. Readers might in turn have attributed agency to the newspaper or journalist by suspending their disbelief and believing that the story was framed fairly and accurately. Furthermore, Canadian society generally attributes a particular kind of agency to its Supreme Court, whereas the parishioners do so with regard to the diocese, the Roman Catholic Church in Rome, and, let us not forget, the Holy Bible.

All these issues imply acts of social valuation with quite consequential effects. Although the authors of the other chapters that comprise this volume each take their own approach on why and how communication should be seen as organizing, it is not difficult to read any of the chapters in light of the ethical view I have presented. Taylor and Cooren's chapter (chap. 7, this volume) on Greimasian narrativity is perhaps most directly amenable to such a read, because it intimates questions similar to the ones I have struck.

As Taylor and Cooren have suggested toward the end of his chapter, Greimas (1987) emphasized the importance of considering the link between narration and valuation in his writings. Taylor and Greimas have both assumed that narration implies the conceptualization, attribution, and appropriation of, indeed, a whole plenum of agencies, involving the enactment of "value *qua* value" (Evens, 1999, p. 4). In this case, questions like the following need to be asked: How is agency conceptualized in narration? Who are abstracted as (micro- or macro-) agents from an ongoing stream of interconnecting activities? How elaborate is the narrated actor network? Why is Agent 1 protagonist, whereas Agent 2 is antagonist? What roles do nonhuman agents play in the unfolding narrative? For what reason is the plot constructed in this way? Do conflicting narratives exist? Why is one privileged over another? Perhaps most important, who narrates (the narrator being an agent who attributes and appropriates agency or agencies)? What is the relation between the narrator and "narratee"? To what extent should this narrator be allowed to appropriate narrative agency in the way he, she, or it appropriates it? That is to say, who participates in the enactment of this particular narrative (language game) by, for example, suspending disbelief and granting the author authority?[6]

Thus, like Cooren's chapter, other chapters in this volume can be read from an early American pragmatist point of view that bridges the ethics–agency divide. For the researcher this implies always keeping the connection between ethics and agency in mind when studying agents' traversing paths. I briefly bring this important matter to the fore before closing this chapter.

IMPLICATIONS FOR THE RESEARCHER AND THE RESEARCHED

So far, I have left one stone unturned by keeping the researcher (myself, others, the Montréal school) at bay as a central agent who engages with others in valuation by conceptualizing, attributing, and appropriating agency. A researcher, perhaps more than any other kind of agent, has "the power to construct" (Shepherd, 2001, p. 248) by enacting a particular kind of ethics in communication. As Deetz (1992), alluding to Dewey and Rorty, has argued, "how we conceptualize and talk about ourselves and others influences what we are and will be." Hence, theories "function to produce responses that produce ourselves, our social interactions, our institutions, and our collective future."[7] Consequently, the theories researchers construct should "be assessed in light of the kind of society [they] wish to produce" (p. 76).

Besides writing about communication as organizing, I believe it is thus necessary to consider how our research actions (my own included) produce conse-

---

[6]Mumby's (1987) article, "The Political Function of Narrative in Organizations," invokes similar questions.

[7]In line with Deetz's conception, as with Dewey's (1929), a theory can be defined as "a coherent grammar, consistent with data, that facilitates professionals' ability to join with others in the cocreation of new affordances and constraints in social action" (Cronen & Chetro-Szivos, 2001, p. 61).

quences in different social spaces, whether academic or nonacademic. Alluding to Berger and Luckmann (1966), Deetz (1992) mentions that an "institution can be thought of as the social equivalent of a personal habit" (p. 126). This idea applies to academic institutions (fields of study like organizational communication studies, universities, departments, or schools of thought like the Montréal school), too. When studying communicative organizing as it occurs in institutional settings, whether our own or another's, it is therefore important to ask: How am I (or are we), as a researching agent, conceptualizing, attributing, and appropriating agency, based on a set of values inhabited by operating in this particular social space? Who am I (or are we) to do so in the first place? What consequences do my (or our) actions yield? That is, do these consequences better the academic and nonacademic spaces in which I (or we) operate?

By taking questions like these, which speak to ethics as they speak to agency, into account in the practice of research (including our textwork), any researching agent, whether an individual, a school of thought, or a field of study, can theorize in ways that do not reinforce a duality between theory and practice (Dewey, 1922). Accordingly, "an alignment of the universe along moral lines, not intellectual ones" (Martel, 2001, p. 70) might be as pragmatic as it is practical, and help us overcome the divide that keeps scholarship from affecting real consequences.

References

Alexander, J. C. (1988). *Action and its environments: Toward a new synthesis*. New York: Columbia University Press.

Alexander, J. C. (1998). *Neofunctionalism and after*. Malden, MA: Blackwell.

Alvesson, M., & Karreman, D. (2000). Varieties of discourse: On the study of organizations through discourse analysis. *Human Relations, 53,*1125–1149.

American Heritage Dictionary (2000). Houghton Mifflin Company. Retrieved November 21, 2005 from http://www.bartleby.com/61/64/00116400.html

Argenti, P. A. (1997). *Corporate communication* (2nd ed.). New York: Irwin/McGraw-Hill.

Artemeva, N., & Freedman, A. (2001). Just the boys playing on computers: An activity theory analysis of differences. *Journal of Business and Technical Communication, 15*(2), 164–194.

Austin, J. L. (1962). *How to do things with words*. Oxford, UK: Oxford University Press.

Barry, D., & Elmes, M. (1996). Strategy retold: Towards a narrative view of strategic discourse. *Academy of Management Review, 22,* 429–452.

Bateson, G. (1979). *Mind and nature: A necessary unity*. New York: Dutton.

Benoit, W. L. (1995). *Accounts, excuses, and apologies: A theory of image restoration discourse/strategies*. Albany: State University of New York Press.

Berger, P. L., & Luckmann, T. (1966). *The social construction of reality: A treatise in the sociology of knowledge*. Garden City, NY: Doubleday.

Blackler, F. (1995). Knowledge, knowledge work and organizations: An overview and interpretation. *Organization Studies, 17*(6), 1021–1045.

Blackler, F., Crump, N., & McDonald, S. (1999). Managing experts and competing through innovation: An activity theoretical analysis. *Organization, 6,* 5–31.

Blackler, F., Crump, N., & McDonald, S. (2000). Organizing processes in complex activity networks. *Organization, 7,* 277–300.

Bloedon, R. V., & Stokes, D. R. (1994). Making university/industry collaborative research succeed. *Research Technology Management, 37,* 44–48.

Boden, D. (1994). *The business of talk: Organizations in action*. Cambridge, UK: Polity Press.

Boje, D. M. (1991). The storytelling organization: A study of story performance in an office-supply firm. *Administrative Science Quarterly, 36,* 106–126.

Boje, D. M. (1995). Stories of the storytelling organization: A postmodern analysis of Disney as "Tamara-land." *Academy of Management Journal, 38,* 997–1035.

Boje, D. M. (1998). The postmodern turn from stories-as-objects to stories-in-context methods. *1998 Academy of Management Research Methods Forum # 3*. Retrieved May 16, 2003 from http://www.aom.pace.edu/rmd/1998_forum_postmodern_stories.html

Boje, D. M. (2001). *Narrative methods for organizational and communication research.* London: Sage.

Boje, D. M., Alvarez, R. C., & Schooling, B. (2001). Reclaiming stories in organization: Narratologies and action sciences. In S. Linstead & R. Westwood (Eds.), *The language of organization* (pp. 132–175). London: Sage.

Bonaccorsi, A., & Piccaluga, A. (1994). A theoretical framework for the evaluation of university-industry relations. *R&D Management, 24,* 229–247.

Bourdieu, P. (1977). *Outline of a theory of practice.* Cambridge, MA: Cambridge University Press.

Bourdieu, P. (1990). *In other words: Essays towards a reflexive sociology* (M. Adamson, Trans.). Stanford, CA: Stanford University Press.

Bourdieu, P. (2000). *Pascalian meditations* R. Nice, Trans.). Stanford, CA: Stanford University Press.

Bourdieu, P., Calhoun, C. J., LiPuma, E., & Postone, M. (1993). *Bourdieu: Critical perspectives.* Chicago: University of Chicago Press.

Bourdieu, P., & Macquant, L. J. D. (1992). *An invitation to reflexive sociology.* Chicago: The University of Chicago Press.

Bromley, D. B. (1993). *Reputation, image and impression management.* New York: Wiley.

Brown, A. D., & Starkey, K. (1994). The effect of organizational culture on communication and information. *Journal of Management Studies, 31,* 807–828.

Brummans, B. H. J. M. (2004). *Dispositional reflections.* Unpublished doctoral dissertation, Texas A&M University, College Station, TX.

Bruner, J. (1991). The narrative construction of reality. *Critical Inquiry, 18,* 1–21.

Burkitt, I. (1998). Sexuality and gender: From a discursive to a relational analysis. *The Sociological Review, 46,* 483–504.

Burrell, G., & Morgan, G. (1979). *Sociological paradigms and organisational analysis: elements of the sociology of corporate life.* London: Heinemann.

Buttle, F. A. (1995). Marketing communication theory: What do the texts teach our students? *International Journal of Advertising, 14,* 297–313.

Buzzanell, P. (1994). Gaining a voice: Feminist organizational communication theorizing. *Management Communication Quarterly, 7,* 339–383.

Callon, M. (1986). Some elements of a sociology of translation: The domestication of the scallops and the fishermen of St. Brieuc Bay. In J. Law (Ed.), *Power, action and belief* (pp. 196–233). London: Routledge & Kegan Paul.

Callon, M., & Latour, B. (1981). Unscrewing the big Leviathan: How actors macro-structure reality and how sociologists help them to do so. In A. V. Cicourel & K. Knorr-Cetina (Eds.), *Advances in social theory and methodology: Towards an integration of micro- and macro-sociologies* (pp. 277–303). Boston: Routledge & Kegan Paul.

Caplow, T. (1968). *Two against one: Coalitions and triads.* Englewood Cliffs, NJ: Prentice-Hall.

Carbaugh, D. (1986). Some thoughts on organizing as cultural communication. In L. Thayer, (Ed.), *Organizationcommunication: Emerging perspectives, 1* (pp. 85–101). Norwood, NJ: Ablex.

Cassirer, E. (1942). The influence of language upon the development of scientific thought. *The Journal of Philosophy, 39,* 309–327.

Chauviré, C. (1995). *Peirce et la signification. Introduction à la logique du vague* [Peirce and meaning: Introduction to the logic of vagueness]. Paris: Presses Universitaires de France.

Chomsky, N. (1957). *Syntactic structures.* The Hague, Netherlands: Mouton.

Chomsky, N. (1965). *Aspects of a theory of syntax.* Cambridge, MA: MIT Press.

Clegg, S. R. (1994). *Frameworks of power.* London: Sage.

Collins, R. (1998). *The sociology of philosophies: A global theory of intellectual change.* Cambridge, MA: Harvard University Press.

Collins, R. (2000). The sociology of philosophies: A précis. *Philosophy of the Social Sciences, 30,* 157–201.

Conrad, C., & Haynes, J. (2001). Development of key constructs. In F. M. Jablin & L. L. Putnam (Eds.), *The new handbook of organizational communication: Advances in theory, research, and methods* (pp. 47–77). Thousand Oaks, CA: Sage.

Cooren, F. (1999). Applying socio-semiotics to organizational communication: A new approach. *Management Communication Quarterly, 13,* 294–304.

Cooren, F. (2000a). The emergent organization: Communication as its site and surface—Book review. *Communication Theory, 10,* 468–475.

Cooren, F. (2000b). *The organizing property of communication.* Amsterdam: John Benjamins.

Cooren, F. (2000c). Toward another ideal speech situation: A critique of Habermas' reinterpretation of speech act theory. *Quarterly Journal of Speech, 86,* 295–317.

Cooren, F. (2001a). Acting and organizing: How speech acts structure organizational interactions. *Concepts and Transformation, 6,* 275–293.

Cooren, F. (2001b). Translation and articulation in the organization of coalitions: The Great Whale River case. *Communication Theory, 11,* 178–200.

Cooren, F. (2004a). The communicative achievement of collective minding. *Management Communication Quarterly, 17,* 517–551.

Cooren, F. (2004b). Textual agency: How texts do things in organizational settings. *Organization, 11,* 373–393.

Cooren, F. (Ed.). (2006). *Interacting and organizing: Analyses of a management meeting.* Mahwah, NJ: Lawrence Erlbaum Associates.

Cooren, F., & Fairhurst, G. (2002). The leader as a practical narrator: Leadership as the art of translating. In D. Holman & R. Thorpe (Eds.), *Management and language: The manager as a practical author* (pp. 85–103). London: Sage.

Cooren, F., & Fairhurst, G. T. (2004). Speech timing and spacing: The phenomenon of organizational closure. *Organization, 11,* 793–824.

Cooren, F., & Fairhurst, G. T. (in press). Dislocation and stabilization: How to scale up from interactions to organization. In L. L. Putnam & A. M. Nicotera (Eds.), *The communicative constitution of organization: Centering organizational communication.* Mahwah, NJ: Lawrence Erlbaum Associates.

Cooren, F., Fox, S., Robichaud, D., & Talih, N. (2005). Arguments for a *plurified* view of the social world: Spacing and timing as hybrid achievements. *Time & Society, 14,* 263–280.

Cooren, F., & Taylor, J. R. (1997). Organization as an effect of mediation: Redefining the link between organization and communication. *Communication Theory, 7,* 219–260.

Cooren, F., & Taylor, J. R. (1998). The procedural and rhetorical modes of the organizing dimension of communication: Discursive analysis of a parliamentary commission. *Communication Review, 3,* 65–101.

Cooren, F., & Taylor, J. R. (2000). Association and dissociation in an ecological controversy: The great whale case. In N. W. Coppola & B. Karis (Eds.), *Technical communication, deliberative rhetoric, and environmental discourse: Connections and directions* (pp. 171–190). Stamford, CT: Ablex.

Corman, S. R., & Poole, M. S. (Eds.). (2000). *Perspectives on organizational communication: Finding common ground.* New York: Guilford.

Craig, R. T. (2001). Dewey and Gadamer on practical reflection: Toward a methodology for the practical disciplines. In D. K. Perry (Ed.), *American pragmatism and communication research* (pp. 131–148). Mahwah, NJ: Lawrence Erlbaum Associates.

Crane, D. (1972). *Invisible colleges: Diffusion of knowledge in scientific communities*. Chicago: The University of Chicago Press.

Cronen, V. E., & Chetro-Szivos, J. (2001). Pragmatism as a way of inquiring with special reference to a theory of communication and the general form of pragmatic social theory. In D. K. Perry (Ed.), *American pragmatism and communication research* (pp. 27–65). Mahwah, NJ: Lawrence Erlbaum Associates.

Czarniawska, B. (1997). *Narrating the organization: Dramas of institutional identity*. Chicago: University of Chicago Press.

Czarniawska, B. (1998). *A narrative approach in organization studies*. Thousand Oaks, CA: Sage.

Czarniawska, B. (1999). *Writing management: Organization theory as a literary genre*. Oxford, UK: Oxford University Press.

Daft, R. L., & Weick, K. E. (1984). Toward a model of organizations as interpretation systems. *Academy of Management Review, 9*, 284–295.

Debackere, K., & Rappa., M. A. (1994). Technological communities and diffusion of knowledge: A replication and validation. *R&D Management, 24*, 355–371.

Deetz, S. (1992). *Democracy in an age of corporate colonization: Developments in communication and the politics of everyday life*. Albany: State University of New York Press.

Deetz, S. A. (1995). *Transforming communication, transforming business: Building responsive and responsible workplaces*. Creskill, NJ: Hampton Press.

Deetz, S. (2001). Conceptual foundations. In F. M. Jablin & L. L. Putnam (Eds.), *The new handbook of organizational communication: Advances in theory, research, and methods* (pp. 3–46). Thousand Oaks, CA: Sage.

Descombes, V. (1996). *Les institutions du sens* [Institutions of meaning]. Paris: Éditions de minuit.

Descombes, V. (2001). *The mind's provisions: A critique of cognitivism*. Princeton, NJ: Princeton University Press. (Original work published 1995)

Dewey, J. (1910). *How we think*. Boston: Heath.

Dewey, J. (1922). *Human nature and conduct*. New York: The Modern Library.

Dewey, J. (1929). *The quest for uncertainty: A study of the relation of knowledge and action*. London: Allen & Unwin.

Dewey, J. (1938). *Logic: The theory of inquiry*. New York: Holt.

Dewey, J. (1939). *Theory of valuation*. Chicago: The University of Chicago Press.

Dewey, J., & Bentley, A. F. (1949). *Knowing and the known*. Boston: Beacon Press.

Diggins, J. P. (1994). *The promise of pragmatism: Modernism and the crisis of knowledge and authority*. Chicago: The University of Chicago Press.

Dill, D. (1990). University-industry research collaborations: An analysis of interorganizational relationships. *R & D Management, 20*, 123–129.

Drucker, P. F. (1973). *Management: Tasks, responsibilities, practices*. London: Heinemann.

Duchon, D., Ashmos, D. P., & Nathan, M. (2000). Complex systems and sensemaking teams. In M. M. Beyerlein, D. A. Johnson, & S. T. Beyerlein (Eds.), *Team performance management* (Vol. 6, pp. 219–238). Stamford, CT: JAI.

Eisenberg, E. M. (1984). Ambiguity as a strategy in organizational communication. *Communication Monographs, 51*, 227–242.

Eisenberg, E. M., & Riley, P. (2001). Organizational culture. In F. Jablin & L. L. Putnam (Eds.), *The new handbook of organizational communication: Advances in theory, research, and methods* (pp. 291–322). Thousand Oaks, CA: Sage.

Elias, N. (1991). *The society of individuals* (M. Schröter, Ed.; E. Jephcott, Trans.). Cambridge, MA: Basil Blackwell.

Elias, N. (2000). Homo clausus and the civilizing process. In P. du Gay, J. Evans, & P. Redman (Eds.), *Identity: A reader* (pp. 284–296). London: Sage.

Emirbayer, M. (1997). Manifesto for a relational sociology. *American Journal of Sociology, 103*, 281–317.

Emirbayer, M., & Mische, A. (1998). What is agency? *American Journal of Sociology, 103*, 962–1023.

Engeström, R. (1995). Voice as communicative action. *Mind, Culture and Activity, 2*, 192–214.

Engeström, Y. (1987). *Learning by expanding: An activity-theoretical approach to developmental research*. Helsinki, Finland: Orienta-Konsultit Oy.

Engeström, Y. (1990). *Learning working and imagining: Twelve studies in activity theory*. Helsinki, Finland: Orienta-Konsultit Oy.

Engeström, Y. (1999). Communication, discourse and activity. *Communication Review, 3*, 165–185.

Engeström, Y. (2000). Activity theory and the social construction of knowledge. *Organization, 7*, 301–310.

Engeström, Y. (2001). Expansive learning at work: Toward an activity theoretical reconceptualizaiton. *Journal of Education, 14*, 133–156.

Engeström, Y., Engeström, R., & Kerosuo, H. (2003). The discursive construction of collaborative care. *Applied Linguistics, 24*, 286–315.

Evens, T. M. S. (1999). Bourdieu and the logic of practice: Is all giving Indian-giving or is "generalized materialism" not enough? *Sociological Theory, 17*, 3–31.

Fairclough, N. (1995). *Critical discourse analysis: The critical study of language*. London: Longman.

Fairhurst, G. T. (in press). *Discursive approaches to leadership*. Thousand Oaks, CA: Sage.

Fairhurst, G. T., & Cooren, F. (2004). Organizational language in use: Interaction analysis, conversation analysis, and speech act schematics. In D. Grant, C. Hardy, C. Oswick, N. Phillips, & L. Putnam (Eds.), *Handbook of organizational discourse* (pp. 131–152). London: Sage.

Fairhurst, G. T., & Putnam, L. L. (1999). Reflections on the organization-communication equivalence question: The contributions of James Taylor and his colleagues. *Communication Review, 3*, 1–20.

Fairhurst, G. T., & Putnam, L. L. (2004). Organizations as discursive constructions. *Communication Theory, 14*, 5–26.

Farace, R. V., Monge, P. R., & Russell, H. M. (1977). *Communicating and organizing*. Reading, MA: Addison-Wesley.

Forester, J. (1993). *Critical theory, public policy, and planning practice: Toward a critical pragmatism*. Albany: State University of New York Press.

Foucault, M. (1972). *The archaeology of knowledge and the discourse on language* (A. M. Sheridan Smith, Trans.). London: Tavistock.

Gabriel, Y. (1995). The unmanaged organization: Stories, fantasies, subjectivity. *Organization Studies, 16*, 477–501.

Gabriel, Y. (1998). Same old story or changing stories: Folkloric, modern and postmodern mutation. In D. Grant, T. Keenoy, & C. Oswick (Eds.), *Discourse and organization* (pp. 84–103). Thousand Oaks, CA: Sage.

Garfinkel, H. (1967). *Studies in ethnomethodology*. Englewood Cliffs, NJ: Prentice-Hall.

Garfinkel, H. (1988). Evidence for locally produced, naturally accountable phenomena of order, logic, reason, meaning, method, etc. in and as of the essential quiddity of immortal society (I of IV): An announcement of studies. *Sociological Theory, 6*, 103–109.

Gergen, K. J. (2000). *The saturated self: Dilemmas of identity in contemporary life*. New York: Basic Books.

Giacalone, R. A., & Rosenfeld, P. (Eds). (1989). *Impression management in the organization*. Hillsdale, NJ: Lawrence Erlbaum Associates.

Giddens, A. (1981). *A contemporary critique of historical materialism: Power, property and the state*. London: Macmillan.

Giddens, A. (1984). *The constitution of society: Outline of the theory of structuration*. Berkeley: University of California Press.

Giddens, A. (1993). *New rules of sociological method: A positive critique of interpretative sociologies* (2nd ed.). Stanford, CA: Stanford University Press.

Gilbert, G. N., & Mulkay, M. (1984). *Opening Pandora's box: A sociological analysis of scientists' discourse*. Cambridge, UK: Cambridge University Press.

Giroux, H., & Taylor, J. R. (2002). The justification of knowledge: Tracking the translations of quality. *Management Learning, 33*, 497–517.

Glynn, M. A. (2002). *The emergent organization: Communication as its site and surface*— Book review. *Administrative Science Quarterly, 47*, 169–172.

Goffman, E. (1944). *Frame analysis: An essay on the organization of experience*. New York: Harper & Row.

Goldberg, A. E. (1995). *Constructions: A construction grammar approach to argument structure*. Chicago: University of Chicago Press.

Gomes da Silva, J. R., & Wetzel, U. (2004). Configurações de tempo e a tentativa de adaptação dos individuos às mudanças organizacionais. *Anais do XXVIII ENPAD* (Encontro Nacional dos Programas de Pós-Graduação em Administração). [Time configurations and individual adaptation to organizational change) Proceedings of the 28th ENPAD (National Conference of Postgraduate Programs in Administration)], (pp. 1–28). Curitiba, Brazil.

Grant, D., Keenoy, T., & Oswick, C. (Eds.). (1998). *Discourse and organization*. London: Sage.

Grayling, A. C. (1988). *Wittgenstein*. Oxford, UK: Oxford University Press.

Greimas, A. J. (1987). *On meaning: Selected writings* (P. J. Perron & F. H. Collins, Trans.). Minneapolis: University of Minnesota Press.

Greimas, A. J. (1993). Préface. In J. Courtès, *Sémiotique narrative et discursive* (pp. 5–25). Paris: Hachette.

Groleau, C. (1995). *An examination of the computerized information flow contributing to the mobility of tasks in three newly computerized firms*. Unpublished doctoral thesis, Concordia University, Montréal, Canada.

Groleau, C. (2002). Structuration, situated action and distributed cognition: Rethinking the computerization of organizations. *Système d'Information et Management, 2*(7), 13–36.

Groleau, C., & Cooren, F. (1998). A socio-semiotic approach to computerization: Bridging the gap between ethnographers and system analysts. *Communication Review, 3*, 125–164.

Groleau, C., & Engeström, Y. (2002, August). *Contradiction as trigger for change: An activity-theoretical approach to computerization*. Paper presented at the Academy of Management Conference, Denver, CO.

Groleau, C., & Taylor, J. R. (1996). Toward a subject-oriented worldview of information. *Canadian Journal of Communication, 21*, 243–265.

Gronn, P. (1983). Talk as the work: The accomplishment of school administration. *Administrative Science Quarterly, 28*, 1–21.

Grosjean, M., & Lacoste, M. (1999). *Communication et intelligence collective: Le travail à l'hôpital* [Communication and collective intelligence: Hospital work]. Paris: PUF.

Habermas, J. (1971). *Toward a rational society*. London: Heinemann.

Habermas, J. (1984). *The theory of communicative action* (T. McCarthy, Trans.). Boston: Beacon Press.

Halliday, M. A. K. (1985). *An introduction to functional grammar*. London: Edward Arnold.

Hardin, P. K. (2001). Theory and language: Locating agency between free will and discursive marionettes. *Nursing Inquiry, 8,* 11–18.

Hardy, C., Lawrence, T. B., & Grant, D. (2005). Discourse and collaboration: The role of conversations and collective identity. *Academy of Management Review, 30,* 58–77.

Harre, R. (1979). *Social being: A theory for social psychology.* Oxford, UK: Blackwell/Rowman & Littlefield.

Harre, R., & Secord, P. F. (1972). *The explanation of social behaviour.* Oxford, UK: Blackwell.

Hasu, M., & Engeström, Y. (2000). Measurement in action: An activity-theoretical perspective on producer–user interaction. *International Journal Human-Computer Studies, 53,* 61–89.

Hawes, L. C. (1974). Social collectivities as communication. *Quarterly Journal of Speech, 60,* 497–502.

Hayek, F. A. (1990). *The fatal conceit: The errors of socialism.* Chicago: University of Chicago Press.

Heath, R. L. (1994). *Management of corporate communication: From interpersonal contacts to external affairs.* Hillsdale, NJ: Lawrence Erlbaum Associates.

Heaton, L., & Taylor, J. R. (2002). Knowledge management and professional work: A communication perspective on the knowledge-based organization. *Management Communication Quarterly, 16,* 210–236.

Henderson, A. M., & Parsons, T. (1947). *Max Weber: The theory of economic and social organization.* New York: Free Press.

Heritage, J. (1984). *Garfinkel and ethnomethodology.* Cambridge, UK: Polity Press.

Herman, D. (2002). *Story logic: Problems and possibilities of narratives.* Lincoln: University of Nebraska Press.

Horton, J. L. (1995). *Integrating corporate communications: The cost-effective use of message and medium.* London: Quorum.

Huberman, M. (1990). Linkage between researchers and practitioners: A qualitative study. *American Educational Research Journal, 27,* 363–391.

Hutchins, E. (1995). *Cognition in the wild.* Cambridge, MA: MIT Press.

Huxham, C., & Vangen, S. (2000). Ambiguity, complexity and dynamics in the membership of collaboration. *Human Relations, 53,* 771–806.

Innis, H. A. (1951). *The bias of communication.* Toronto, Canada: Toronto University Press.

Jarzabkowski, P. (2003). Strategic practices: An activity theory perspective on continuity and change. *Journal of Management Studies, 40,* 23–55.

Johansen, J. D. (1993). *Dialogic semiosis: An essay on signs and meaning* (Vol. 1). Bloomington: Indiana University Press.

Johnson, P., & Duberley, J. (2000). *Understanding management research: An introduction to epistemology.* London: Sage.

Katambwe, J. M. (2004). *La nature du lien organisationnel: Une étude de cas selon une approche discursive* [The nature of the organizational link: A case study using a discursive approach]. Unpublished doctoral dissertation, Université de Montréal, Montréal, Canada.

Keenoy, T., Oswick, C., & Grant, D. (1997). Organizational discourses: Texts and context. *Organization, 4,* 147–157.

Kenny, A. (1973). *Wittgenstein.* London: Allen Lane.

Kerosuo, H., & Engeström, Y. (2003). Boundary crossing and learning in creation of new work practice. *Journal of Workplace Leaning, 15,* 345–351.

Kersten, A. (1986). A critical-interpretive approach to the study of organizational communication: Bringing communication back into the field. In L. Thayer (Ed.), *Organization-communication: Emerging perspectives 1* (pp. 85–101). Norwood, NJ: Ablex.

Ketner, K. L. (Ed.). (1995). *Peirce and contemporary thought: Philosophical inquiries.* New York: Fordham University Press.

Klapper, J. T. (1960). *The effects of mass communication.* New York: Free Press.

Krugman, H. E. (1965). The impact of television advertising: Learning without involvement. *Public Opinion Quarterly, 29,* 349–356.

Krugman, H. E. (1977). Meaning without recall, exposure without reception. *Journal of Advertising Research, 17,* 7–12.

Kuutti, K. (1996). Activity theory as a potential framework for human–computer interaction research. In B. A. Nardi (Ed.), *Context and consciousness: Activity theory and human–computer interaction* (pp. 17–43). Cambridge, MA: MIT Press.

Kvale, S. (1996). *Interviews: An introduction to qualitative research interviewing.* Thousand Oaks, CA: Sage.

Labov, W., & Fanshel, D. (1977). *Therapeutic discourse: Psychotherapy as conversation.* New York: Academic.

Lacoste, M. (2000). Les objets et le travail en collectif [Objects and collective work]. In P. Delcambre (Ed.), *Communications organisationnelles: Objets, pratiques, dispositifs* (pp. 23–34) [Organizational communications: Objects, practices, technology]. Rennes, France: Presses Universitaires de Rennes.

Langer, R. (1999). Towards a constructivist communication theory? Report from Germany. *Nordicom Information, 1–2,* 75–86.

Latour, B. (1986). The powers of association. In J. Law (Ed.), *Power, action and belief: A new sociology of knowledge?* (pp. 264–280). London: Routledge & Kegan Paul.

Latour, B. (1987). *Science in action.* Cambridge, MA: Harvard University Press.

Latour, B. (1993). *We have never been modern* (C. Porter, Trans.). Cambridge, MA: Harvard University Press

Latour, B. (1994). On technical mediation: Philosophy, sociology, genealogy. *Common Knowledge, 3*(2), 29–64.

Latour, B. (1996). On interobjectivity. *Mind, Culture, and Activity, 3,* 228–245.

Latour, B. (1999). *Pandora's hope: Essays on the reality of science studies.* Cambridge, MA: Harvard University Press.

Latour, B. (2004). *Politics of nature: How to bring the sciences into democracy.* Cambridge, MA: Harvard University Press.

Latour, B., & Woolgar, S. (1986). *Laboratory life: The construction of scientific facts.* Princeton, NJ: Princeton University Press.

Law, J. (Ed.). (1991). *A sociology of monsters: Essays on power, technology and domination.* London: Routledge.

Law, J. (2000). *Objects, spaces, others.* Lancaster, UK: Center for Science Studies and the Department of Sociology, Lancaster University. Retrieved January 10, 2004 from http://www.comp.lancs.ac.uk/sociology/soc027jl.html

Law, J., & Mol, A. (2001). Situating technoscience: An inquiry into spatialities. *Environment and Planning D: Society and Space, 19,* 609–621.

Lawrence, P. R., & Lorsch, J. W. (1969). *Organization and environment: Managing differentiation and integration.* Homewood, IL: Irwin.

Lawrence, T. B., Hardy, C., & Phillips, N. (2002). Institutional effects of interorganizational collaboration: The emergence of proto-institutions. *Academy of Management Journal, 45,* 281–290.

Lawrence, T. B., Phillips, N., & Hardy, C. (1999). Watching whale watching: Exploring the discursive foundations of collaborative relationships. *Journal of Applied Behavioral Science, 35,* 479–502.

Leont'ev, A. N. (1978). *Activity, consciousness and personality.* Englewood Cliffs, NJ: Prentice-Hall.

Levin, M. R. (2000). *Cultures of control*. London: Harwood.

Lévi-Strauss, C. (1963). *Structural anthropology* (C. Jacobson & B. Schoepf, Trans.). New York: Basic Books. (Original work published 1958)

Lewis, J. D., & Smith, R. L. (1980). *American sociology and pragmatism*. Chicago: The University of Chicago Press.

Lyotard, J.-F. (1984). *The postmodern condition: A report on knowledge*. Minneapolis: The University of Minnesota Press.

Makin, K. (2004, March 26). Supreme court: Roman Catholic diocese responsible for priest's years of sexual abuse. Implications for other organizations. *The Globe and Mail*, p. A4.

Manning, P. K. (1992). *Organizational communication*. New York: Aldine de Gruyter.

Mantovani, G. (1996). *New communication environments: From everyday to virtual*. London: Taylor & Francis.

Markham, A. (1996). Designing discourse: A critical analysis of strategic ambiguity and workplace control. *Management Communication Quarterly, 9*, 389–421.

Martel, Y. (2001). *Life of Pi: A novel*. Toronto: Vintage Canada.

Maturana, H. R. (1988). Ontology of observing: The biological foundations of self consciousness and the physical domain of existence. In *Conference workbook: Texts in cybernetics*. American Society of Cybernetics Conference, Felton, CA, 18-23 October. Retrieved November 23, 2005 from http://www.inteco.cl/biology/

Maturana, H. R. (1991). Science in daily life: The ontology of scientific explanations. In F. Steier (Ed.), *Research and reflexivity: Self-reflexivity as social process* (pp. 30–52). Newbury Park, CA: Sage.

Maturana, H. R. (1997). *La objetividad: un argumento para obligar* [Objectivity: A compelling argument]. Santiago, Chile: Dolmen.

Maturana, H. R., & Varela, F. J. (1987). *The tree of knowledge: The biological roots of understanding*. Boston: Shambhala.

May, S., & Mumby, D. K. (2005). Thinking about engagement. In S. May & D. K. Mumby (Eds), *Engaging organizational communication theory & research: Multiple perspectives* (pp. 1–14). Thousand Oaks, CA: Sage.

McDaniel, R. R., Jr. (1997). Strategic leadership: A view from chaos and quantum theories. In W. J. Ducan, P. Ginter, & L. Swayne (Eds.), *Handbook of healthcare management* (pp. 339–367). Oxford, UK: Blackwell.

McHugh, P., Raffel, S., Foss, D. C., & Blum, A. (1974). *On beginning social inquiry*. London: Routledge & Kegan Paul.

McPhee, R. D. (1985). Formal structure and organizational communication. In R. D. McPhee & P. K. Tompkins (Eds.), *Organizational communication: Traditional themes and new directions* (pp. 149–177). Beverly Hills, CA: Sage.

McPhee, R. D. (1989a). Commentary on Cheney and Tompkins. On The facts of the "facts of the text". In J. A. Anderson (Ed.), *Communication yearbook* (Vol. 11, pp. 482–493). Beverly Hills, CA: Sage.

McPhee, R. D. (1989b). Organizational communication: A structurational exemplar. In B. Dervin, L. Grossberg, B. J. O'Keefe, & E. Wartella (Eds.), *Rethinking communication* (Vol. 2, pp. 199–212). Newbury Park, CA: Sage.

McPhee, R. D. (2004). Text, agency, and organization in the light of structuration theory. *Organization, 11*, 355–371.

McPhee, R. D., & Poole, M. S. (2001). Organizational structures and configurations. In F. M. Jablin & L. L. Putnam (Eds.), *The new handbook of organizational communication: Advances in theory, research, and methods* (pp. 503–543). Thousand Oaks, CA: Sage.

McPhee, R. D., & Seibold, D. R. (1999). Responses to the finalist essays. *Management Communication Quarterly, 13*, 327–336.

McPhee, R. D., & Trethewey, A. C. (2000). *The emergent organization: Communication as its site and surface*—Book review. *Management Communication Quarterly, 14,* 328–334.

McPhee, R. D., & Zaug, P. (2000). The communicative constitution of organizations: A framework for explanation. *Electronic Journal of Communication/La Rvue Énique de Communication, 10*(1–2), 1–16.

Mead, G. H. (1934). *Mind, self, & society from the standpoint of a social behaviorist.* Chicago: The University of Chicago Press.

Menand, L. (Ed.). (1997). *Pragmatism: A reader.* New York: Vintage.

Menz, F. (1999). "Who am I gonna do this with?": Self-organization, ambiguity and decision-making in a business enterprise. *Discourse & Society, 10*(1), 101–128.

Merriam-Webster's Collegiate Dictionary (10th ed.). (1998). Springfield, MA: Merriam-Webster.

Miller, K. (1999). Widening the lens: Using historical data in organizational communication theorizing. In P. Salem (Ed.), *Organizational communication and change* (pp. 175–206). Cresskill, NJ: Hampton.

Miller, K. (2002). *Communication theories: Perspectives, processes, and contexts.* Boston: McGraw-Hill.

Mills, C. W. (1940). Situated actions and vocabularies of motive. *American Sociological Review, 5,* 904–913.

Mintzberg, H. (1973). *The nature of managerial work.* New York: Harper & Row.

Mumby, D. K. (1987). The political function of narrative in organizations. *Communication Monographs, 54,* 113–127.

Mumby, D. (1988). *Communication and power in organizations: Discourse, ideology, and domination.* Norwood, NJ: Ablex.

Mumby, D. (2001). Power and politics. In F. M. Jablin & L. L. Putnam (Eds.), *The new handbook of organizational communication: Advances in theory, research and methods* (pp. 585–623). Thousand Oaks, CA: Sage.

Mumby, D. K., & Stohl, C. (1996). Disciplining organizational communication studies. *Management Communication Quarterly, 10,* 50–72.

Nair, C. T. S., Apichart, K., & Enters, T. (1998). Forestry research: Changing times and times for change. In T. Enters, C. T. S. Nair, and K. Apichart (Eds.), *Emerging institutional arrangements for forestry research* (pp. 1–10). Bangkok, Thailand: FORSPA-FAO.

Newcomb, T. (1953). An approach to the study of communicative acts. *Psychological Review, 50,* 393–404.

Orlikowski, W. J. (2002). Knowing in practice: Enacting a collective capability in distributed organizing. *Organization Science, 13,* 249–273.

Orr, J. E. (1996). *Talking about machines: An ethnography of a modern job.* Ithaca, NY: Cornell University Press.

Oswick, C., Keenoy, T., Grant, D., & Marshak, B. (2000). Discourse, organization, and epistemology. *Organization, 7,* 511–512.

Parker, L. E. (1992). *Industry-university collaboration in developed and developing countries* (World Bank's PHREE Background Paper Series, No. PHREE/92/64). Education and Employemnt Division, Population and Human Resources Department, The World Bank.

Peirce, C. S. (1955). *Philosophical writings of Peirce.* New York: Dover.

Peirce, C. S. (1960). *Collected papers.* Cambridge: Belknap Press. (Original work published 1934)

Peirce, C. S. (1965). *Collected papers: Vol. V. Pragmatism and pragmaticism* (Vol. 5–6). Cambridge, MA: Belknap Press. (Original work published 1934)

Peirce, C. S. (1992). *Reasoning and the logic of things.* Cambridge, MA: Harvard University Press.)

Peirce, C. S., Houser, N., Kloesel, C. J. W., & Peirce Edition Project. (1992). *The essential Peirce: Selected philosophical writings: Vol. 1.* Bloomington: Indiana University Press.

Penman, R. (2000). *Reconstructing communicating: Looking to a future.* Mahwah, NJ: Lawrence Erlbaum Associates.

Perry, D. K. (Ed.). (2001). *American pragmatism and communication research.* Mahwah, NJ: Lawrence Erlbaum Associates.

Phillips, N., Lawrence, T. B., & Hardy, C. (2000). Inter-organizational collaboration and the dynamics of institutional fields. *Journal of Management Studies, 37,* 23–44.

Pickering, A. (1995). *The mangle of practice: Time, agency & science.* Chicago: University of Chicago Press.

Propp, V. J. (1968). *Morphology of the Folktale* (2nd ed.). Austin: University of Texas Press. (Original work published 1928)

Putnam, L. L. (1983). The interpretive perspective: An alternative to functionalism. In L. L. Putnam & M. E. Pacanowsky (Eds.), *Communication and organizations: An interpretive approach* (pp. 31–54). Beverly Hills, CA: Sage.

Putnam, L. L. (2001). Shifting voices, oppositional discourse, and new visions for communication studies. *Journal of Communication, 51,* 38–51.

Putnam, L. L., & Cooren, F. (2004). Alternative perspectives on the role of text and agency in constituting organizations. *Organization, 11,* 323–333.

Putnam, L. L., & Fairhurst, G. T. (2001). Discourse analysis in organizations: Issues and concerns. In F. M. Jablin & L. L. Putnam (Eds.), *The new handbook of organizational communication: Advances in theory, research, and methods* (pp. 78–136). Thousand Oaks, CA: Sage.

Putnam, L. L., & Pacanowsky, M. E. (1983). *Communication and organizations: An interpretive approach.* Newbury Park, CA: Sage.

Putnam, L., Phillips, N., & Chapman, P. (1996). Metaphors of communication and organization. In S. Clegg, C. Hardy, & W. Nord (Eds.), *Handbook of organizational studies* (pp. 375–408). London: Sage.

Pye, A. (1993). "Organizing as explaining" and the doing of managing: An integrative appreciation of processes of organizing. *Journal of Management Inquiry, 2,* 157–168.

Rappa, M. A., & Debackere, K. (1992). Technological communities and the diffusion of knowledge: A replication and validation. *R&D Management, 22,* 209–220.

Reed, M. (1999). Organizational analysis as discourse analysis: A critique. In D. Grant, T. Keenoy, & C. Oswick (Eds.), *Discourse and organization* (pp. 193–213). London: Sage.

Reed, M. (2000). The limits of discourse analysis in organization analysis. *Organization, 7,* 524–530.

Ricoeur, P. (1984). *Time and narrative* (Vol. 1, K. McLaughlin & D. Pellauer, Trans.) Chicago: University of Chicago Press.

Robichaud, D. (1999). Textualization and organizing: Illustrations from a public discussion process. *Communication Review, 3,* 103–124.

Robichaud, D. (2000). *The organizing property of communication*—Book review. *Management Communication Quarterly, 14,* 317–322.

Robichaud, D. (2001). Interaction as a text: A semiotic look at an organizing process. *American Journal of Semiotics, 17,* 141–161.

Robichaud, D. (2002). Greimas' semiotics and the analysis of organizational action. In P. B. Anderson, R. J. Clarke, K. Liu, & R. K. Stamper (Eds.), *Coordination and communication using signs: Studies in organizational semiotics* (pp. 129–149). Boston: Kluwer Academic.

Robichaud, D., Giroux, H., & Taylor, J. R. (2004). The meta-conversation: The recursive property of language as the key to organizing. *Academy of Management Review, 29,* 617–634.

Ruscio, K. (1984). University-industry cooperation as a problem in interorganizational relations. In B. Bozeman, M. Crow, & A. Link (Eds.), *Strategic management of industrial R&D* (pp. 171–185). Lexington. MA: Lexington Books.

Sacks, H. (1992). *Lectures on conversations* (Vol. 1 & 2, G. Jefferson, Ed.). Oxford, UK: Blackwell.

Salk, J. (1973). *The survival of the wisest.* New York: Harper & Row.

Saussure, F. de. (1974). *Course in general linguistics* (W. Baskin, Trans.). London: Fontana.

Schank, R., & Abelson, R. (1977). *Scripts, plans, goals and understanding.* Hillsdale, NJ: Lawrence Erlbaum Associates.

Schlenker, B. R. (1980). *Impression management.* Monterey, CA: Brooks-Cole.

Schön, D. A. (1983). *The reflective practitioner: How professionals think in action.* London/New York: Temple Smith/Basic Books.

Schonbach, P. (1990). *Account episodes: The management or escalation of conflict.* Cambridge, UK: Cambridge University Press.

Schramm, W. A. (1948). *Mass communications.* Urbana: University of Illinois Press.

Schramm, W. A. (1971). The nature of communication between humans. In W A. Schramm & D. F. Roberts (Eds.), *The process and effects of mass communication* (pp. 3–54). Urbana: University of Illinois Press.

Schumacher, E. F. (1995). *A guide for the perplexed.* London: Vintage.

Schutz, A. (1973). *Collected papers I : The problem of social reality.* The Hague, Netherlands: Martinus Nijhoff.

Scott, M. B., & Lyman, S. M. (1968). Accounts. *American Sociological Review, 33,* 46–62.

Scott, W. R. (1995). *Institutions and organizations.* Thousand Oaks, CA: Sage.

Searle, J. R. (1969). *Speech acts: An essay in the philosophy of language.* London: Cambridge University Press.

Searle, J. R. (1989). How performatives work. *Linguistics and Philosophy, 12,* 535–558.

Shannon, C. E., & Weaver, W. (1963). *The mathematical theory of communication.* Urbana: University of Illinois Press. (Original work published 1949)

Sharrock, W., & Anderson, B. (1986). *The ethnomethodologists.* Chichester, UK: Ellis Horwood.

Shepherd, G. J. (2001). Pragmatism and tragedy, communication and hope: A summary story. In D. K. Perry (Ed.), *American pragmatism and communication research* (pp. 241–254). Mahwah, NJ: Lawrence Erlbaum Associates.

Shotter, J. (1984). *Social accountability and selfhood.* Oxford, UK: Basil Blackwell.

Sigman, S. J. (1995). *The Consequentiality of Communication.* Mahwah, NJ: Lawrence Erlbaum Associates.

Simonson, P. (2001). Varieties of pragmatism and communication: Visions and revisions from Peirce to Peters. In D. K. Perry (Ed.), *American pragmatism and communication research* (pp. 1–26). Mahwah, NJ: Lawrence Erlbaum Associates.

Smith, R. C. (1993, May). *Images of organizational communication: Root-metaphors of the organization-communication relation.* Paper presented at the annual meeting of the International Communication Association, Washington, DC.

Spinosa, C., Flores, F., & Dreyfus, H. L. (1997). *Disclosing new worlds: Entrepreneurship, democratic action and the cultivation of solidarity.* Cambridge, MA: MIT Press.

Star, S. L. (1996). Working together: Symbolic interactionism, activity theory and information systems. In Y. A. D. M. Engeström (Ed.), *Cognition and communication at work* (pp. 296–318). Cambridge, MA: Cambridge University Press.

Stohl, C. (in press). Bringing the outside in: A contextual analysis. In F. Cooren (Ed.), *Interacting and organizing: Analyses of a management meeting.* Mahwah, NJ: Lawrence Erlbaum Associates.

Strauss, A. L. (1978). A social world perspective. *Studies in Symbolic Interaction, 1,* 119–128.

Suchman, L. (1987). *Plans and situated action: The problem of human–machine communication.* Cambridge MA: Cambridge University Press.

Suchman, L. (1996). Constituting shared workspaces. In Y. Engeström & D. Middleton (Eds.), *Cognition and communication at work* (pp. 35–60). Cambridge, UK: Cambridge University Press.

Taylor, J. R. (1993). *Rethinking the theory of organizational communication: How to read an organization.* Norwood, NJ: Ablex.

Taylor, J. R. (1995). Shifting from a heteronomous to an autonomous worldview of organizational communication: Communication theory on the cusp. *Communication Theory, 5,* 1–35.

Taylor, J. R. (1999). What is "organizational communication"? Communication as a dialogic of text and conversation. *Communication Review, 3,* 21–64.

Taylor, J. R. (2000a). Apples and orangutangs: The worldviews of organizational communication. *Saison Mauve, 3,* 45–64.

Taylor, J. R. (2000b). Is there a "Canadian" approach to the study of organizational communication? *Canadian Journal of Communication, 25,* 145–174.

Taylor, J. R. (2001). Toward a theory of imbrication and organizational communication. *American Journal of Semiotics, 17,* 1–29.

Taylor, J. R. (2005). Engaging worldview: My pursuit of an explanation of communication as organizing. In S. May & D. Mumby (Eds.), *Engaging organizational communication theory and perspectives: Multiple perspectives* (pp. 197–221). Thousand Oaks, CA: Sage.

Taylor, J. R., & Cooren, F. (1997). What makes communication "organizational"? How the many voices of a collectivity become the one voice of an organization. *Journal of Pragmatics, 27,* 409–438.

Taylor, J. R., Cooren, F., Giroux, N., & Robichaud, D. (1996). The communicational basis of organization: Between the conversation and the text. *Communication Theory, 6,* 1–39.

Taylor, J. R., Flanagin, A. J., Cheney, G., & Seibold, D. R. (2001). Organizational communication research: Key moments, central concerns, and future challenges. *Communication Yearbook, 24,* 99–137.

Taylor, J. R., & Giroux, H. (2005). The role of language in self-organizing systems. In G. Barnett & R. Houston (Eds.), *Self-organizing systems* (pp. 131–168). New York: Hampton.

Taylor, J. R., Groleau, C., Heaton, L., & Van Every, E. (2001). *The computerization of work: A communication perspective.* Thousand Oaks, CA: Sage.

Taylor, J. R., & Gurd, G. (1996). Contrasting perspectives on non-positivist communication research. In L. Thayer (Ed.), *Organization–communication: Emerging perspectives III* (pp. 32–73). Norwood: NJ: Ablex.

Taylor, J. R., Gurd, G., & Bardini, T. (1997). The worldviews of cooperative work. In G. Bowker, L. Gasser, S. L. Star & W. Turner (Eds.), *Social science research, technical systems and cooperative work* (pp. 379–413). Mahwah, NJ: Lawrence Erlbaum Associates.

Taylor, J. R., & Lerner, L. (1996). Making sense of sensemaking: How managers construct their organization through their talk. *Studies in Cultures, Organizations and Societies, 2,* 257–286.

Taylor, J. R., & Robichaud, D. (2004). Finding the organization in the communication: Discourse as action and sensemaking. *Organization, 11,* 395–413.

Taylor, J. R., & Van Every, E. J. (1993). *The vulnerable fortress: Bureaucratic organization and management in the information age.* Toronto: University of Toronto Press.

Taylor, J. R., & Van Every, E. J. (2000). *The emergent organization. Communication as site and surface*. Mahwah, NJ: Lawrence Erlbaum Associates.

Thatchenkery, T. J. (2001). Mining for meaning: Reading organizations using hermeneutic philosophy. In R. Westwood & S. Linstead (Eds.), *The language of organization* (pp. 112–131). London: Sage.

Tiercelin, C. (1993). *C. S. Peirce et le pragmatisme* [C. S. Peirce and pragmatism]. Paris: Presses Universitaires de France.

Tompkins, P. K., & Cheney, G. (1983). Account analysis of organizations: Decision making and identification. In L. L. Putnam & M. E. Pacanowsky (Eds), *Communication and organizations: An interpretive approach* (pp. 123–146). Beverly Hills, CA: Sage.

Van der Meer, W., Trommelen, G., Vleggaar, J., & Vriezen, P. (1996). Collaborative R & D and European industry. *Research Technology Management, 39,* 15–18.

Van Every, E. J., & Taylor, J. R. (1998). Modeling the organization as a system of communication activity: A dialogue about the language/action perspective. *Management Communication Quarterly, 12,* 127–146.

Van Maanen, J. (1996). On the matter of voice. *Journal of Management Inquiry, 5,* 375–381.

van Riel, C. B. M. (1995). *Principles of corporate communication*. London: Prentice-Hall.

Vickers, G. (1983). *Human systems are different*. London: Harper & Row.

Vygotsky, L. S. (1978). *Mind in society: The development of higher psychological processes*. Cambridge, MA: Harvard University Press.

Wacquant, L. (1993). Bourdieu in America: Notes on the transatlantic importation of social theory. In C. Calhoun, E. LiPuma, & M. Postone (Eds.), *Bourdieu: Critical perspectives* (pp. 235–262). Chicago: The University of Chicago Press.

Weber, M. (1962). *The methodology of the social sciences*. New York: Free Press. (Original work published 1949)

Webster's New World Dictionary of the American Language. (1964). Cleveland & New York: The World Publishing Company.

Weick, K. E. (1979). *The social psychology of organizing*. New York: Random House.

Weick, K. E. (1983). Organizational communication: Toward a research agenda. In L. L. Putnam & M. Pacanowsky (Eds.), *Communication and organizations: An interpretive approach* (pp. 13–29). Beverly Hills, CA: Sage.

Weick, K. E. (1989). Organized improvisation: 20 years of organizing. *Communication Studies, 40,* 241–248.

Weick, K. E. (1993). The collapse of sensemaking in organizations: The Mann Gulch Disaster. *Administrative Science Quarterly, 38,* 628–652.

Weick, K. E. (1995). *Sensemaking in organizations: Foundations for organizational science*. London: Sage.

Weick, K. E. (2001a). *The emergent organization: Communication as its site and surface*—Book review. *Contemporary Psychology, 46,* 166–168.

Weick, K. E. (2001b). *Making sense of the organization*. Oxford, UK: Blackwell Business.

Weick, K. E. (2001c). Organizational redesign as improvisation. In K. E. Weick (Ed.), *Making sense of the organization* (pp. 57–91). Oxford, UK: Blackwell Business.

Weick, K. E., & Browning, L. D. (1986). Argument and narration in organizational communication. *Yearly Review of Management, 12,* 243–259.

Weick, K. E., & Roberts, K. H. (1993). Collective mind in organization: Heedful interrelating on flight decks. *Administrative Science Quarterly, 38,* 357–381.

Wenger, E. (2002). *Communities of practice: Learning, meaning, and identity* (7th ed.). Cambridge, UK: Cambridge University Press.

Westwood, R., & Linstead, S. (Eds.). (2001). *The language of organization*. London: Sage.

Wittgenstein, L. (1953). *Philosophical investigations* (G. E. M. Anscombe, Trans.) Oxford, UK: Blackwell.

Woodward, W. (2001). Transactional philosophy and communication studies. In D. K. Perry (Ed.), *American pragmatism and communication research* (pp. 67–88). Mahwah, NJ: Lawrence Erlbaum Associates.

Xie, C. (2002). *The organizing property of communication*—Book review. *Studies in Language, 26,* 181–215.

Zilber, T. B. (2002a). Institutionalization as an interplay between actions, meanings, and actors: The case of a rape crisis center in Israel. *Academy of Management Journal, 45,* 234–254.

Zilber, T. B. (2002b, July). *Stories of conflicts and conflict between stories: Politics, narration, and board-decision making.* Paper presented at the 18th Conference of the European Group for Organization Studies, Barcelona, Spain.

Author Index

Subject Index